One of Morgan's Men

ONE OF
MORGAN'S MEN

MEMOIRS OF
LIEUTENANT JOHN M. PORTER
OF THE NINTH KENTUCKY CAVALRY

Edited by
KENT MASTERSON BROWN

THE UNIVERSITY PRESS OF KENTUCKY

Scholarly publisher for the Commonwealth,
serving Bellarmine University, Berea College, Centre College of Kentucky, Eastern
Kentucky University, The Filson Historical Society, Georgetown College, Kentucky
Historical Society, Kentucky State University, Morehead State University, Murray
State University, Northern Kentucky University, Transylvania University, University
of Kentucky, University of Louisville, and Western Kentucky University.
All rights reserved.

Editorial and Sales Offices: The University Press of Kentucky
663 South Limestone Street, Lexington, Kentucky 40508-4008
www.kentuckypress.com

15 14 13 12 11   5 4 3 2 1

Frontispiece: Lieutenant John Marion Porter, from an ambrotype probably taken
while he was a prisoner of war. (Courtesy of Cora Jane Spiller, Bowling Green,
Kentucky.)

All maps prepared by the editor.

Library of Congress Cataloging-in-Publication Data

Porter, John Marion, 1839-1884.
  One of Morgan's men : memoirs of Lieutenant John M. Porter of the Ninth
Kentucky Cavalry / edited by Kent Masterson Brown.
     p. cm.
  Includes bibliographical references and index.
  ISBN 978-0-8131-2989-1 (hardcover : alk. paper)
  ISBN 978-0-8131-2990-7 (ebook)
  1. Porter, John Marion, 1839-1884. 2. Confederate States of America. Army.
Morgan's Cavalry Division. 3. Confederate States of America. Army. Kentucky
Cavalry Regiment, 9th. 4. United States—History—Civil War, 1861-1865—Personal
narratives, Confederate. 5. Kentucky—History—Civil War, 1861-1865—Personal
narratives, Confederate. 6. Soldiers—Kentucky—Biography. I. Brown, Kent
Masterson, 1949- II. Title.
  E547.M8P67 2011
  973.7'82—dc22

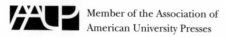 Member of the Association of
American University Presses

To all the wonderful and generous people
who form the community known as
Apostles Anglican Church, Lexington, Kentucky,
I very proudly dedicate this book.

K.M.B.

CONTENTS

ILLUSTRATIONS

FIGURES

ILLUSTRATIONS

ILLUSTRATIONS

MAPS

ACKNOWLEDGMENTS

There are many individuals who helped make the publication of Lieutenant John M. Porter's war memoirs a reality. First and foremost, Steve Carson of Lexington, Kentucky, gave me the typescript of the war memoirs and the permission to publish it. Steve is a descendant of Thomas Carson of Prince Edward County, Virginia, who married Anna Porter, the sister of John Marion Porter's grandfather, Francis Porter. Thomas and Anna Carson settled near Sugar Grove in Butler County, Kentucky. Thank you, Steve, for your great interest in history and your warm friendship.

Colonel Robert Spiller and his dear wife, Cora Jane Spiller, of Bowling Green, Kentucky, provided magnificent archival material, including the Hines genealogies, Porter's own sketch of his family history, various manuscript materials relating to the Porter and Hines families, and Porter's wartime photograph. Cora Jane is the granddaughter of none other than John Marion Porter Hines, the fifth child of Lieutenant Edward Ludlow Hines, who rode with Porter in the Ninth Kentucky Cavalry and came back to Kentucky from Georgia with him in 1865. Edward Ludlow Hines was a cousin of Thomas Henry Hines. Cora's grandfather was named in honor of none other than Lieutenant John Marion Porter. The Spillers are terrific people who love history. I am very grateful for all they did to make the publication of Porter's war memoirs possible and for their great friendship.

ACKNOWLEDGMENTS

My secretary, Sharon Howard of Georgetown, Kentucky, patiently typed draft after draft of the war reminiscences; she was always cheerful and interested in the story. David Hicks of Lexington, Kentucky, my law clerk, helped me prepare all the maps. He is computer savvy; I, of course, am not. The result of David's efforts are the wonderful maps that chronicle Porter's incredible odyssey. Thank you, Sharon and David.

My two good friends James Ramage, professor of history at Northern Kentucky University, and Edward McKenzie "Mac" Coffman, professor emeritus of history at the University of Wisconsin, and now of Lexington, Kentucky, were most helpful. Jim read—and made critical comments about—the typescript of Porter's war reminiscences, giving me a roadmap to edit it. Mac provided me with his master's thesis on the life of Thomas Henry Hines, and then helped me crystallize my thoughts about the project during our Sunday afternoon discussions after church and during our regular lunches. Jim and Mac are terrific historians; more than that, they are great people who dearly love history. I am very grateful to them.

Michael Courtney at Black Swan Bookstore in Lexington was very helpful, locating for me long out-of-print books that provided important narratives which helped bring Porter's story to life. Michael is a longtime friend; our friendship spans at least fifty years.

William Marshall, Jim Birchfield, and, especially genealogical specialist Phyllis V. Spiker, all at the University of Kentucky Special Collections, were more valuable than words can tell. Phyllis is a treasure; she patiently explored computer databases with me, finding, in the end, the identities of literally every person mentioned by Porter in his war reminiscences. That was quite a feat. I cannot say enough about Phyllis Spiker. For permission to use the photographs from the Hunt Morgan and Lafayette Studio Collections at the University of Kentucky Special Collections, I am most appreciative.

B. J. Gooch of the Transylvania University Library was very helpful. She opened up J. Winston Coleman Jr.'s photographic collection to me, and then patiently converted those photographs to digital form for me twice! I am very grateful. I must say, it was wonderful going through Coleman's collection. I remember viewing so much of it as a lad. Winston Coleman was a great friend. He would frequently call me up, and I would ride my bicycle to his house and spend the day with him looking at his vast collections and just "talking history." It was such great fun. I am proud that some of his magnificent photographs adorn this book. I will never forget Winston Coleman.

I also want to thank the Filson Historical Society, the Kentucky Historical Society, the Southern Historical Collection at the University of North Carolina at Chapel Hill, and the Alabama Department of Archives and History for permission to use the wonderful illustrations from their collections.

My good friend and college classmate Dr. Dan Rush, of Kingsport, Tennessee—formerly from Fern Creek, Kentucky—traveled with me on tours of Morgan's great raids, along with his brother, Dr. Neil Rush of Cynthiana. Dan provided me with the transcript of *The Vidette*, a newspaper printed by Morgan's command in Hopkinsville, Kentucky, on October 28, 1862, recounting the action at "Ashland." Save for Basil W. Duke's recounting of the action in his *History of Morgan's Cavalry*, it is to my knowledge the only Confederate version of the brief encounter ever printed. Dan also provided me with valuable information about Major George Washington Morgan, who was mortally wounded at "Ashland." My longtime friend Bill Penn of Cynthiana provided a wonderful stream of material on the Battle of Cynthiana. Even more remarkable than those materials, he located

ACKNOWLEDGMENTS

a copy of the *Louisville Daily Journal* of July 26, 1862, that included a memoir of Morgan's command entering Midway, Kentucky. It must be the only such memoir in existence. Thank you, Dan and Bill.

I also want to thank Laura Sutton and Stephen Wrinn at the University Press of Kentucky for their faith in this project and their tireless efforts in its realization. Their efforts made a critical difference.

Finally, my dear wife, Genevieve, proofread the manuscript time and time again, making needed suggestions. Moreover, her patience and the patience of my three little ones—Annie, Philip, and Thomas—was wonderful. All of you are my greatest blessings.

NOTE ON THE EDITORIAL METHOD

The original typescript of Porter's war memoirs must have been prepared in the late nineteenth century; it was a literal transcription. A retyping of the original typescript was accomplished in 1927. It was this second typescript that was given to me to publish. It contained some errors that were quickly determined to be typists' mistakes. Most of those were misspellings of words that included extra letters or excluded letters, clearly indicating keystroke errors. Once those typographical errors were corrected, the manuscript still had some problems: there were errors of grammar; some sentences ran for nearly a page or more in length and were very complicated; there were run-on sentences, and some sentences were incomplete; there were numerous paragraphs that had multiple subjects and literally ran on for two or three pages; there was one missing page and another noticeable gap in the narrative for which substitutes and missing fragments were never found; and some individuals were improperly identified or their names were misspelled. Most individuals were identified by Porter only by their surnames, and there were many of them in the manuscript. It seemed as though Porter believed his descendants would know who all those individuals were. To anyone other than those who actually knew the people in the area where Porter lived and with whom he campaigned, the use of only surnames made the manuscript very difficult to read, understand, or even appreciate.

I could not edit the manuscript so much that Porter's wonderful means of expression would be lost. I had to make sure Porter told his own story as he wanted to tell it. The University Press of Kentucky and I called upon Professor James Ramage of Northern Kentucky University, John Hunt Morgan's biographer and a historian who was familiar with the Porter typescript, to provide guidelines for the editing of the manuscript. He graciously provided detailed written recommendations.

Following Ramage's recommendations, I corrected all the misspellings and glaring errors in grammar. That included inserting, where necessary, commas, semicolons, and even periods. It also included the occasional inserting or changing of words to correct the grammar, such as adjusting the verb tense, inserting omitted articles and prepositions, and the like. I separated sentences that were too long and complicated, and disconnected overly lengthy paragraphs. I recrafted the last paragraph of the page before the one missing page and the first paragraph of the page following it, so the story would properly flow, and added two sentences to fill the gap of the second break in the narrative. It was not difficult, as the narratives on the pages before and after the missing page and before and after the second gap were very clear.

I then identified all the individuals mentioned by Porter by locating all of them in the census records of 1850, 1860, and even 1870 when necessary, as well as in the Porter and Hines family histories or in the extant military records, to make sure they were the persons actually referred to by Porter. All individuals mentioned were given their full names and, where appropriate, their correct military ranks held at the times referenced by Porter. I also spelled out abbreviations of titles, regimental numbers, and dates. I also added words to complete some sentences. In those cases, the context of the narrative made the completion of those sentences simple. There were some sentences I rephrased in order to make the meaning more understandable. I also corrected the spelling of names of persons and places where it was necessary.

I broke the manuscript down into fourteen chapters and then annotated it with endnotes so that the reader would be able to fully understand who the individuals Porter mentions were, what roads (keyed to present-day highways and roads) Porter was traveling, and the context in which the events Porter narrates must be placed. At the beginning of each chapter, I wrote an introduction that appears in italics in order that the reader might understand the context of each episode of Porter's narrative. Hopefully, these edited memoirs retain much of Porter's writing style but are given context, completeness, and readability.

INTRODUCTION

John Marion Porter was born at Sugar Grove in eastern Butler County, Kentucky, in 1839. The month and day of his
birth were never recorded. The Sugar Grove settlement
grew up along Little Muddy Creek, a tributary of the Barren
River. Porter was the second child and first son of Reverend
Nathaniel Porter and his second wife, the former Sarah Elizabeth Helm. Altogether, there were nine children born to
the Porters. Three died in infancy; the others, Mary Thomas,
Nancy Virginia, Martha Cullie, Elizabeth Margaret Alice, and
Nathaniel Anthony—along with Francis and Sarah Ann, the
children of Reverend Porter's first marriage—grew up with
John M. Porter on a farm located at Sugar Grove, not far
from the Little Muddy Cumberland Presbyterian Church
where their father was the preacher.[1]

Porter's grandfather, Francis Porter, was a Virginia yeoman farmer. He and two of his four brothers moved to Kentucky from Prince Edward County, Virginia, around 1800.
Francis Porter's brothers, William and John, were veterans
of the Revolutionary War. William Porter, a first lieutenant,
had been wounded at the Battle of Cowpens; John Porter
had attained the rank of colonel. Porter's grandfather, Francis Porter, had something else in common with his brother
William, besides being his sibling; the two brothers married
sisters. Francis married Sallie Carson, and William married
Susan Carson back in Virginia. If that is not enough, Fran-

cis's and William's sister, Anna, married Thomas Carson, brother to Sallie and Susan. Little else is known about them. John M. Porter's knowledge of his ancestors was scant, and the fact that there were no records or writings about them was of great regret to him.[2]

As was so common in the settlement of the lands beyond the Cumberland Mountains, Little Muddy Creek was settled by not only the three Porter brothers and their wives and growing families, but by large numbers of their extended families. The Little Muddy Creek area became the settlement for the Porter, Carson, and Helm families, among others. There, those families flourished, and subsequent generations frequently intermarried. As the years passed, the area became home to a bewildering array of uncles, aunts, cousins, and "kinfolk."

It seems some of those families, like many Virginians who settled Kentucky, were slaveowners. They brought their slaves with them to Kentucky, and they and their slaves, together, cleared the lands, built their houses, and planted and harvested their crops. How many slaves were owned by any of those families was never recorded, but the number was probably very small, as they had little financial resources and the lands they farmed were generally not as large as those in central Kentucky, where slaveowning was on a somewhat larger scale.[3]

John M. Porter's father, Nathaniel Porter, was born on February 8, 1797. Before his marriage to his first wife, Martha Ann Chapman, he became swept up in the great revival movement of the early 1800s. The Porters, like their neighbors, were Presbyterians. As a result of a great revival, Nathaniel Porter became a Cumberland Presbyterian at Mount Moriah Church in Logan County in 1819. The next year, he placed himself under the tutelage of the Logan Presbytery as a candidate for the ministry. Nathaniel was ordained in 1829, three years after his first marriage. It was hardly coincidental that his first wife's father, Reverend Alexander Chapman, was also a Cumberland Presbyterian minister.

For the next fifty years, Reverend Nathaniel Porter preached on a circuit that, at times, included Ohio, Daviess, Breckinridge, and Grayson counties, as well as counties along the upper Green River. For much of that ministry, Nathaniel was the preacher at Little Muddy Cumberland Presbyterian Church, a one-and-one-half-story structure just north of Sugar Grove made entirely of large chestnut logs.[4]

Reverend Nathaniel Porter was a very enterprising man. He successfully operated a dry goods store with his brother, Frank Porter, and his wife's brother, Owen Helm, out of a log structure he constructed in 1844 on his farm at Sugar Grove. Nathaniel farmed parts of more than 1,200 acres of land. It was Reverend Nathaniel Porter who gave Sugar Grove its name, and the village still bears that name today.[5]

Nathaniel would live until 1871; his second wife, Sarah Elizabeth, died the next year. They both joined many of their kinfolk who had predeceased them in the little graveyard alongside Little Muddy Cumberland Presbyterian Church. Those not buried there had joined the earliest settlers of Porters, Carsons, and Helms in the old family graveyard at Sugar Grove.[6]

Little is known of John M. Porter's childhood. Neither Porter nor any family member left any record of it. One has to assume he spent it helping his family farm the land. If he wasn't working in the fields, he was helping with the dry goods store. He fished, hunted, and went swimming in the creeks and the Barren and Green rivers. Many of his social interactions probably came about through functions held at the Little Muddy Cumberland Presbyterian Church.

As with many deeply religious families, reading the Bible was the evening routine for the Porters. John M. Porter reflected fondly on that aspect of his life at Sugar Grove in his war reminiscences. His reading skills undoubtedly enabled him to study law. In the census of 1860, John M. Porter was still living in his parents' house, but he was listed as a "law student." He studied law under Vincent S. Hay, Esq., in Morgantown, Kentucky, the county seat of Butler County. By 1860, Porter may well have joined the local Masonic lodge; he seems to intimate that he was a Freemason when he recalls his months as a prisoner of war.[7]

War interrupted Porter's plans to become a lawyer. He joined the cause of the fledgling Confederate States. Unlike many families in Butler County, the Porters were slaveowners, as were many of their immediate neighbors in Sugar Grove. Maybe because of that, but most likely because so many of his family members and friends in and around Sugar Grove and in neighboring Logan, Simpson, and Warren counties supported the Southern cause, Porter identified with those in the seceding states. Porter, however, never articulated exactly why he fought for the Confederacy, other than to say he fought for freedom and against tyranny. To say more than what has been written by Porter here would be pure speculation. Interestingly, most people in Butler County were pro-Union, a fact that must have made Porter's decision to fight for the Confederacy all the more difficult for him and his family.

Porter joined the Confederate Army at nearby Bowling Green, in Warren County, Kentucky. He entered the service with his friend and kinsman Thomas Henry Hines. The Hines family hailed from Campbell and Charlotte counties in Virginia. The first Hineses to settle in Kentucky found lands in Butler and Warren counties. They too were Revolutionary War veterans. Like the Porters, the Hineses were mostly Presbyterians, although some were Methodists. Also like the Porters, the Hineses were modest slaveowners.[8]

Thomas Henry Hines was born on October 9, 1838, to Warren Walker Hines and his wife, the former Sarah Jimeson Carson of Woodbury, Butler County, Kentucky. Woodbury was, and is, a small hamlet on the Green River only a few miles north of the Little Muddy Cumberland Presbyterian Church. It was through the Carson family that John Marion Porter and Thomas Henry Hines were related.[9]

John Marion Porter and Thomas Henry Hines knew one another well before the Civil War. They were almost inseparable during the war as commissioned officers in Company E of the Ninth Kentucky Cavalry, part of John Hunt Morgan's command. Porter was a lieutenant; Hines was a captain.

Hines would lead an almost larger-than-life role after he and most of John Hunt Morgan's command were captured in eastern Ohio in July 1863. Hines became the mastermind behind Morgan's escape from the Ohio State Penitentiary in Columbus, Ohio, in November 1863, and then, from Canada, he became the organizer of a conspiracy among Confederate operatives and anti-Lincoln "Copperheads" in Illinois and Indiana to free Confederate prisoners of war at Camp Douglas Prison and Rock Island Prison in Illinois and Camp Morton Prison in Indiana, and to take over the governments of Illinois, Indiana, and Ohio. Although the conspiracy collapsed, Hines gained the reputation of being "the most dangerous man in the Confederacy."[10]

John M. Porter was a prisoner of war at Johnson's Island Prisoner of War Depot in Sandusky Bay, Ohio, for nineteen months; he returned to his native Butler County at war's end. Porter married Mary Bell Burch of Hart County, Kentucky. The couple had one daughter, Minnie Bell, who, wrote Porter later, was "the light of [his] life." Porter's wife died on July 11, 1868, probably from complications due to childbirth. He buried her alongside her family members at Mt. Gilead Church in Hart County, the same site he visited as a cavalryman during Morgan's famous "Christmas Raid" in December 1862. One gets the idea that Porter was never very well after the war, and the death of his wife was almost more than he could bear.[11]

Porter was admitted to the practice of law in Morgantown, the county seat of Butler County, in 1868, and he began practicing there. Two years later he moved to Bowling Green and entered into a partnership with none other than his wartime comrade and kinsman Thomas Henry Hines. That partnership was probably initiated by Hines in an effort to aid his ailing and grieving cousin. In Bowling Green, though, lived Porter's two sisters, Martha Cullie Porter McKay and her family and Elizabeth Margaret Alice Porter, a spinster, as well as his young unmarried brother, Nathaniel Anthony Porter. Porter's sisters and brother must have also encouraged his move. In due time, Thomas Henry Hines and his wife, the former Nancy Sproule of Woodbury, would have two children, a daughter, Alice, and a son, William.[12]

Porter was elected commonwealth's attorney for Warren County and briefly served in that capacity. Hines was elected to the Kentucky Court of Appeals, then Kentucky's highest court, in 1878 and served as chief justice from 1884 to 1886.[13]

John M. Porter died on June 26, 1884; he was only forty-five years of age. Although there is no record of the circumstances surrounding Porter's death, one has to suspect that his nineteen-month incarceration at Johnson's Island Prisoner of War Depot and his exposure to the frigid and crowded conditions there were contributing factors. Porter was buried in the McKay family plot in Fairview Cemetery in Bowling Green. Fourteen years later, on January 23, 1898, Thomas Henry Hines died. He, too, was buried in Fairview Cemetery, just across the narrow lane from Porter. In death, as in life, the two were inseparable.[14]

Porter wrote his war reminiscences, entitled "A Brief

Account of What I Saw and Experienced During the War for Southern Independence," in, probably, 1872, while he was living in Bowling Green and practicing law with Thomas Henry Hines. That his family's history had been lost and his own service during the Civil War would be lost if he did not write his memoirs were of great concern to him. "To address this defect as to my own military service, so far as I can, is one motive behind this memoir," Porter wrote in the preface to his war reminiscences. Thus, so future generations of his own family would know what he did during the war, Porter penned these memoirs. That they are published here for a twenty-first-century world to read would probably be beyond Porter's wildest dreams.

Although Porter appears to have been a very humble and modest man, he does extol the prowess and virtues of his fellow Confederates, and of the men in Morgan's command in particular. Even though his war reminiscences were not written to be published, Porter, nevertheless, frequently interjects in them his belief in the justness and rightness of the cause for which he fought. He clearly wanted his descendants to understand that his motives to fight for the Confederacy were just.

Porter paints the Civil War as a conflict between right (his cause) and wrong, freedom (for which he fought) and tyranny. In that sense, Porter wrote like so many other Confederate veterans who penned reminiscences; he wrote them to uphold what he believed were the virtues of the Confederacy and those who fought for it and to rebut the writings of the victors, which hailed the Civil War as a victory over the wrongs of slavery. These reminiscences may thus be understood by some to be Porter's small, very private contribution to what David W. Blight refers to as the "literary wars" of memory that marked memoirs written by veterans of both sides of the conflict in post–Civil War America.[15]

Porter's war reminiscences are positively authentic. The copy provided to me by Steve Carson of Lexington, Kentucky, a collateral descendant of Porter, is one of four that I know to exist. One copy is owned by Porter's collateral kin Cora Jane Spiller of Bowling Green, Kentucky, another is in the collections of Western Kentucky University, while a fourth is in the collection of the Tennessee State Library and Archives in Nashville.

The authenticity of Porter's war reminiscences can be found in the text itself. Every individual named by Porter—and there are many—was found. If the person was in the army, he was located in the correct military unit as related in the story. If he or she was a civilian, the location of his or her residence mentioned by Porter matches the records. Porter's kinship to many of the individuals mentioned by him was ultimately confirmed in every instance. Porter's reminiscences of his travels during his military operations are readily traceable by the use of modern-day Kentucky county roadmaps. Where Porter identifies dates for specific military operations, they are correct. Frankly, I found Porter's memory of names, dates, and the details of his military exploits to be absolutely remarkable.

John Marion Porter's war reminiscences form a remarkable record of the Civil War in Kentucky and Tennessee. Apart from that, they represent one of the very few war reminiscences extant that were penned by members of Morgan's command. That and the stirring events about which Porter writes make his memoirs so extraordinarily valuable and compelling.

PREFACE

I propose to place upon record a narrative of events, commencing during the year 1861, continuing through the sanguinary years of 1861–1865, embracing the period of the War for Southern Independence, and closing with the final surrender of the Confederate Armies to the forces of the United States. I propose to present how, in a few brief months, the whole country was roused to arms; how, in a short time, the citizens of every hill and valley, every plain and mountain, every city and town in Kentucky, from the Big Sandy to the mouth of the Tennessee River, from Kentucky's mountain gaps to her lowlands, were driven to almost frantic excitement by the near approach to her borders of hostile armies. I propose to present how her citizens, deluded by the cry of "neutrality," deemed that they were secure from the Confederate army upon the one side and from the armies of the United States upon the other, until, bound too securely, they found her borders trod at almost the same moment by troops in Southern and Northern uniforms, in whose bosoms rankled the bitterest hate towards each other.

And, while I shall give an account of many things which shall be personal to myself and concerning those who were and are still dear to me by reason of an association of four long and eventful years, I trust that the charge of egotism will not be made or inferred from the manner in which I write, and from the frequent use of the first person. To make this record what I desire it to be necessitates the style of composition I adopt. Julius Caesar, in giving to his countrymen—and through them to the world and to us—his excellent and incomparable history of the Gallic Wars speaks always of himself in the third person and thus avoids any idea of egotism. If that course is not adopted here it is because it cannot be done so as to render this record all that I wish it to be.

It should be the desire of every one to preserve for his family everything of importance which has occurred and which is occurring. I have often regretted that I know so little of the family, or, I should rather say, of the ancestry whose name I bear. Farther back than the war of the Revolution in 1776, my knowledge is meager and vague indeed. That some of my ancestors, not more than one generation removed, were participants in that war is undoubtedly true. But, beyond this, the information in my possession is limited, except that they were of Scotch-Irish descent and emigrated at an early day to the Colony of Virginia, and settled in the vicinity of the Staunton River and Appomattox River. This want of information exists because there has been no record kept, so far as I know, by any member of a very numerous and now widely dispersed family.

To supply this defect, so far as I can, is one motive to this attempt. If those who come after me are in any wise gratified with this record, or if they are by this means made familiar with the stirring events which occurred while I served in the Confederate States Army, and if they take an interest in reading what I have here written, all my desires will be satisfied.

I dedicate these pages to those whom I love tenderly and of whom I am proud, feeling confident that their charity as a mantle will cover all its defects, and that their interest in it will prompt them to preserve it and hand it down as an heirloom, as it were, to those who come after them.

John M. Porter

1

TO THE MILITARY
I SUBMITTED MYSELF

The election of Abraham Lincoln in November 1860 plunged Kentucky into turmoil. John M. Porter became caught up in the political furor. His home county of Butler was divided, but most people in the county were staunchly pro-Union. Porter and most of his family members and friends in the southeastern Butler County village called Sugar Grove, though, were decidedly pro-Southern. In January 1861, during the height of the secession crisis, Kentucky's pro-Southern governor, Beriah Magoffin, called the state legislature into special session for it to consider Kentucky's joining her "sister" Southern states and seceding from the Union. After months of legislative stalemate, news arrived in Kentucky of the surrender of Fort Sumter and of Lincoln's call for 75,000 troops to "suppress the rebellion." Tennessee seceded from the Union and began arming its border with Kentucky after Governor Magoffin declared Kentucky's neutrality on May 20. Magoffin had not been able to muster the votes for secession. Fort Henry on the Tennessee River, Fort Donelson on the Cumberland River, and the fort at Island Number 10 on the Mississippi River—all situated just below the Kentucky border—were constructed to defend Tennessee.

Simon Bolivar Buckner, a native of Hart County, Kentucky, commanded the pro-Southern Kentucky State Guard before the war. He and most of his officer corps, honoring Kentucky's neutrality, went to Clarksville,

11

Tennessee, where they raised elements of at least four Kentucky infantry regiments and a battery of Kentucky artillery for Confederate service.

General Albert Sidney Johnston, a native of Mason County, Kentucky, and one of the most respected and senior military commanders in the nation on the eve of the Civil War, assumed command of Confederate Department No. 2, which included Kentucky, with headquarters at Nashville, Tennessee, in September 1861. Major General Leonidas Polk moved his Confederate force protecting west Tennessee to Columbus, Kentucky, on the Mississippi River, early that month; Brigadier General Ulysses S. Grant countered by moving his Federal army from Cairo, Illinois, to the mouths of the Tennessee and Cumberland rivers at Paducah and Smithland, Kentucky, respectively. Johnston then ordered newly commissioned Brigadier General Buckner to move his division from Clarksville to Bowling Green, Kentucky, a key center on the Louisville and Nashville Railroad.

At Bowling Green Porter joined a company of couriers and scouts at General Buckner's headquarters known as "Buckner's Guides." Buckner moved elements of his division along the L&N as far north as the southern bank of the Green River at Woodsonville, Kentucky. Buckner was soon joined at Bowling Green by another Confederate division under the command of newly commissioned Major General William J. Hardee. Bowling Green became General Johnston's headquarters. Kentucky was the front line of a civil war, and Kentuckians were playing dominant roles in the drama.

To enter into the details of the contest for the establishment of the Confederate States of America, to speak of the causes and consequences of that contest, or even to speak minutely of affairs in Kentucky during 1861 and the four following years, would seem to be a work of supererogation. No such general features will be given here for the reason that all those facts can be learned from the history of the times; only a few words will be said, enough only to afford a starting point. All else must needs be gathered from sources within the reach of all.

The first divisions among the states, which afterwards assumed greater proportions and grew wider, occurred during the Presidential canvass of the year 1860. Four candidates were then before the people for that position. Three of these, John Cabell Breckinridge, Stephen A. Douglas and John Bell, had each a respectable party both in numbers and influence in Kentucky. The other, Abraham Lincoln, had very few adherents. The friends of the first three were zealous and active for the success of their respective candidates, and all were equally hostile and unfriendly to the election of Lincoln. The result of the contest throughout the entire United States left the friends of the first three beaten, disappointed and chagrined. What course were the three defeated candidates to pursue? Would they favor the South? Or, would they still cling to the Union? The friends of Breckinridge, with great unanimity, chose to lend their aid and give their sympathies to the cause of the South. A very considerable number of Douglas and of Bell adherents also were in favor of the South and her principles; others were for the Union and the doctrine of neutrality. Thus Kentucky, in a short time, was in such a commotion as had never before been, and which I hope may never again be, witnessed.[1]

To say that I was ardently attached to the South would be only indicative of my subsequent career. Even from the time of the election of Lincoln, and especially from the time of the fall of Fort Sumter, I had determined, in the event of war, to join the standard of the South. Surrounded in my native county of Butler by men who, by a very large majority, were opposed to the action of the Southern States, excitement was of course high and feelings were anything but amicable.[2]

Upon one occasion, I think it was in August 1861, the Unionists assembled in several companies at Morgantown for the purpose of drilling and receiving instructions in military tactics under the direction and leadership of Pierce B. Hawkins, afterwards a colonel in the Federal army. Notwithstanding our great minority, some forty or fifty Southern sympathizers determined to meet and drill as cavalry in the same town at the same time. Our presence upon the parade ground, within one hundred yards of those who could then be considered our enemies, was evidence that we were not being intimidated nor driven from our purpose.[3]

Upon the countenances of all could be seen evidence of great dissatisfaction, but their prudence bade them to beware, and no hostile demonstrations were made toward us. We were commanded by Thomas E. Puckett, an old Virginia militia officer, and at present living in Butler County. This organization was maintained for some time, but was finally disorganized by reason of the loss of those of its members who gradually seemed disposed to remain at home to enjoy the society and smile of their friends rather than undergo the dangerous consequences of entering the contest which all felt would be terrible in its nature.[4]

I have no word of complaint to utter against those who did not enter the army, and I have no animadversions to put down. It was simply a question which each had to decide for himself, and each did of his own volition decide the issue. I have no regrets at my course, and were the same circumstances to again arise, the same course would be pursued, conscious of its justice and rectitude, and with a feeling of pride such as then moved me.

The seventeenth day of September 1861 will long be remembered by the people of southern Kentucky. On that day, Brigadier General Simon Bolivar Buckner advanced by the Louisville and Nashville Railroad with a Confederate force from Camps Boone and Trousdale in Tennessee to Bowling Green, occupying that place, and sending a por-

Brigadier General Simon Bolivar Buckner of Hart County, Kentucky, John M. Porter's first commander. Buckner surrendered the Confederate forces at Fort Donelson on February 16, 1862. (Library of Congress.)

tion of his army farther up on the railroad to Green River bridge at Munfordville. Great indeed was the rejoicing of the Southern sympathizers, and greater was the dismay of the Union-neutrality element. Many of the latter party hastily left their homes and sought places beyond Confederate control, while daily were seen the other class winding their way from all parts of the country to see the Southern soldiers, give them of their plentiful stores, and speak words of commendation. Every neighborhood was in confusion. It was not infrequently the case that persons on their way to join the Federal army were met by others on their way to enlist in the cause of the South.[5]

A few days after Bowling Green had been occupied by the Confederates under General Buckner, he started a portion of his army westward to Rochester, in Butler County, for the purpose of engaging in battle or frightening away a small camp of Federals at that place under command of Colonel P. B. Hawkins. That camp had been formed a few weeks previously, and the men there were actively engaged in recruiting and drilling. General Buckner advanced from Bowling Green with a brigade infantry, about three hundred cavalry and a few pieces of artillery. He headed toward the Green River and, at "Frank Jackson's," moved on with his command by "Lewis's" and "Captain Ben Davis's" places. He halted at Berry's Lick where the men rested a day or so. By the time he reached Berry's Lick he had learned that there was no probability of having an engagement at Rochester, for the gallant defenders and protectors of the "Old Flag," having deemed the north side of the Green River safer than the south side, had crossed over, and were on their way, "a la Gilpin," towards a more *advantageous position*.[6]

After remaining at Berry's Lick for a short time enjoying the hospitality of some of the good citizens, General Buckner moved on to Rochester, crossed the Mud River, and, after

Federal troops of the Army of the Ohio on the north bank of the Green River in the fall of 1861. (From a woodcut in *Frank Leslie's Illustrated Newspaper,* January 18, 1862, Martin F. Schmidt Collection of Kentucky Views, 2004.41, Kentucky Historical Society, Frankfort, Kentucky.)

partially destroying the lock and dam on the Green River at that place, proceeded with his army by way of Greenville to Hopkinsville. From there, in a week or two, he moved back to Bowling Green. Although no opportunity was offered to measure Buckner's strength with the enemy, the expedition was by no means unproductive of good. It dispelled the idea, which until then prevailed in the minds of many persons, that Southern soldiers were a set of murderers and cut throats. Furthermore, it was an opportune time for those who were desirous of joining the army to do so, and many did. It is proper to say that no evil demonstrations were made; no persons were arrested for trivial causes and thrown into prison, but protection was given to all so far as could be done. Forage and commissary stores were bought at a fair price and paid for punctually. Anything which citizens had

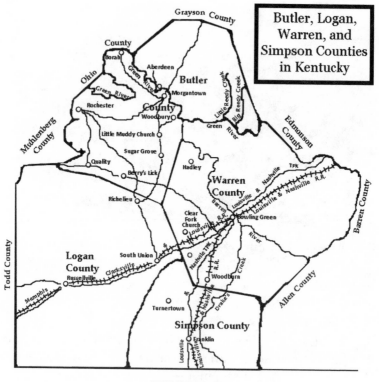

Butler, Logan, Warren, and Simpson Counties in Kentucky

to sell commanded a good price. Horses, cattle, hogs, wheat, corn and other goods were collected, and, in many cases, farmers received in exchange purses of gold. Such an army as this was not likely to make enemies even in an unfriendly country, but rather friends. A great contrast surely compared with some Federal commanders who ruled in Kentucky at a time subsequent to this.[7]

About the second day of November 1861, I enlisted as a soldier of the Confederate States of America by taking an oath to bear true and faithful allegiance to the name. I was sworn into service by Captain James W. Johnson of First Kentucky Cavalry (C.S.A.), which was at the time camped in "Underwood Grove."[8]

Captain Alonzo Ridley, afterwards colonel, having come from California to Richmond, Virginia, in company with General Albert Sidney Johnston, and who had followed the general to Bowling Green, was at this time recruiting a company whose duty it should be to act as guides and scouts for the army. He brought to his position much experience obtained from his mode of life in the far west. Added to this was a mind that was naturally strong, though self-educated; it fitted him well for the station. He was of fine form and handsome appearance, though rough in manners and in conversation. At the time he first recruited his company and for some time afterwards I had no particular regard for him. But afterwards, when I met him in 1863 in prison at Johnson's Island, Ohio, I learned his nature more perfectly than I had before known, and came to think well of him. He was a brave and gallant man, and of a strong, native mind.[9]

To the military discipline of such a man I submitted myself about November 2, 1861. His company, known as "Buckner's Guides," was officered as follows: Alonzo Ridley, Captain; Thomas H. Hines, First Lieutenant; J. H. Burnam, Second Lieutenant; John A. Warfield, Third Lieutenant; John H. Hines, Orderly Sergeant; and, as Forage Master, W. P. Roberts, whose duty it was to provide forage for our horses. As the object of the organization was to furnish guides and scouts for the army, it received the name as above given, which it retained till it was disbanded. To attain as far as possible the object desired, one or more men from various counties were received into its ranks.

For the sake of preserving the company register as nearly accurate as may be, I insert here the names of all whom I now

General Albert Sidney Johnston, the first Confederate commander in the trans-Appalachian west, who died at Shiloh, April 6, 1862. (Library of Congress.)

remember and also their respective counties. Warren County: Thomas Buckner, Thomas Robinson, R. N. Heard, W. Curtis May, William Adams, Richard Sublett, Thomas Biggs, Ward McDonald, George W. Logan, John Starks, Edward L. Hines,

J. W. Rasdell and Henry C. Hines, Hiram V. Dulaney, and Tubal S. McDaniel; Butler County: Andy Kuykendall, Hezekiah I. Kuykendall, Reuben M. Johnson, Dempsey Burton Bailey and John M. Porter; Hardin County: Joseph S. Gray; Nelson County: George W. Gregg and James M. Cook; Bullitt County: Henry C. Magruder; Meade County: John Morrow; Lincoln County: Porter Crow and Thomas Shanks; Boyle County: Samuel McBride; and Ohio County: William Hines, and William Skinner from New Mexico or California, a Confederate who journeyed with Captain Ridley. There were a number of others whose names have passed from my memory. Many of the above names attained an enviable reputation for gallantry on more than a score of bloody fields throughout the South.[10]

Five persons from the above list were from Butler County and were privates in this company. Of course, when any important scout was necessary to be made westward from Bowling Green some or all of that number were required to go. That was a very important flank of the army and was watched very closely by the generals commanding the Confederate forces. Many and many a night was I roused from sleep in my tent with orders to repair at once to headquarters for instructions about the mission I should undertake. And, after having received the necessary orders with an injunction of caution, the countersign would be whispered in my ear, and the next moment the sentinel at the door would receive orders to pass me out. Then three or four of us, mounted upon fleet and spirited horses, would dash out into the darkness toward the Morgantown Road. A stern command of "Halt" would greet our ears a few miles out of town. After approaching and giving the pickets the countersign, we would ride on and be alone in the darkness and our own thoughts. How can I, or any one, describe the thoughts which would rush through the minds of such as are on duty at once so dangerous and so important? One moment our spirits were in keeping with the cause we were serving, but then a presentiment passed before our minds that perhaps it was our last ride over that road. We would, for a time, remain silent, each busy with his own reflections, but intent upon serving his country in any way in which he might perchance be ordered.

Our destination was often Morgantown, Woodbury and Rochester, and though it was attended with no very great open danger, it was by no means devoid of peril. Anyone familiar with the sentiment of that portion of the country at that time, must and will confess that there was enough danger in those expeditions to give a relish to those of an adventurous mind and daring spirit. Man is buoyed up and carried to the cannon's mouth by pride and excitement. In the heat of the action he may, perhaps, rather like the fray, or it may be that he does not care to think of his *danger*, but rather of his *duty*. Now and then, when out on these trips, we would call and see our friends at home, eat at a table and use a knife and fork, a towel, take off our hats and act like we had previously done.

The assistance rendered to the army and to the commanders by means of these scouts was very great. In every direction, from Bowling Green towards the enemy, these parties were continually away on the outposts and very frequently entirely within the lines of the enemy. Many sharp skirmishes, among the first fighting in the State, were brought on by assistance given the cavalry in piloting detachments to the enemy's positions. At times our company was called on to escort General Albert Sidney Johnston, or Major General William J. Hardee, or General Buckner to different positions in and around the Confederate lines. Several points on the Barren River were visited with a view of fortifying them against the enemy.[11]

2

YOU HAVE CROWNED YOURSELVES WITH GLORY

General Grant moved elements of his Federal army—soon to be known as the "Army of the Tennessee"—on troop transports up the Tennessee River from Paducah, Kentucky, with Flag Officer Andrew H. Foote's armada of gunboats in early February 1862. On February 6, Foote's naval forces bombarded Fort Henry on the east bank of the Tennessee, forcing its surrender by Brigadier General Lloyd Tilghman within seventy-nine minutes. Grant disembarked his land forces at Fort Henry and moved them twelve miles east to besiege Fort Donelson, situated on the west bank of the Cumberland River, while a fleet of gunboats ascended the Cumberland from Smithland, Kentucky, to bombard the fort. General Johnston called upon Buckner, with elements of his division then at Russellville, Kentucky, to reinforce Fort Donelson while the rest of the Confederate army evacuated Kentucky. Buckner ordered John M. Porter to accompany him. Porter thus found himself in Fort Donelson.

Grant's army arrived in front of the outer works of Fort Donelson on February 12. In command of the Confederate forces there, about 18,000 strong, was Brigadier General John B. Floyd of Virginia. Brigadier General Gideon J. Pillow of Tennessee and General Buckner commanded the two divisions forming the garrison. The Confederate lines extended more

23

than three miles, from just east of Dover, Tennessee, on the river, all the way around Fort Donelson to nearly one mile west of it, also on the river.

The Confederate defenders turned back a Federal naval assault on February 14. Confederate ground assaults on February 15 actually broke through the Federal lines and gained possession of the Charlotte and Forge roads to Nashville, but General Pillow ordered the troops withdrawn. That night General Pillow and General Floyd left the fort, fearing what would happen to them if captured, leaving General Buckner to surrender the garrison. The surrender conference took place on February 16 in the Dover Tavern, Buckner's headquarters in Dover, Tennessee, between Buckner and Grant, former classmates at the U.S. Military Academy. Grant demanded that Buckner surrender "unconditionally," which Buckner reluctantly agreed to do. Porter became a prisoner of war. General Johnston withdrew his Confederate forces from Kentucky altogether. They first occupied Nashville and then Murfreesboro, Tennessee.

It became necessary toward the last of December 1861, around Christmas, to strengthen the Confederate forces at Fort Henry on the Tennessee River and Fort Donelson on the Cumberland River, both of which were menaced by Federal troops. General Buckner moved with a few thousand men to Russellville. The ostensible object of the move was to be in a position from which he could move, as soon as the roads were passable, to attack Brigadier General Thomas L. Crittenden, then in command of a considerable force of the enemy at Calhoun, on the Green River. But the real purpose was to be within aiding distance of Fort Donelson, if it should become necessary to reinforce that position.[1]

The wisdom and necessity of this movement was soon made obvious. Already, the enemy had profited by some experience and resorted to famous flank movements, the only way for them to force General Johnston from his position at Bowling Green. A formidable fleet of vessels under the command of Flag Officer Andrew Foote and a large Federal army under Brigadier General Ulysses S. Grant, in February 1862, ascended the Cumberland River for the purpose of reducing Fort Donelson. Brigadier General Lloyd Tilghman had been forced to surrender the Confederate forces at Fort Henry on the Tennessee River, only twelve miles west of Fort Donelson. The rivers were only some twelve miles apart at those points. Upon General Buckner learning that the Federals were moving on Fort Donelson, he moved his command from Russellville as expeditiously as possible to the fort, which was destined, in a few days, to witness bloody and terrible scenes.

Before General Buckner left Bowling Green, he detached from the "Guides" Joseph S. Gray, Dempsey Burton Bailey, Thomas Robinson, J. W. Rasdell, Reuben M. Johnson and myself, to proceed with him to Russellville. After remaining for two or three weeks at Russellville, scouting very often in the vicinity of the enemy at Calhoun and South Carrollton, we were ordered to move with the army to Fort Donelson. Arriving at Clarksville, we halted a few days, and then, crossing the Cumberland River on coal barges, we proceeded over the rough country to the fort, where we arrived on Wednesday, February twelfth, at about two o'clock in the afternoon.[2]

The fight had already begun, but only the cavalry had been engaged, commanded by Lieutenant Colonel Nathan Bedford Forrest. For some two or three hours before we got there, we had heard the firing and knew that the crisis was at hand, and we eagerly hurried forward to take part in whatever might occur. The Federal lines were closing in on every side, and but little space intervened between the Federal right wing and the Confederate left, which reached to the river. Through that narrow space on the Confederate left, growing still narrower every hour, we rode, and when once inside the lines of the Confederates, we then appreciated

Brigadier General Ulysses S. Grant as he appeared in the winter and early spring of 1862. (Library of Congress.)

the situation. The Cumberland River, very high from recent rains, was in our rear, and an army three times the size of our own was in our front, extending from a point on the river below the fort, in a semi-circular form, to a point on the river above it. Added to this was a large fleet of vessels just down the river, ready to advance and bombard the fort and reduce it by their enormous guns. This was the situation of affairs.[3]

Our troops were disposed in excellent order, and through the openings in the woods could be seen the movements of the enemy as if in confusion and haste. The country there is very broken, hill after hill arises in irregular order, with timber upon all the soil. From one hill I could see the enemy upon another, a deep hollow between, with a thick *abatis* separating the hostile forces. The weather for a few days previous had been pleasant, but on the night of the twelfth it became extremely cold, and on the morning of the thirteenth our army found itself half frozen, with the enemy in large numbers just in front.[4]

Our line extended in a semi-circular form from the fort below to a point on the Cumberland River, above the town of Dover, Tennessee. The arc was about three miles in length; the river was in a swollen stage in the background. The line of the enemy assumed the same shape, their left resting on the river below our right, and connecting with their fleet of gunboats and transports; their right wing was above our left and rested on the head of a slough which ran at right angles to the river. The little town of Dover at once became full of bustle and confusion, which was greatly increased about dark on the evening of the twelfth, by a few shots from the enemy's batteries upon land which came whistling through the air, some striking houses, some going beyond the town and plunging in the angry waters of the river, some falling in the rifle pits among the soldiers or plowing up the ground nearby. The night became quiet after a time. During the long weary hours nothing was heard, save now and then a shot from the faithful sentinels ever on the alert.

It was extremely cold, and in the early hours of the night a gentle snow fell. The ground was frozen hard. I think it was the brave and daring Thomas Robinson and Dempsey Burton Bailey who, with myself, threw a blanket over a brush pile, and, by tearing away an opening large enough, crept under it and occupied a very small space. There we passed the night in a freezing way, not more than ten paces from our works. Ever and anon during the long and dreadful night the sharp reports of firearms told us that the enemy too was out on his line of defense.[5]

Slowly and gloomily the hours passed away. Morning came and we arose from our bed to look upon our first battlefield. The batteries of the Confederates under the command of Captain Rice E. Graves and Captain Thomas K. Porter had been placed in fine positions, and about this time sent forth their first hostile greetings toward the enemy. Ere long, the conflict began, and, for the first time, but by no means the last, we heard the music of the battlefield, the buzzing of small balls, the screaming of shells, the rumbling explosion and the shrieks of the unfortunate. One would almost have to ask himself if he were not dreaming before he could at first realize the situation. It was no dream, but a reality, a contest between Freedom and Tyranny. It was a shock of arms in which right was battling against wrong. The day wore on. We gained it. Would that we could have maintained it.[6]

Friday the fourteenth came, clear though cold; still, the snow in a measure had disappeared. No general fighting occurred during the day along the line, only skirmishing and sharpshooting. Attention was directed away from the front and centered on the river and the fort. The gunboats were ascending to attack the fort. Would it be able to repel the attack? That was the all important question. It did repel the attack. The close of the day showed two or three of the vessels disabled, and all of them driven off; they retired to a secure spot down the river out of reach of the guns of the fort. The night passed with nothing of interest except that the enemy was massing his forces and bringing up reinforcements.[7]

Saturday the fifteenth dawned, and many who saw the sun rise on that morning beheld its rising beams for the last time. Ere the rays cast from its western pathway fell upon the slanting hillsides around Dover, the spirits of many had gone up from a field red with carnage to the God of Battles. It was a fearful day, a day of terrible fighting. Dead bodies, here, there and almost everywhere round told how hard and severe had been the contest, how they had fought, and how they had died with their faces to the foe, and their guns to their faces. For two or three miles upon our right the enemy had been driven in great confusion and with immense loss. Outnumbered on our right five to one, a portion of our line at night-fall was in the possession of the enemy. Darkness found us thus situated. We had gained the day; we had driven the enemy, but had not sufficient force to maintain our success. Reinforcements were constantly coming to the enemy, while we were getting no aid.[8]

No longer could the contest be waged. A vague idea of surrendering passed in the minds of many who banished it in a moment, and, grasping their weapons with a firmer hand, they begged to be again led forth to battle with the enemy. Gloomy indeed were the reflections when it became almost certain that the morrow's sun would arise on a defeated and imprisoned, though by no means a conquered, army.

Tennessee was there in the person of her gallant sons who felt the proud satisfaction that their duty had been heroically performed. The Mississippians, with tearful eyes, looked towards the far-off South, their own home, conscious that the pristine valor of their State had been maintained upon that field, as twenty years before it had been maintained on the plains of Buena Vista. Virginia, too, from the summit of her western ridges, felt that the spirit of George Washington and Patrick Henry were hovering over the hills around Dover. Kentucky, with General Buckner and Colonel Roger Weightman Hanson at the head of the Second Regiment of Infantry, felt a pride akin to that of the ancient Spartans in praising the chivalry of Leonidas and his brave band at the historic pass of Thermopylae. Beating hearts told the deep feeling within, while the compressed lips and defiant eyes spoke louder than words: "Give us one more chance to press our way out upon the left; let us drive back the enemy once more and gain the open country, or find a resting place on the hard fought field." His eyes streaming with tears, General Buckner bid them be content, saying it was folly to sacrifice so many lives to save a few, and added: "You have crowned yourselves with glory" . . . "A prison will not, cannot, tear from your brows the laurels entwined here today."[9]

A few feet in the rear of our line of works on the crest of a hill was a tent which had been put up by Major Samuel K. Hays, brigade quartermaster. Two or three of us were ordered to report to Hays's tent at about, perhaps, nine or ten o'clock at night. Several officers were assembled there and, from them, we learned the surrender of the fort would soon take place a mile distant. One was sent with pieces of breastworks, a token of surrender, to avoid the firing as soon as it should become light enough in the morning.[10]

I was sent with a dispatch to an officer in Dover. The dangerous condition of the road, owing to the ice and deep declivities and darkness and also the desultory firing from the enemy's guns which kept up a continual business during the night, rendered the ride extremely hazardous. My horse fell on a bad piece of road and caught my leg and disabled me for more than two weeks. Even with this mishap, I per-

Colonel Roger Weightman Hanson. (Library of Congress.)

formed my duty and returned in the darkness to my post, after more than once hearing the bullets "zip" by me with the peculiar noise which they make and which is not easily forgotten. The remainder of the night was consumed in similar duties, and morning came, the saddest I had up to that time experienced during my military service, having been only about four or five months in the army.[11]

During the dark hours just preceding the dawn, the shrill sound of "parley" was heard, and the conference between the commanders began. It ended ere long, and Oh! What feelings can be compared to those we experienced when we knew all was done. He who had not slept for four nights lay down by his trusty gun to snatch a moment's well-earned repose to dream of *home* and the loved ones there, of country, liberty, and the *right*. The sun rose joyously, but shone upon sad hearts. Soon long lines of gleaming bayonets, borne by the enemy, came on toward our works. One after another of the gallant regiments of the Confederates were marched out and arms were grounded. Murmurs deep, not loud, ran all round.

Our party of "Guides" wended our way to the little village of Dover, about one mile distant. We all met in town, although we had been engaged during the battle on different parts of the field. Dismounting, we tied our trusty horses— and I might say we loved our horses—and threw ourselves by their sides to await the turn of events. Visions of prisons were before our eyes. One soldier prepared to swim the wide and angry river in our rear, but it was given up as too dangerous. Another proposed that we all mount and swim our horses and escape by that means. But the question was: could our horses stem the swift current and carry us safely over? It was thought not. It was finally agreed, after discussing every possibility of escaping, to calmly await the development of affairs.

Just then a sound broke upon our ears. It was the music

The surrender flag appears on the parapet of Fort Donelson, February 16, 1862. (Editor's collection.)

of the advancing victorious army, and never did music sound to us so much like the wails of the dying. Nearer and still nearer the sound approached, and then up the street a few hundred yards from where we were, we beheld the head of a Yankee regiment with streaming banners, making for the center of the town. We held our place and *looked*. It was, I think, the Forty-fourth Indiana Infantry Regiment. Then a sound from the river indicated that a boat was coming up. It finally approached and landed, and from it came Flag Officer Andrew Foote, the Federal naval officer. He met in the street the colonel of the Indiana Regiment which had just arrived. A body of horsemen came next, comprising General Grant and his staff. General Buckner had already come to town and was at his headquarters.[12]

Flag Officer Foote and General Grant met amid the yells of the enemy's troops. Never during the entire war did the Yankees learn how to utter a decent yell. Their attempts at it were simply ridiculous, not to say hideous. The Confederates, on the other hand, were experts and adept at it; they could not be excelled. Grant and Foote went immediately to the house to meet General Buckner. We saw them meet. It was formal, though after the style of military men. We heard no conversation, and we saw no more of them afterwards.

A large quantity of military stores were thrown open to the Confederates when it was ascertained that a surrender was inevitable, and many soldiers found everything they desired, even whiskey, the soldier's greatest enemy. Sugar was abundant and it was not unusual to see a barrel of whiskey with one head burst out and buckets of the contents taken out, and large quantities of sugar put in. Thus, many soldiers got under the influence of the sweetened dram to a considerable extent. But the sequel can be gathered from what goes before.

About four o'clock in the afternoon of that memorable Sunday, February 16, 1862, we were ordered on board the steamer, *Memphis,* to be convoyed, we knew not where. From one thousand to twelve hundred weary Confederates, crowded together, composed her passengers, or, rather, I should say, *freight,* for there was nothing to remind us of being passengers in the sense it is used. The boat dropped down the river a short distance and remained till next morning. We found but a sorry place to rest, and slept in a damp and filthy part of the vessel. It was damp on account of the vapor and steam, and filthy because it had been used in transporting Federal troops. Sleep, however, *in any place*, is sweet to those who need its refreshing effects, and the night went by without our knowledge.

We went when morning came and moved on down the Cumberland River with many other boats, all bearing prisoners. At Smithland, Kentucky, we entered the Ohio River and then went on down to Paducah, Kentucky, and Cairo, Illinois. It was known that St. Louis was our destination. In due time we ascended the Mississippi and were at St. Louis. There we were anchored in the river opposite the city for some days; I have forgotten how long.

A chance of escaping the fate of being confined in prison was presented, and so Joseph S. Gray, Dempsey Burton Bailey and Dr. Frank Porter and myself availed ourselves of it and fortunately succeeded. Our hope of success was indeed little. A good many civilians had been made prisoners at Fort Donelson and conveyed with the soldiers to St. Louis. Major General Henry Halleck, the Federal commander, whose headquarters were at that time in the city, directed that all the citizens should be sent back to the place of capture and there released. One day a Yankee officer came on the boat and required all the citizens to give him their names to be taken to headquarters and acted upon. By chance, one of our party heard the officer make that announcement, and he immediately proposed that we should all try the chance. Three objected, and the four of us before named consented to the plan, wrote our names on a slip of paper, and gave it to the officer, having very little hope that we would ever again hear anything about it more.[13]

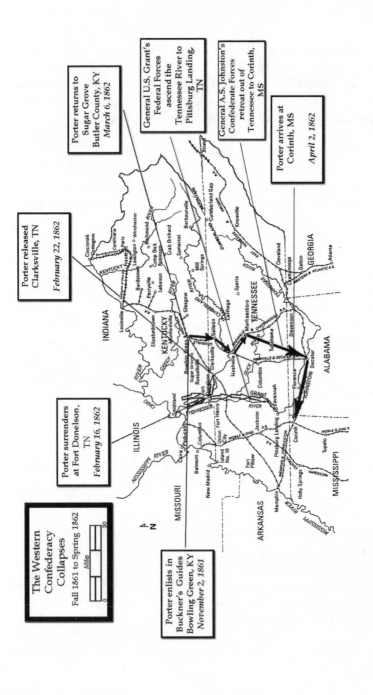

The Western Confederacy Collapses

Fall 1861 to Spring 1862

Miles

Porter released
Clarksville, TN

February 22, 1862

Porter surrenders
at Fort Donelson,
TN

February 16, 1862

Porter enlists in
Buckner's Guides
Bowling Green, KY

November 2, 1861

Porter returns to
Sugar Grove
Butler County, KY

March 6, 1862

General U.S. Grant's
Federal Forces
ascend the
Tennessee River to
Pittsburg Landing,
TN

General A.S. Johnston's
Confederate Forces
retreat out of
Tennessee to Corinth,
MS

Porter arrives at
Corinth, MS

April 2, 1862

Three days afterwards we were on a boat coming back to Fort Donelson. Our names had been included in the number to be released, and when we were called, we gladly responded. No oath of any kind was required, and we took none. I do not deny that it was dissembling and deceiving the enemy, but I am firm in my convictions that we were justified in our action, and am utterly astonished, when I reflect upon it, that more did not make the attempt as we did. Nothing was easier. I venture such an opportunity given a year later would have been crowded with eager applicants. Very few tried it; only four, as I think.

3

IT WAS LITERALLY A LEAP
IN THE DARK

*From the time of John M. Porter's capture at Fort Donelson and his release
to his reaching General Albert Sidney Johnston's army, the strategic picture
in the trans-Appalachian west changed dramatically. With the fall of Forts
Henry and Donelson, General Grant's Federal forces controlled the Tennessee and Cumberland rivers and could move into the interior of the Confederacy at will. General Johnston had no alternative but to withdraw below
those rivers. He selected Corinth, Mississippi, as the site where the widely
scattered elements of his army and other Confederate forces in the Gulf states
could converge. Corinth was the site of the crossing of the north-south Mobile
and Ohio Railroad and the east-west Memphis and Charleston Railroad;
moreover, it was situated below the great bend of the Tennessee River. Covering the rear of Johnston's army as it retreated from Nashville to Murfreesboro
and from Murfreesboro to Decatur, Alabama, and on to Corinth, was Captain John Hunt Morgan's squadron of Kentucky cavalry.*

*After secreting himself home upon his release from captivity, Porter fol-
lowed on horseback in the wake of the retreating Confederate army all the
way to northern Alabama in an effort to rejoin his comrades. All of Kentucky and all of west and central Tennessee were occupied by Federal troops
by then, making Porter's travels perilous.*

In a few days we were again at Dover in view of the field of recent strife. But how different was the scene from the appearance of it when we arrived there from Clarksville on the twelfth of February before. The boat we were on was bound for Nashville, and had a regiment of Yankee cavalry on board. By a little strategy we remained on the boat till we got to Clarksville, although they wanted us to get off at Dover.

When we went ashore at Clarksville we proceeded to a hotel and, although without any money except Confederate currency, the proprietor told us we could stay till morning, it being late in the evening. The proprietor was of the name of Spurrier, the same who keeps at this time the Spurrier House in Louisville. We gave him some Confederate money for his pay, which he was even then willing to take although its circulation had been interdicted by the Yankees, of whom there were, at that time in the city, some nine thousand and perhaps more.[1]

The night was spent at the hotel, and morning found us in no very desirable position. Our desire was to make our way out of the city and get to our homes. The Red River footbridge in the suburbs of Clarksville was strictly picketed by Yankee troops and there was no other means out than over that bridge. The waters were high; all canoes, skiffs, and boats were guarded, and we were compelled to cross that bridge.

Partly by strategy and partly by the influence of friends and by making the impression that we were wood choppers and wanting to go over the river for the purpose of cutting cord wood, we obtained a pass from the officer in command. Thus equipped, we were permitted to go over the bridge and were then ferried across the water from the end of the bridge to the hill on the side next to Russellville, the entire bottom being over-flowed several feet in depth.

After being safely ferried over by the Yankee guards we were on a good turnpike, and, once again, felt free. We felt as if we could walk to our homes during the day and before its close.

We walked on as speedily as possible and continued until, becoming very much fatigued, we halted for the night near Camp Boone at the house of a Mr. Mimms where we were kindly and hospitably entertained by that family who were ardent Southerners. The Mimms's house is on the pike from Clarksville to Russellville.[2]

The next morning Dr. Porter was too unwell to proceed further, and, at the urgent solicitation of the kind family, he concluded to remain until he got better. He remained until he was able to travel, and then went to Cousin Jane Porter's near Elkton, Kentucky. Gray, Bailey and I started on towards Russellville and soon found a wagon going to that place, and, as it was not loaded, we were permitted to ride on it.[3]

At about sunset, we reached the suburbs of Russellville. We had been stationed there for some weeks before going to Fort Donelson, and were afraid of being recognized by someone and then arrested by the soldiers who were garrisoning that town. We were very cautious and had reason for it. Dismounting from the wagon at the edge of town, each of us took a different route through town, one going by one street and another by another, agreeing as we separated to meet on the Morgantown Road on the opposite side of town, and if one got through and waited a certain time without hearing from the others, he was to take care of himself, being satisfied of the capture of the others. We fortunately passed through without being interrupted, and all met as per agreement and proceeded about three or four miles to the house of a Mr. Withers where we spent the night, representing ourselves as workmen who had been engaged on the railroad near the Tennessee River, and were going north.[4]

The next day we walked on in the snow and slop and mud, the march being very tiresome. When we got to the

Pleasant Hill Church, near the old tanyard of Mr. Anderson, we went in and lay down on the benches for the purpose of resting ourselves and remained there for some time. Bailey left us near there and went to his cousin Eaton Davis's home nearby.[5]

Joseph Gray and I went to Uncle Moody's, who lived only a few miles from the church. We remained there till after supper and he kindly furnished us a horse a piece, and we rode home to Sugar Grove, arriving there about ten o'clock at night. It was the night of March 6, 1862, that we got home. Rumors of various kinds had been put in circulation in regard to our detection and probable arrest. We had been seen and recognized indeed before we got home. The report of it had been circulated, and fortunately we heard it and prepared to leave as soon as possible. Gray was sent on his way to his home in Hardin County near Elizabethtown. This left Bailey and myself alone to make our way out to the Confederate army which had retreated from Bowling Green and at that time was moving on toward Corinth, Mississippi.[6]

I spent the day of the seventh of March at home, and at dark, Bailey sent me a message, saying he would meet me at midnight at a Mr. Proctor's, in Logan County, about twelve miles distant. Bidding our home ones farewell, I set out in the darkness upon a journey the length of which I had no idea of, nor did I scarcely know by what route I would go. The army was in retreat, I knew. But where it was, where it would stop, and how and when I should reach it were matters of which I could form no idea. It was literally taking a leap in the dark. That the trip would be full of peril and adventure, I well knew, yet Bailey and I were determined to rejoin our command.[7]

At about eleven o'clock that night, the seventh of March, I arrived at Mr. Proctor's. The family had gone to bed not knowing that Bailey and I were to meet there. I awoke the family and made known to them the object of my unseasonable visit, and as Bailey had not yet got there, I lay down to take a few moments sleep. I had not been more than an hour in bed when Bailey, true to his promise as he always was, aroused me for the night's ride. Saying farewell again, I went to the gate and found Bailey and several friends who had come to see us start. Among them were Hickman Gray, Frank Bailey and, I believe, Calvin Kuykendall, Jerry Bailey and perhaps some others whom I do not now remember. They had ridden ten or fifteen miles, and were going to return to their homes before day to avoid being seen by the pro-Federal citizens.[8]

After a few minutes conversation, we bade them good night and rode off on our long and uncertain journey. It was quite cold and the ground hard frozen. Wind was keen and cutting, and it seemed that our horses made more than common noise going over the frozen ground. We went up the Franklin Road till we got near the South Union Depot, and, as we had learned at Mr. Proctor's that the enemy was there in a body, we turned to the right about half a mile from the station and crossed the railroad south of it, and went directly to the house of Mr. John McCutchen in order to warm ourselves, as by this time we were extremely cold. It was before day, but we aroused the family and were received kindly. We remained there till after an early breakfast, when we again set out.[9]

After cautiously feeling our way, and traveling neighborhood roads, we reached, at night-fall, Dickson Beard's home on the edge of Tennessee. The family was "loyal," but being acquaintances, we were secure. A good night's rest for us and our horses was succeeded by another day's march, or rather ride, through a section of country that, at that time, was full of Major General Don Carlos Buell's Federal forces on their march in pursuit of the retreating Confederate army under General Albert Sidney Johnston. This was in that part of Kentucky and Tennessee between Franklin in the former and Gallatin in the latter State. We traveled by-roads, except the Louisville and Nashville Turnpike, and also the Louisville and Nashville Railroad. After being almost in the midst of the Yankees several times during the day, we, at night, found another safe retreat at the hospitable house of Mr. Thomas Dobbins, a relative of our family who lived at that time, and at this date, near Gallatin, Tennessee.[10]

This day was Sunday, but "Sunday shone no Sabbath day to us." Bailey was here taken quite sick with diphtheria, and as a consequence of which we remained for two or three days, the Yankees all the time passing down two roads near us. As soon as he was able to ride, although before he got well, we again set out, going north and east of Gallatin, and, reaching the Cumberland River at Canoe Branch Ferry, we crossed over and proceeded directly and rapidly to Lebanon. We expected to encounter the enemy at Lebanon but found none there, as they had not ventured up that far east of Nashville.

Here we debated as to whether we should go by way of Alexandria and McMinnville and thence to New Market, Alabama, or to go directly to Murfreesboro, and at that place fall in the rear of the Confederate army. The last named route was extremely dangerous, while the other, being further east, was quite safe, although circuitous. We at length determined to go by way of Murfreesboro, and run all risk of encountering the enemy.

Our progress was not very rapid, as we felt our way cautiously and with a good deal of discretion. We had learned to take affairs calmly and were prepared for any emergency. Near Black's Shop we spent the night, and in the morning of the next day we rode into Murfreesboro and found the last of the Confederate soldiers leaving the town. This body of men

Major General Don Carlos Buell, commander of the Army of the Ohio. (Library of Congress.)

was the cavalry squadron commanded by John H. Morgan, who at that time was a captain. Here we learned for the first time definite information about the whereabouts of the Confederate army and the place of concentration.[11]

After leaving Murfreesboro we traveled leisurely, going

about thirty miles a day, passing through the towns of Shelbyville and Fayetteville, and on in the direction of Huntsville, Alabama. Then, when we arrived at a point about twelve miles, I think, from Huntsville, we were compelled to stop a day or two on account of rains and high water, the streams being impassable. We concluded, after waiting a few days, during which time the rain continued to fall, to go directly to Decatur, Alabama, on the Tennessee River, and, accordingly, we did so. During the next three days we made our journey to Decatur. We swam a good number of angry streams and had calamities enough to, in some degree, try our nerves. I remember we stayed overnight with a family in a section of the country known as "Nubbin Ridge," because, I suppose, corn grew in "nubbins" on account of the land being poor, and it *was* poor too. The next night we stayed with a wealthy planter named, I believe, Bibb, a son, perhaps, of an ex-governor of Alabama. At both of these places we were kindly taken care of, and every attention was paid to us. Bibb lived only a few miles from Decatur, near a place called Mooresville. The day we left Mr. Bibb's we reached Decatur, crossing the Tennessee River on horseback over the railroad bridge which had been prepared for the use of the retreating army.[12]

We found our old company, the "Guides," encamped in the suburbs of the place, and once more, amid shouts and cheers, greeted our comrades. Well do I remember the joy which filled my bosom in again seeing my friends, and the pleasure it afforded us all to recount to each other the events which each had experienced during the previous two months. We carried to them the latest information from their friends at home. We told them all we knew about how the Federals were doing in Kentucky and what had transpired after they had left Bowling Green. We told them how we had been captured, how we had escaped, our travels, and everything connected with ourselves from the time of our separation. They in turn told us what had occurred on their retreat, how and what they did at Nashville and everywhere they had stopped. Altogether we had a perfect "jollification."

The army was at this time concentrating at Corinth, Mississippi. A few days after we arrived at Decatur we proceeded on our march to Corinth, which occupied us some three or four days or perhaps five days, passing through the towns of Tuscumbia, Courtland, Barnesville, and others, where we camped and had a good time generally. We finally got to Corinth and went into camp. It was evident that a serious battle would soon be fought. Troops were rapidly concentrating at that place.[13]

The object of the organization of our company, as given in the first part of this sketch, being that of guides, it was evident that we could no longer be of service in that capacity, inasmuch as we were wholly and entirely unacquainted with the country in which we had been thrown by the stern fortunes of war. Consequently, the company was disbanded by order of General Johnston, and the members were left free to act as they chose and were at liberty to attach themselves to any company or command they might select.

Of course, it was but natural that we should seek to place ourselves under the command of Captain John Hunt Morgan, who had at this time won very considerable fame. And, although all of our company did not at once join Morgan, still a large majority of the "guides," in a few weeks, were in his command.

It cannot, I think, be said that it is egotism when I affirm that each and every one of that gallant company won more or less notoriety before the war closed. And, they contributed their full share toward making up that glorious and undying record of gallantry and daring which Morgan's cavalry afterwards won. As officers and private soldiers, they share the largest in the honors given now and which shall be given

Youthful John Hunt Morgan, as he appeared when he commanded Morgan's Squadron of Kentucky Cavalry in the fall of 1861 and spring of 1862. (Hunt-Morgan House Deposit Photographic Collection, University of Kentucky Special Collections.)

in the future history of our country to the fame of that cavalry command which attracted the eyes of the civilized world and the likes of which has never been witnessed. It would be a pleasure to write down the names and deeds of each one, but it would comprise so much that it cannot be done. For a complete history of Morgan's Cavalry, reference is made to its history as written by Basil W. Duke, though in it many deeds and acts of individual daring and bravery are, as a matter of course, omitted.[14]

The Battle of Shiloh was fought and won, and lost. That is to say, it was won on the first day and lost on the second, and the army again fell back to Corinth, from which place it had gone to battle. To describe the conditions of the roads and the country is not my purpose, more than to say that the route of the retreating army from Shiloh to the town of Corinth, some twelve or thirteen miles distant, was the worst that perhaps ever was traveled.[15]

4

WE STRUCK OUT ON
OUR OWN RESPONSIBILITY

John M. Porter reached Corinth, Mississippi, although he never was able to join John Hunt Morgan's command there or even participate in the Battle of Shiloh, where General Johnston was mortally wounded and the Confederate Army of the Mississippi was hurled back after two days of fierce fighting. After the Army of the Mississippi withdrew back to Corinth and on to Tupelo, Porter set out to find Morgan. John Hunt Morgan had already left the Army of the Mississippi after the Battle of Shiloh and had proceeded to central Tennessee, around Murfreesboro. He then rode on to Chattanooga, and soon moved to Knoxville to confer with the commander of the Confederate Department of East Tennessee, Major General Edmund Kirby Smith. Informed by Smith of the likelihood of an invasion of Kentucky later that summer, Morgan was instructed to enter Kentucky for the purpose of destroying rail lines, telegraph lines, and government stores in the central part of the state and capturing and forcing the withdrawal of as many Federal troops as possible, all to support a Confederate invasion, the objective of which was to hold central Kentucky.

Now commanding the Second Kentucky Cavalry (C.S.A.) Regiment, along with a battalion of Texans under Major Richard M. Gano, newly commissioned Colonel John Hunt Morgan left Knoxville and moved to Sparta, Tennessee. A regiment of Georgia partisan rangers under Major F.

M. Nix was added to the command. From Sparta Morgan moved to Tomp-kinsville, Kentucky, and arrived at Glasgow on July 10, where he destroyed government stores along the Louisville and Nashville Railroad (L&N) Glasgow Branch. Morgan pressed on to Lebanon, tearing up L&N tracks, bridges, and rolling stock and seizing and burning government stores along the Lebanon Branch on July 12.

From Lebanon, Morgan moved his command to Springfield and Har-rodsburg and on to Lawrenceburg. Crossing the Kentucky River at Shryock's Ferry, Morgan's command entered Versailles on July 14. The next day, Morgan and his men rode to Midway, where they destroyed tracks, bridges, and telegraph wires of the Lexington and Frankfort Railroad. They then rode on to Georgetown, skirting Lexington because of a large Federal force there.

All the while, John M. Porter was trying to locate Morgan and his com-mand. Porter embarked upon his odyssey while Morgan was still in central Tennessee. Porter journeyed from north Alabama all the way to central Kentucky. He was ultimately joined in Kentucky, near Winchester, by Lieuten-ant Thomas H. Hines, the Butler County native and kinsman who would become his lifelong friend and law partner after the war. Along the way, they found refuge in the homes of those who sympathized with the Confeder-ate cause.

It was at Georgetown, on July 15, that Porter joined Company C of the Second Kentucky Cavalry (C.S.A.) in Morgan's command; he would ride with Morgan for the remainder of his military service. Morgan's next target—and Porter's first pitched battle alongside Morgan's men—would be Cynthiana, an important rail center on the Kentucky Central Railroad between Covington and Lexington.

A few days after the Battle of Shiloh, Andy Kuykendall, some others and I boarded, for the time being, with a man by the name of Davenport, near Jacinto, Mississippi. William L. Dulaney was one of our party at this place. After we had spent perhaps two weeks at that house, Andy Kuykendall and I rode to Tuscumbia, Alabama, and there we met the Texas Rangers, the Eighth Texas, Colonel Benjamin Franklin Terry's old regiment, and in the same vicinity was Colonel Benjamin Hardin Helm's First Kentucky Cavalry (C.S.A.). The First Kentucky had campaigned through Tennessee and as far as Cave City, Kentucky, having left the army at Corinth while we were at the Davenports', which fact prevented our being with it, and which was the cause of our being away from Morgan's command until about July of that year.[1]

When we arrived at Tuscumbia, we found the Eighth Texas Cavalry and First Kentucky Cavalry regiments were about ready to move across the Tennessee River at Lamb's Ferry for the purpose of ridding that part of Alabama of the Federals, who, under Brigadier General Ormsby M. Mitchel, had occupied it, and were at that time traversing the whole country about Florence, Athens and Rogersville. Andy and I, at once, took our place in the ranks of a company of the Texas regiment, to which Andy's brother belonged, and the command proceeded to the Tennessee River. By means of an improvised boat, we succeeded, in about two days, in crossing the river which, at that point, was quite wide. About two miles from the river we camped, and a scouting party was sent out for some distance, and it had a considerable fight with the enemy in which some Texans and Kentuckians were killed and wounded. Captain Charles T. Noel, Company C, First Kentucky Cavalry, of Daviess County was killed there.[2]

A few days later, the commands all advanced into the country infested with the enemy, leaving a small guard at camp for the purpose of protecting the boats and securing a way of retreat if it became necessary. The object, however, was not accomplished so fully as was desired, for a very large force of the enemy came upon those of us who were left at camp, and dispersed us to the four winds. The coming of the Federals was so sudden that time was not given to re-cross the river and, as a matter of course, after a fair show of the fight with little of the reality, we retreated down the river in the direction of Florence. There was no one to command, no one to obey, and, in short, it was a stampede. We did not cross the river, but were scattered around through the country in squads of from two to six just as we happened to be thrown together.

Andy and another person and I were together, and, for a day or so, were in the woods and roads and everywhere, first trying to find out, if we could, where the Yankees were, and, next thing, finding them uncomfortably close. At one time we ran upon a few of them at a short turn of the road. Both parties were alarmed and both retreated in "good order." At another time they gave chase and pursued us for a mile or more at full speed. No one, I think, but Andy and myself were thus chased. Finding it not in our power to find the main body of the command, the whereabouts of which we had not heard for some days, we determined to strike out on our own responsibility in the direction of Tennessee, for at that particular time, it was useless to remain where we were and almost as useless to attempt to return toward the Tennessee River.

We did not know where Morgan was, but expected to find him in middle Tennessee. In this we were disappointed, however. We fell into the hands of the Yankees at Pulaski, Tennessee, and were detained for a day or so, when we came on to Nashville by way of Columbia and Franklin. We had determined to go directly to Kentucky to see our friends, and had attired ourselves as citizens so as to pass unmolested. After some days riding, we got to Logan County, Kentucky, where, after night, we proceeded in order to prevent anyone from seeing us. This was, I am of the opinion, some time about the middle or latter part of May 1862. Andy and I remained at our homes for a day or two, and then we determined to leave and go to the central part of the State, Clark County, where Andy had relatives.[3]

Attiring ourselves in the dress of citizens, we started from

The covered bridge over the Dix River at King's Mill. John M. Porter crossed the bridge on his way to Bryantsville, Kentucky, three miles distant, and Lexington to join Morgan's command. (J. Winston Coleman, Jr. Photographic Collection, Transylvania University Library.)

our homes for our destination. The entire State through which our route lay was full of Federal soldiers. Our journey was through Warren, Barren, Hart, Green, Taylor, Marion, Boyle, Jessamine, Fayette, and Clark Counties. Passing ourselves, sometimes, as stock traders and sometimes as agents for purchasing supplies for the Yankee army, as the emergencies suited us, we made our trip without being arrested, although we encountered frequent bodies of soldiers. One night I remember we stayed at a tavern not far from Dix River Bridge, where there was a company of cavalry which regarded us suspiciously.[4]

The Old Burnt Tavern, Bryantsville, Kentucky. John M. Porter stopped at the tavern on his way to Lexington to join Morgan's command. The tavern burned in 1956. (J. Winston Coleman, Jr. Photographic Collection, Transylvania University Library.)

We were received at Mr. David Hays's, four miles from Winchester, on a beautiful Sunday afternoon, and were hospitably welcomed, Mr. Hays and his wife being the uncle and aunt to Andy. There were a good many persons at Mr. Hays's when we arrived there, neighbors who had come in to spend the afternoon. I was an entire stranger to the family as well as their visitor, but was introduced to the family as a relative from western Kentucky, and the intimation was given that Andy and I were only on a visit to see kinfolk.[5]

As soon as the company had gone, we told the Hays our reason for being there and on what business we were bent, as well as what we had been doing the preceding eight or ten months. The family were true friends of the South and naturally very kind and hospitable. There were, however, a good many Union people in that section, and some very close neighbors were of that number. It was highly important that our views and designs should not be known to any except true and trusty friends. We soon came to be looked on in the neighborhood as suspicious persons, and it was even whispered around that we were rebel soldiers in disguise. The surmises were pretty accurate to say the least.

We remained at Mr. Hays's for a few days under the pretense of resting from our fatiguing ride, when, in reality, we were accustomed to riding constantly and great distances without rest. Then, after we had been there a few days, we visited around in the neighborhood with members of the family and attended picnics and gatherings of all kind. We went to church on Sundays and frequently went to Winchester. About twice we entered Lexington, which was filled with Federal troops, and returned in safety to our country retreat. We remained in this quarter till about July 1, 1862, when we were joined by Lieutenant Thomas H. Hines, who had been in the Green River section and had heard where we were and had hunted us up. This was about the time newly commissioned Colonel John Hunt Morgan entered the State on his first great raid. We were already expecting to hear from him when Hines came and gave us definite news in regard to it.[6]

Hines and I then drove to Lexington, eighteen miles distant, in order to ascertain what we could about the number of troops there and the means of defending the city. We stopped at a hotel, and, while at dinner, heard a conversation between two Yankee officers by which we learned that great preparations were being made to defend the city, and that they expected an attack within twenty-four hours by Colonel Morgan, who really was some distance away but no one knew

Thomas Henry Hines, John M. Porter's kinsman, compatriot during the war, and law partner after the war. The photograph was taken after the war. (Thomas H. Hines Papers, Filson Historical Society Collections, Louisville, Kentucky.)

precisely where. After dinner we drove around the city and out to the cemetery and observed everything which afforded us any idea of the force there. When we came back to the hotel in the afternoon, perhaps four o'clock, we found Home Guards were arriving in large numbers from all the surrounding country, and at the same time we received information that in a very few minutes, or quite a short time, all persons would be prevented from leaving the city, and perhaps would be forced to take up arms to defend the place from the anticipated attack. This information, which was given to us by a friend to whom we had made ourselves known, was rather startling, and immediately we were in our buggy and driving at full speed out the Winchester Road in order to clear the limits of the city before pickets were sent out. This we succeeded in doing, although the pickets were in view behind us coming on their posts. We had made our escape by the narrowest, and made our way back to Mr. Hays's that night for supper. We had learned that Colonel Morgan would, in a short time, be in the vicinity of Lexington, but we did not know whether he would attack the city or not. Indeed, he was expected to attack that very night, and great consternation was visible among the soldiers when we left town.[7]

Hines, Andy Kuykendall and myself, after taking supper at Mr. Hays's and remaining till the family of negroes on the place had gone to bed or become quiet and we were satisfied all was well, bid "goodbye" to the kind friends who had entertained us, and started out for the purpose of getting with Colonel Morgan, believing we would find him somewhere in the vicinity of Lexington, Versailles or Georgetown.[8]

The night was a pleasant one, and having a pilot with us who knew the country very well, we traveled neighborhood roads and avoided the more public ones. About three o'clock in the morning, our guide, Mr. Colby Hays, who afterwards was a gallant soldier in our command, left us and returned home

Main Street, Lexington, Kentucky, looking east toward the corner of Main and Limestone streets, circa 1860. The three-story building in the center of the photograph is the Phoenix Hotel, where John M. Porter and Thomas Henry Hines inquired about the whereabouts of Morgan's command on July 14, 1862. (Lafayette Studio Photographic Collection, University of Kentucky Special Collections.)

in order to reach there before daylight. We were then alone in a strange locality with nothing familiar, no roads over which we had ever gone over, no acquaintances in all that section and no definite news of the whereabouts of the command.[9]

After we three had consulted, we concluded to approach Lexington and ascertain if any attack would be or had been made. We knew if the attack occurred, it would probably be about daylight, and we at once moved forward and in a short time entered a pike which, from its direction, we judged led into the city. Rapidly riding this pike, which I believe was called the Tate's Creek Pike, about daylight we came within one mile of the city and halted in sight of Yankee pickets on that road. We remained there in a position to observe their movements and where we could easily discover whether any fight had begun or not.[10]

The sun rose and there were no indications of a fight. We were satisfied that Colonel Morgan was not in the immediate vicinity. Our course was then changed, and we turned our attention to find some way of getting around towards the Kentucky River, and, by way of Nicholasville and some other points, reach Versailles. We did not dare go on a direct route, fearing we would meet some of the numerous scouting parties of the enemy, as we well knew they were all through the country. After riding until about ten o'clock in the forenoon we called at a house and asked to remain for dinner and have our horses fed. This favor was granted by the lady whose husband was absent when we got there. This lady, Mrs. Martin, was a friend to our cause, but whereas she did not know us, neither did we, at the time, know her views. She was inquisitive and we were inquisitive, and in a short time we found her "cut," and had no hesitancy in telling who and what we were.[11]

In the meantime, her husband came in, and, just as dinner was announced, it was discovered that three Yankees were dismounting at the gate. Here was a dilemma. We could easily have taken them prisoners because they did not know we were there. The family was very much frightened, and, to quiet their fears, we bid the husband to meet the Yankees in the front yard and conduct them in to dinner, while we would remain in the parlor and be ready for any emergency. The officers, for such they were, were accordingly taken in a different room and then sat down to eat the dinner which had been prepared for us by Mrs. Martin. As soon as they were well at work on the viands, we walked out and went to

61

the stable, mounted our horses, and rode away. We walked by their horses and did not interrupt them, because we knew Mr. Martin and his family would be arrested and persecuted if we were known to have been there. For their sakes alone, these three Yankees were permitted to go unmolested, to eat *our* dinner, while we fasted.

We rode a few miles and halted in a woods till nightfall. While we were in this woods, we saw one or two parties of Yankees pass along a road at no great distance from us. At night we again set out, and morning found us near a village called Keene, I think, and here or near it, we encountered about one or two hundred Yankee Home Guards. We met them in the road, they on their way to Lexington and we, by chance, going in the direction of Shyrock's Ferry on the Kentucky River. We out-talked the officer in command, passed the entire party unmolested, and, as soon as they had disappeared from our view, we changed our direction and rode rapidly away. We carried beneath our coats side arms which were not visible to the casual observer. The day closed and still we had not found Colonel Morgan, nor even heard of his whereabouts.[12]

Night again came on, and, by circuitous routes, we reached the farm of Abram Buford, soon to be a brigadier general, by breakfast time, and from him heard that Morgan had gone in the direction of Midway and Georgetown. A day's ride in a dangerous locality brought us late in the evening to Georgetown, and soon we had overtaken the command and were again free and easy.[13]

During the trip from Mr. Hays's in the vicinity of Winchester to the command of Colonel Morgan at Georgetown, we encountered a good many obstacles, and were frequently in dangerous situations. We each had papers on our person which would have been sufficient to have told what our politics were, and early one morning, when on a turnpike which

Keene Springs Tavern and Hotel, Jessamine County, Kentucky, as it looked at the time of the Civil War. John M. Porter passed the hotel on his way from Nicholasville, Kentucky, to Versailles to join Morgan's command. (J. Winston Coleman, Jr. Photographic Collection, Transylvania University Library.)

led into Lexington, and only a few miles from the city, we concluded to destroy our papers and letters. We called at a black smith shop about sunrise after a night's travel and asked for a shoe to be repaired on a horse. While the desired work was being done, we walked about thirty yards away and, lighting a match, burned everything which could lead to our identity. We returned to the shop and conversed freely with the wondering smith for a short time and then rode away, leaving him in a bewildering state of mind as to what we meant

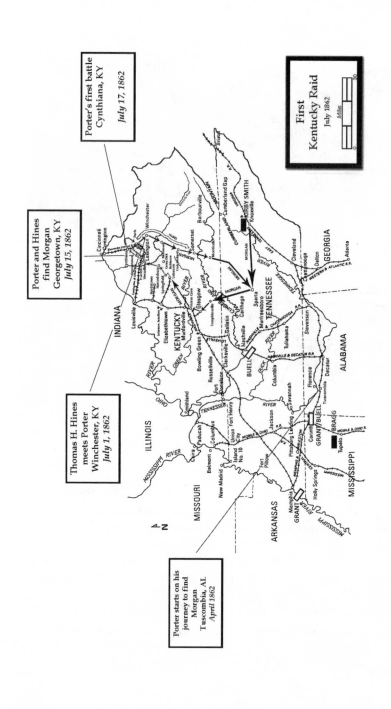

Porter's first battle
Cynthiana, KY
July 17, 1862

Porter and Hines
find Morgan
Georgetown, KY
July 15, 1862

Thomas H. Hines
meets Porter
Winchester, KY
July 1, 1862

Porter starts on his
journey to find
Morgan
Tuscombia, AL
April 1862

First
Kentucky Raid
July 1862

Miles

A rarely published carte de visite photograph of Brigadier General Abraham Buford taken at the time he joined the Confederate Army, fall 1862. (Courtesy of the Alabama Department of Archives and History.)

and who we were. I venture to say that that black smith has thought a thousand times since about the three strange— and doubtless to him, suspicious—persons whom he saw that morning. From our appearance, he must have known that we had ridden all night, and, in those days of the war, every stranger was regarded with distrust.[14]

5

A PERFECT TORNADO OF SHOTS WAS FIRED AT US

Within two days of joining Morgan's command, John M. Porter saw combat in the Battle of Cynthiana, one of the most vicious engagements of the war for the size of the opposing forces involved. At Cynthiana, the Kentucky Central Railroad, connecting Covington, Kentucky, and Lexington, crossed the South Fork of the Licking River. Large amounts of government stores, rolling stock, and railroad equipment were kept there for use by Federal occupation troops, including the sizable force in Lexington.

Morgan's men were in the saddle early on July 17, 1862, riding on the road between Georgetown and Cynthiana. The Georgetown Road entered Cynthiana by means of a 320-foot covered bridge over the Licking River. Federal troops, mostly Home Guards from the area and detachments from the Eighteenth Kentucky Infantry (U.S.A.) and Seventh Kentucky Cavalry (U.S.A.) regiments, filled the buildings in Cynthiana on either side of the covered bridge and manned barricades in the streets. They were supported by a twelve-pound brass howitzer manned by members of a Cincinnati, Ohio, police detachment, set up in the Harrison County Courthouse lot.

Dismounting his troopers, Morgan positioned elements of the Second Kentucky Cavalry (C.S.A.) on either side of the bridge, while Major Richard M. Gano's command crossed the river and struck Cynthiana from the high ground to the east and Major F. M. Nix's command crossed the river and attacked the town's defenders from the west and north. Finally, Porter's own Company C of the Second Kentucky stormed through the covered bridge on horseback. Soon, all of the Kentuckians were across the river, driving the Federal defenders to the railroad depot. It was a bloody fray.

The town was seized, along with hundreds of Federal soldiers. Morgan burned all of the government stores he didn't confiscate, destroyed the Kentucky Central Railroad bridge over the Licking River, ripped up track, and destroyed rolling stock. His men were soon back in the saddle, heading toward Tennessee after one of the most successful raids of Morgan's career.

We found many of our old comrades when we reached the command at Georgetown, and right glad were we to shake hands again with them after a separation of about two months. Our company, or that to which we were to unite and to which nearly all of the old "Guides" belonged, was off on a scout at the time we overtook the command, and for this reason, we "fell in" with Company C, commanded by Captain James W. Bowles, afterwards Colonel Bowles. Company D, commanded by Captain John B. Castleman, would be our company thereafter.[1]

The command moved on in due time towards Cynthiana in Harrison County, which was, at the time, garrisoned with a force of Federals commanded by Lieutenant Colonel John J. Landrum, I believe. About two o'clock in the afternoon the advance reached the vicinity of the town and encountered the Yankee pickets, who were quickly driven in. An immediate advance was ordered, and, at once, the entire force of Colonel Morgan moved towards the town, which is situated on the north side of Licking River. A portion of the force was sent to the right of the road we were on, with directions to cross the railroad bridge over the river and enter the town from that direction. Another force, with like directions, was sent to the left of the road, each of which were compelled to pass across the river. The bridge was covered. Up and down

The covered bridge over the South Fork of the Licking River at Cynthiana, Kentucky, as it would have looked in 1862. The bridge stood until 1946. (J. Winston Coleman, Jr. Photographic Collection, Transylvania University Library.)

the river were houses and a street with business houses that ran parallel with the river and at right angles with the bridge. A large brick building stood directly in front of the mouth of the bridge, not more than twenty feet from the bridge. In order to reach the Kentucky Central Railroad depot, it was necessary, after the bridge was crossed, to turn to left and go twenty or thirty yards and then turn right down a street which led directly past the depot.[2]

Our company, having approached to within about three hundred yards of the bridge, was ordered to halt for a moment. By this time, the two parties on the right and left were hotly engaged. We were ordered to charge the depot from which a terrific fire was issuing, and, at the command,

Woodcut of the Battle of Cynthiana, Kentucky, July 17, 1862, showing the attack of Company C, Second Kentucky Cavalry, through the covered bridge over the South Fork of the Licking River. (J. Winston Coleman, Jr. Photographic Collection, Transylvania University Library.)

the company dashed forward and crossed the bridge. In doing so, we found ourselves jammed up against the brick house I have spoken of above, which up to that time had not been discovered. No one knew which way to go in order to reach the depot. We knew the direction, but where was the street which led to it?[3]

In the momentary confusion which ensued, Colonel George St. Leger Grenfell came galloping up, having crossed the river at another point, and directed Captain Bowles how to reach the depot street. The charge was again ordered and the company, surrounded on all sides by the enemy in houses, charged on horseback toward the depot, which was filled with Yankee infantry. The enfilading fire was very severe and the single company of Captain Bowles lost heavily in the charge.[4]

The firing from the depot was checked somewhat by our reckless charge, and, as it was impossible for horsemen to ride into the building, we continued our ride entirely through the town, subject all the time to a severe fire from every side of us. After getting through the town, we dismounted and returned in line on foot, and the other two parties, having by this time advanced on two sides—we coming up from the opposite side—the three parties closed around, and, after a severe fight for some time, the Yankees surrendered, except a few who made their escape early in the action.[5]

It was a hard-fought engagement, but we conquered the game. The scenes here were as horrible as any I had at that time ever witnessed. Most of the enemy who were killed were in the upper rooms, and shot through windows as they were in the act of firing on our men. They lay in every shape, some wounded and others dead. The fight closed late in the evening, and, after it was over, every luxury which the good people of the town could command was set before us. We were literally wined and dined. The houses were thrown open and general invitations for all the Confederate soldiers were extended to come and eat. Some gallant soldiers died there covered with honor.[6]

The command camped there during the night and till the afternoon of the next day, when we moved off in the direction of Paris, which we reached, I think, that night. We encountered no enemy at Paris, the garrison there having gone to Lexington, expecting that city would be the next point of attack.

After remaining at Paris for nearly twenty-four hours, we moved off in the direction of Winchester, just as a large Federal force was approaching. We moved slowly, expecting to have an engagement, but, instead of that, as soon as they discovered that Morgan had moved slowly in the direction of Winchester, they made good speed back to Lexington

Woodcut of Morgan's command at Paris, Kentucky, July 18, 1862, after the Battle of Cynthiana. (Hunt-Morgan House Deposit Photographic Collection, University of Kentucky Special Collections.)

for fear Morgan would get there first. By slow and leisurely marches, we arrived at Winchester where we found our Company D, which had been detached on a scout for some days, and which had been causing great consternation in the vicinity of Lexington, Paris and Winchester.[7]

Some few soldiers, mostly Home Guards, were captured at Winchester. Here we were, within four miles of Mr. Hays's, whose house we had left some eight or ten days or two weeks before, and we were glad to meet some of the family in town who came to see Colonel Morgan and his men.

From Winchester, the march was made by way of old Boonsboro on the Kentucky River to Richmond in Madison County, which we reached some time during the night, and captured a very large wagon train and some soldiers. I remember it was a pleasant night, and we marched on foot a good distance in order to surprise the Yankee wagon guards, almost all of whom were asleep in the wagons and, of course, were easily captured.[8]

From Richmond, the march was by Crab Orchard, which we passed at daylight, worn down by fatigue and want of rest. A large force of Yankee Cavalry, commanded by Brigadier General Green Clay Smith, was in pursuit. We were not fooling away any time in playing, although it was evident that the Yankee general was not trying very hard to overtake Morgan. The march south was not marked by anything of particular note. No organized body of soldiers met us, although we were very considerably annoyed by bushwhackers who, from hillsides and behind trees, fired on us frequently.[9]

We passed out through Monticello and Pulaski County, going through the county seat, Somerset, and passing in the vicinity of the Fishing Creek battleground where Brigadier General Felix K. Zollicoffer of Tennessee was killed in January 1862. After reaching the Tennessee line, we passed through a rough, rugged country and did not halt for any length of time until we had reached Livingston in Overton County, where we remained a few days and rested, having been for a long time almost continually in the saddle. Of course, in giving this imperfect account of the first great raid of Colonel Morgan into Kentucky, I have not attempted to give a complete and full history of it, because it would require many pages to write down every incident which transpired in that long, daring and dangerous campaign.[10]

After remaining at Livingston a few days for the purpose of resting men and horses, the command was ordered to Sparta, Tennessee, where there was more forage for the horses and provisions for the men were more plentiful. Around Sparta we had what we usually called a "good time." That is to say, we had a sufficiency of provisions and corn for men and animals, and a few days of genuine rest from the arduous and fatiguing duties.

We were not long to remain at complete rest, however, for the Yankees, who at that time held all of Middle Tennessee, were in considerable force at McMinnville, about twenty or twenty-five miles distant, and, as a consequence, they came up in large force to know why we were at Sparta. We went out on the road leading to McMinnville and, having met them, gave *them* our *reasons* for being in that vicinity. The reasons seemed satisfactory, for after an engagement, they rapidly returned to McMinnville and we still remained at Sparta.

The Yankees were reported again in a day or two to be advancing, and Lieutenant Colonel Basil W. Duke took about fifteen men, Andy Kuykendall and myself being of the number, and went out on the McMinnville Road intending to go as far as the bridge over a stream, about four miles, I think, from Sparta. The bridge was a covered one, and, when we got in sight of it, we thought, from all indications, that the enemy was not far off and perhaps just beyond the bridge, hid from our view by the trees on the bank of the creek.[11]

We went up to within about three hundred yards of the bridge and discovered the enemy some distance on the other side, and Colonel Duke thought he would go up a little closer. The road was not straight which went up to the bridge, and, consequently, we could not see in at the entrance, but had only a sort of side view of it. Suspecting that the bridge was full of Yankees, Colonel Duke told us to be prepared for any emergency, and we cautiously and slowly advanced until we got within a short distance of the mouth of the bridge when, sure enough, they dashed out and at us like an avalanche in numbers about forty, and those were followed by two hundred or three hundred more on the far side who rapidly came charging over. Things were rather uncomfortable, to say the least, and, after firing a volley at them, the colonel ordered a retreat.

Then occurred one of those exciting and lively chases

that a cavalryman is so accustomed to. Our horses were of the best that Kentucky afforded and, by apt use of the spur, we were soon beyond the reach of the enemy, but not until we had gone about one and a half or two miles. As a matter of course, under those circumstances, it did not take long to go that distance. We had an ambuscade prepared and hoped to draw them in it, but in this we failed, as they ceased their pursuit before they reached it. Immediately, the entire command was mounted and the pursuit was given, but the enemy fled back to McMinnville and gave us no fight. This was truly an exciting race. No one was hurt, although a perfect tornado of shots was fired at us. The cause, doubtless, of no one being hurt was the rapid gait at which the Yankees were riding, which prevented them from firing with accuracy. I do not know whether we did any injury to them by our volley. We did not wait just then to see.

In the midst of the race, when every man was straining his horse to its highest speed, someone's horse fell in the road, dashing its rider far out in the dust along with two other horses with their riders, one of whom was Andy Kuykendall. He fell over the first horse and such another mixture of horses, men, guns, pistols, and so forth was wonderful to see, and still more wonderful, all recovered their feet, remounted and rode away, while the rest checked the Yankees for the moment. It was truly marvelous that some of them were not killed by the fall! Many and many were the laughs we afterwards enjoyed about this race. I wish I could remember the names of each one of our party, but I cannot now call to mind any except Jim Cook in addition to Andy.[12]

We remained in possession of Sparta and the country around there for some two or three or perhaps four weeks. Colonel Morgan having gone to Knoxville, we were under Colonel Duke, who needs no praise nor eulogy from me to add to his fame.

6

IT WAS A GRAND AND
IMPOSING OVATION

*Probably no single month in John Hunt Morgan's military career was more
filled with action and success than August 1862. After returning from his
wildly successful first Kentucky raid, Morgan settled his command in and
around Hartsville, Tennessee, a small town in Trousdale County, about fifteen miles east of Gallatin.*

*As General Braxton Bragg, the recently named commander of the Confed-
erate Army of the Mississippi, was shifting his troops from Tupelo, Mississippi,
to Chattanooga, Major General Don Carlos Buell was pushing his Federal
Army of the Ohio from Corinth, Mississippi, back toward Nashville, the vital
railroad center supplying the Federal occupation forces in Tennessee. Elements
of Buell's forces moved east of Nashville, occupying the outlying towns in order
to protect the city from attack and to probe Confederate movements.*

*Gallatin, Tennessee, about twenty miles north of Nashville, became
the focal point of Morgan's operations. As Major General Edmund Kirby
Smith was marching his army into Kentucky from Knoxville and Bragg's
army was preparing to march from Chattanooga to central Tennessee and,
possibly, Kentucky, Morgan struck Gallatin on August 12, 1862, capturing Colonel William P. Boone and his wife, along with a large number of
Boone's soldiers in the Twenty-eighth Kentucky Infantry Regiment (U.S.A.)
who had garrisoned the town. Morgan struck Gallatin again on August*

19 and 20. This time he destroyed the Louisville and Nashville Railroad bridges and tracks between Gallatin and Edgefield Junction, Tennessee, seriously crippling the flow of supplies to General Buell's occupation forces. Then, in a wild fight on August 21, Morgan captured Brigadier General Richard W. Johnson of Kentucky, who had marched his Federal brigade into Gallatin, vowing to bring Morgan back "in a band-box!" Johnson's whole brigade was scattered; many were captured. Porter, then riding with Company D of the Second Kentucky Cavalry (C.S.A.), had vivid memories of those exciting actions.

Morgan soon moved ahead of Bragg's army into Kentucky, entering Lexington on September 4, 1862. There, he divided his force. He sent Lieutenant Colonel Basil W. Duke and the Second Kentucky Cavalry north to near Covington to screen one of General Smith's divisions, and he took the rest of his command, including John M. Porter, who had been elevated to the rank of lieutenant and transferred to Major William Campbell Preston Breckinridge's battalion, into eastern Kentucky to harass Brigadier General George W. Morgan's Federal forces that evacuated Cumberland Gap on September 16 and were marching toward Greenupsburg, Kentucky. It was a harrowing experience for Porter.

After the pivotal Battle of Perryville, two of Morgan's newly raised regiments protected Bragg's and Smith's retreating armies, while Morgan, with Duke's Second Kentucky Cavalry, Breckinridge's Battalion, Gano's Battalion, and Captain C. C. Corbett's section of mountain howitzers, moved behind Buell's army and captured Lexington on October 18. They then rode toward Versailles and Lawrenceburg, Kentucky, on the way back into Tennessee.

After we remained for some time at Sparta, Colonel John Hunt Morgan returned and we started on an expedition which finally brought us to Hartsville and Gallatin. The first afternoon after leaving Sparta was spent in slowly wending our way toward Chestnut Mound, a spot which every one of Morgan's command will recollect. We went into camp and, on that night, we were joined by some recruits from Kentucky, and, among them, I was delighted to see Virgil Gray who had but a few days before left home for the purpose of hunting up Morgan. These all fell in with different companies on the next morning and we moved on in high spirits towards the Cumberland River which we crossed, and, without encountering any enemy, we finally arrived at Hartsville where we were very kindly received and were provided food for ourselves and our horses, the very best that was in the town and country.[1]

Of course our movements were known to the enemy on the other side of the river; at Lebanon, Murfreesboro, Nashville and even Gallatin, they knew where we were. Gallatin was the

Colonel John Hunt Morgan as he would have looked during the Confederate invasion of Kentucky in September 1862. Note his civilian dress, particularly the purple and black plaid shell jacket. (Lafayette Studio Photographic Collection, University of Kentucky Special Collections.)

point we were after, as by capturing the garrison at that town we would be in a position to destroy the Louisville and Nashville Railroad, burn out the tunnels near there, and materially interrupt communications between Louisville and Nashville.[2]

At about midnight we reached the vicinity of Gallatin. The command was halted in the pike and scouts were sent in the advance, who succeeded in getting between the pickets and the town and captured all of them, which permitted us an uninterrupted march into the town, which was done about daylight.

The officer commanding the Yankees was captured in bed at his headquarters asleep with his wife. Virgil Gray was of the party who captured this officer, who was Colonel William P. Boone of Twenty-eighth Kentucky Infantry (U.S.A.). The Yankee force was camped in the Fair Ground on the side of town next to Nashville and knew not that Morgan was near until they heard their commander was already a prisoner. Boone agreed at his headquarters to surrender his forces, and we rode on in view of the Yankee camp about sun-up and saw them surrender their arms and themselves prisoners without us having fired a gun.[3]

Of course this was gratifying to us, as we were spared a fight, but, if it had been our own men, a fight would have been the word and not a surrender. Colonel Morgan was not so easily caught napping as Colonel Boone. I think the Reverend Hiram A. Hunter, a distinguished Cumberland Presbyterian minister, was chaplain to this Yankee Regiment and, of course, was compelled to see his regiment give up its banner.[4]

We destroyed the military stores, the railroad, the tunnel, and so on, and sent scouts out toward Nashville and in other directions. We spent all day and night in and around Gallatin, camping on the same grounds and sleeping near the same place that the Yankees did the night previous.

The Yankees at Lebanon, Nashville and Murfreesboro

knew of our whereabouts, and a select body of twenty-four hundred cavalry under Brigadier General Richard W. Johnson of Kentucky was sent out by way of Carthage, crossed the Cumberland River, came down by Hartsville, and went on to Gallatin to catch Morgan and his men. As he rode through Hartsville, General Johnson claimed that he would bring Morgan *back in a cage* in a few hours. I will now proceed to tell how he tried to fulfill his promise and what came of it.[5]

About day-light on the morning after the capture of Colonel Boone and his command, we were all aroused and ordered at once to count and form as the enemy was approaching from the direction of Hartsville. It was General Johnson's picked force. We marched through Gallatin and took position near the forks of the Hartsville and Scottsville Pikes, and, at about sunrise, encountered the enemy.

Company D of the Second Kentucky Cavalry (C.S.A.), led by Captain John Breckinridge Castleman, to which our boys then belonged, and one other Company were in position in a woods, and advanced to meet the enemy who were in large force on horseback in an open farm. We were dismounted. After skirmishing for a little time, we advanced to the edge of the open field and the enemy made a charge which we repulsed. Another charge was attempted, but our fire was so destructive that that portion of them in our front was driven from the field in great confusion and we continued in close pursuit. In the meantime, our other detachments had been equally successful and had driven the enemy from every position which it had occupied. Our horses were immediately ordered up and we mounted and pursued them, they by this time having fled in the greatest confusion toward the Cumberland River. Our pursuit was so rapid and pressing that a large number, including General Johnson himself, were captured.

General Johnson was a prisoner instead of his having

Colonel Morgan *in a cage.* This was the result of the gigantic effort made to capture Morgan and his command. I have no doubt that Johnson fully expected to annihilate our command, but he found it not easily overcome. The opinion in the Yankee mind was that Morgan's force would not fight; that they would dodge and evade a struggle. But the result of this day's work gave them to understand that Morgan, with his eleven hundred men, could whip twenty-four hundred

Captain John B. Castleman, commander of Company D, Second Kentucky Cavalry. He was born and raised on what is now Castleton Farm near Lexington, Kentucky. (Hunt-Morgan House Deposit Photographic Collection, University of Kentucky Special Collections.)

and capture their general and many of his men. I have said we had eleven hundred men, but the truth is we had, I suppose, no more than eight hundred all told in the fight. Our loss was severe in killed and wounded, some of our best men. The loss of the enemy was much greater than ours. After this, we were not molested much by the enemy. We held Gallatin and the surrounding country until about the first of September.

The day before this fight was one of great excitement. I have said that this fight occurred the day succeeding the capture of Colonel Boone, but in this I am, upon reflection, mistaken. After Boone's capture we returned to Hartsville, and remained two or three days when we heard that the enemy was at Gallatin. The command at once moved rapidly in the night to Gallatin, arriving about daylight to find the utmost excitement. The Yankees had come from Nashville in considerable force and arrested every man and boy in the place and had a few hours before marched them off toward Nashville on foot. When we entered the town at daylight, the women and children were in the greatest distress, weeping and bewailing the fate of their fathers, husbands and brothers.

The command was immediately put in motion at "Double quick" in pursuit, in order if possible to overtake and rescue our friends. I can safely say that I never, during my entire soldier life, saw as much excitement in our command. The circumstances and everything combined to render them perfectly furious, and a fixed determination seized every one to hazard all things in the attempt to rescue the enfeebled old men and small boys whose wives and mothers and sisters had bid us "God speed" as we rode through the streets of Gallatin in the dim light of dawn. They came in their night clothing to the pavements, and, as we rode by, uttered fervent prayers for our success.

An extraordinary march brought us up with the rear of the enemy about twelve miles from Gallatin and the fight began. We gave them no time for forming. We rode on and over and among them. We scattered them to the four winds. The cornfields were full of them and the woods were full. We rode them down and captured a good many and rescued nearly all of our friends. Some of the enemy who were in front succeeded in reaching a stockade on the railroad, and, as we had no artillery, we did not capture them. We lost some good men in attempting to capture the stockade by a charge with our small arms.[6]

We abandoned the attack, and, after driving all the other uncaptured ones into Nashville, we returned to Gallatin at night with all the rescued prisoners, and the women and children shed tears of joy over our success. That night was spent there, and, the next morning, the battle with General Johnson, which I have related, took place.

Gallatin was the theater of some of Colonel Morgan's most brilliant achievements, and, I dare say, every one of Morgan's "old" command remembers with the kindest feeling the hospitable people there. We remained about Gallatin and Hartsville until about the last days of August 1862, when we began our march toward Kentucky once more. No one but ourselves can describe the feelings of each of us whenever we started for our own State. We did not know our precise destination, but we did know that every expedition in Kentucky was attended with great excitement and danger which caused us to be the more delighted at having an opportunity of encountering them all for the sake even of temporarily relieving our friends from the despotism which bore them down. Our homes were here, our friends were here, and our own firesides were all the more dear to us because of our inability to permanently rescue them from the hands of an unscrupulous enemy.

We marched from Hartsville one day and came in the direction of the Kentucky line. Major General Edmund Kirby

Smith and his army was at the time advancing in the State towards Big Hill and Richmond, and General Braxton Bragg was also on his way with his army from Chattanooga toward the State, but we were ignorant of those facts. Colonel Morgan was, of course, advised of it.[7]

I do not now remember where we spent the night after leaving Hartsville. The second day brought us to Scottsville, Kentucky. Then we moved on to Columbia, Adair County, where we remained for some three or four days waiting for

Major General
Edmund
Kirby Smith,
commander of
the Provisional
Army of
Kentucky.
(Library of
Congress.)

our artillery to come up from Knoxville, Tennessee. At this place we were put in possession of the fact that General Smith was already in the State. We moved on by easy marches and were not disturbed by the Yankees, who had more than they could manage with the army of General Smith. We went by way of Liberty, Hustonville, Danville, and finally reached Nicholasville in Jessamine County.[8]

In the meantime, General Smith had beaten the enemy at Richmond and Big Hill, and had advanced and occupied Lexington and had even marched some of his troops as far as in sight of the spires of Cincinnati. At Nicholasville, we camped all night and formed in line in the morning, prepared by our appearance to make it a proud day for Colonel Morgan as well as for ourselves by marching into his own city, Lexington, the place of his residence. He had gone from it about a year before with scarce a dozen true and tried men, escaping in the darkness to avoid capture. Now he returned with as fine a body of cavalry as ever answered a bugle sound. No wonder his heart swelled within him.[9]

We entered the city in perfect order and precision about ten o'clock in the morning and marched through the principal streets of the place. The streets were full of people; men, women and children, in vast numbers and from every direction, had come in to town to welcome Morgan and his men. It was a grand and imposing ovation. I doubt that Morgan ever had a prouder day of his life.[10]

We went into camp near the city and were permitted to rest from our toils and severe hardships for a short time. Our duty for some weeks before had been arduous, and rest was needed and hugely enjoyed.

While in the camp at Lexington, Mr. and Mrs. Martin came to see us. It will be recollected that it was at their house we, Thomas Hines, Andy Kuykendall and I, encountered the Yankee officers, and by their appearance, we missed our dinner as I have related before. We were very glad to meet the Martins, and related at their request our adventures after leaving their house on the occasion referred to. They brought with them in their carriage a very sumptuous dinner and we partook of it with them on the grass, picnic fashion.

Before we had left Hartsville on our trip into Kentucky, Thomas Hines had received permission from General Morgan to go into the County of Butler in order to recruit a company of which he was to be captain. Some days before the command moved from Tennessee, he left on this mission. In consequence of this, he did not reach Lexington for a few days after we arrived there. He came, however, with a part of a company, raised in Butler, Logan and Warren Counties. He received about thirty or forty recruits from the vicinity of Lexington, and fifteen of our old Company "D" were also transferred, at our request, to his company, which made up the required number. Edward L. Hines and I were appointed Lieutenants of the company.

Our company was made part of the battalion commanded by Major William Campbell Preston Breckinridge, which was composed of four companies, our letter being "E." This was a fine company, and I write it not for the purpose of self-praise when I say it won celebrity throughout the entire command and many of its members won individual praise and mention from Colonel Morgan in special orders from headquarters.[11]

General Braxton Bragg and his army were in Kentucky by this time. General Kirby Smith and his forces held all of the country about Lexington. The Yankees were confined at Louisville and Cincinnati. We had possession of nearly all the State. The Federal Brigadier General George W. Morgan, however, held Cumberland Gap with about ten thousand men. He was cut off from his supplies, and his only alternative was to surrender or retreat to the Ohio River, through the mountains, by way of Big Sandy River. He chose to retreat, or

Major William Campbell Preston Breckinridge. Breckinridge would become the commander of the Ninth Kentucky Cavalry. (Hunt-Morgan House Deposit Photographic Collection, University of Kentucky Special Collections.)

General Braxton Bragg, commander of the Army of the Mississippi and the Army of Tennessee during most of Lieutenant John M. Porter's military service. (Library of Congress.)

Brigadier General Humphrey Marshall. (Library of Congress.)

rather march, his command through the rugged country to Ohio River. When his departure from the "Gap" was made known at Lexington, Colonel Morgan was ordered to proceed with our battalion and a few other troops, about eight hundred in all, and retard his progress through the mountains until Brigadier General Humphrey Marshall should move up with infantry from Lexington.[12]

Forced marches by way of Richmond and Irvine brought us, in about two days, in contact with the advance of the Yankees in the vicinity of Hazel Green. The route by which the Yankees returned was extremely rough and mountainous, sparsely populated and scant of provision and forage. We harassed the enemy very greatly. We fought them in front. The Yankees barricaded the mountain passes by felling timber, then, while they were removing it, we would dash around in the rear and attack them. We captured a large drove of cattle which they were driving with them for the purpose of eating. We relieved them of their wagons. We captured their men. We killed and wounded Yankee soldiers more or less every day and night. We fought them from sunrise to sunrise. We retarded their march so much that, some days, they could travel only two or three miles. Thus, day after day, for seven days, we were continually fighting them. We prepared ambuscades, and they marched in and found themselves suddenly fired on in the darkness of the night. They knew not how to move or where to turn, for, at every step, they encountered some portion of our small command. Their cavalry dared not encounter us and their infantry seemed in a demoralized state. In a word, eight hundred of us were a match for ten thousand for seven days. But those days were severe ones.[13]

We had no provisions, only paw-paws and raw meat, such as we could find, and that without salt. It was a trying time. The fighting was every day, every hour, and it was almost continual, and the idea of a possibility, even a strong probability, of being killed and put away in some dark mountain gorge where the sun's rays scarcely ever penetrated was enough to try the courage of the best and bravest. Many daring deeds were performed. But, I will particularize none. In many instances the contest was almost hand to hand.

Night engagements are the worst of all, darkness adds something to a fight which is never experienced in daylight. You know not how near you are, or may be, to an enemy. You can't take advantage of position, for you can see nothing but flash after flash. It requires more nerve for a night fight than for a daylight encounter.

We remained at our post and performed that for which we were sent, but the infantry we expected did not arrive. Day after day we expected General Humphrey Marshall, and, day after day, we were disappointed. In the central part of the State, our armies and General Buell's Yankee army were com-

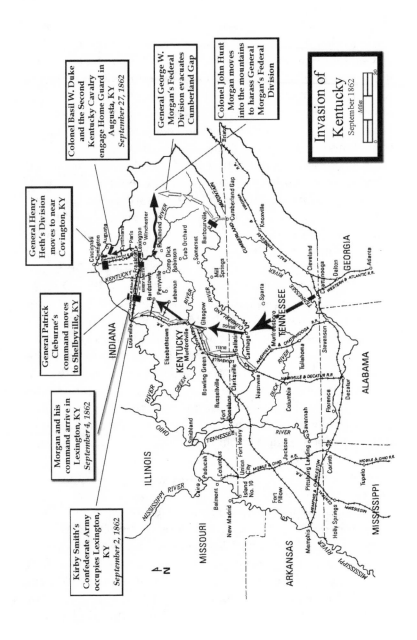

Invasion of Kentucky

September 1862

Colonel Basil W. Duke and the Second Kentucky Cavalry engage Home Guard in Augusta, KY *September 27, 1862*

General George W. Morgan's Federal Division evacuates Cumberland Gap

Colonel John Hunt Morgan moves into the mountains to harass General Morgan's Federal Division

General Henry Heth's Division moves to near Covington, KY

General Patrick Cleburne's command moves to Shelbyville, KY

Morgan and his command arrive in Lexington, KY *September 4, 1862*

Kirby Smith's Confederate Army occupies Lexington, KY *September 2, 1862*

ing to a crisis, and General Marshall was ordered hastily back to Lexington before he reached us. Finally, when we had harassed the enemy until we had got almost to the Ohio River and found no support, Colonel Morgan received a dispatch from General Smith ordering him to march by rapid movements forthwith to Lexington, and we abandoned the enemy who proceeded on unmolested to the mouth of the Big Sandy.[14]

I am of firm opinion that if we had had two thousand infantry, we could have captured the entire force of General George W. Morgan. But we failed to do so, and, after seven days of the most arduous duty, during which we tasted bread not more than once, we left his front and drew off to a little town called Grayson, in Carter County, where we spent the night and got something to eat, both for ourselves and horses that were as much worn out as the men. We left Grayson, and by very rapid marches, moved on to Owingsville in Bath County, passing through Morehead in Rowan County.

During the day that we made the march from Grayson to Morehead, we were continually fired at by parties from the hillsides, and some of the men and horses were wounded, and, as a measure of retaliation, we were forced to burn the houses of the citizens for a distance of about fifteen miles. The people had all fled to the sides of the mountains, and, in groups, poured a terrible volley at us every few hundred yards. It was utterly impossible for us to catch them, for they disappeared in the mountain fastnesses as soon as our details were sent after them.[15]

At night we went into camp for a few hours between two large hills, our men being strung along in the valley. We built fires, for it was frosty, and lay down for a few hours' sleep. Suddenly, a perfect shower of balls came from all the hills around, creating quite an amusing scene in camp. As soon as possible the fires were extinguished, and we again lay down in the darkness, and took our rest, not unmindful of our danger from their almost continual firing during the night. Morning came, but no enemy was to be seen. All the firing was from citizens and regular "bushwhackers." That day, however, they did not molest us, having been taught a terrible lesson from the occurrences of the day before.

By extraordinary marches, we reached Lexington in a worn-out and fatigued state, but only to participate in more stirring events. We had won the confidence of our commander, while the other portion of his command under Colonel Duke had likewise added to its renown by the severe duty it had been employed in in the vicinity of Covington, Falmouth, Augusta and other points. Duke's command had sustained heavier losses in men than we had, although our duty had been more arduous.[16]

The entire command met at Lexington and was prepared to participate in any movements necessary. We remained there a day or perhaps longer and then moved in the direction of Perryville, where a battle was imminent. In the vicinity of Lawrenceburg, we were engaged in diverse maneuvering with the cavalry of the enemy, but had no contest. The maneuvering of troops just before a battle is worth the study of any one, and, in and about Perryville, we did a great deal of it. We were not in the battle regularly, but were in and around and about it all; in a word it seems to me we were everywhere in that entire vicinity, day and night.

The cavalry commands of Morgan and Wheeler united in the evening of the day of battle, and were spread out in a line of about ten thousand in number, in the fields and groves about Perryville. The whole affair was, and is now, an enigma to me. What was expected to be done I never have known. It was one of those movements that no one comprehends, except those in command, and to others it is mysterious. We fought no Yankees that evening. We marched and counter-marched. We formed line-of-battle after line-of-battle. We galloped from one

The Henry Clay Home as it would have looked in 1862. Behind and around the house, Morgan trapped two battalions of Ohio cavalrymen on October 18, 1862. (J. Winston Coleman, Jr. Photographic Collection, Transylvania University Library.)

position to another. We marched through fields and woods, over fences and ditches, and yet we saw no enemy. At night we camped near the field and we awoke all the time expecting something we knew not what. One camping on a battlefield sees, or fancies he sees, something or nothing.

Bragg's army finally retreated, and Colonel Morgan covered the rear of the army on one road, and, from there to Gum Spring, beyond Lancaster, we had our hands full. The Yankees were pressing us, and, at all hazards, we had orders to protect the rear of the retreating and foot-sore infantry. To do this, we were constantly fighting back the Yankees, day and night, hour after hour. We fought them and moved on again in the rear of the army. Finally, after reaching Gum Spring, the enemy gave up the pursuit. We remained a day or so at the place and were not molested. The enemy had withdrawn.[17]

Colonel Morgan then decided to go out of Kentucky in his own way and by his own route, and, to this end, he determined to make a strike at Lexington, and, accordingly, we marched rapidly. In about twenty-four hours we reached Lexington at daylight one morning. The Yankees in considerable force were camped on the "Ashland" premises. The command, at this time, consisted of the Second Kentucky Cavalry (C.S.A.) under Colonel Duke, Colonel Richard Gano's Battalion, and our battalion under Major W.C.P. Breckinridge.[18]

An attack was made about daylight and after we had a sharp view of the enemy positions behind the home of Henry Clay. The city was occupied and held for a few hours, when we bid "adieu" to that locality for the time being and moved away on the Versailles Pike.[19]

7

THE WHISKEY WAS
STILL ABUNDANT

While General Bragg's army slowly withdrew from Kentucky by way of Cumberland Gap to Knoxville and then to Murfreesboro, and General Buell's army marched west of Bragg on direct routes to Nashville, John Hunt Morgan set out for Tennessee on roads west of Buell's line of march. Returning to Tennessee was no easy matter. Morgan and his command, Duke's Second Kentucky Cavalry (C.S.A.), Breckinridge's Battalion, Gano's Battalion, and Captain C. C. Corbett's section of mountain howitzers, rode from Lexington to Versailles, crossed the Kentucky River at Shryock's Ferry, and rested near Lawrenceburg on October 18.

At Lawrenceburg, Morgan's men discovered the presence of two Union infantry divisions—Brigadier Generals Joshua H. Sill's and Ebenezer Dumont's of Major General Alexander McDowell McCook's Corps—operating out of Frankfort, Kentucky. Morgan quickly put his command on the road toward Bardstown. They were in the saddle day and night, and rode around Bardstown to avoid the Federal garrison there. Reaching Elizabethtown, they tore up the Louisville and Nashville Railroad tracks there and a few of the trestles near Muldraugh, Kentucky. They then continued south to Leitchfield, Kentucky.

At Leitchfield, Lieutenant John M. Porter and his friend Captain Thomas Hines, along with Company E of Breckinridge's Battalion, were sent on their first detached mission, toward Woodbury in Porter's and Hines's home county of Butler. It was Porter's first taste of what would become Morgan's practice of detaching elements of his command to their home counties for purposes of scouting, recruiting, and damaging Federal logistical support systems, such as bridges, railroad rolling stock, tracks, dams, and river transportation facilities. Porter briefly reunited with his family and neighbors in Butler County while at the same time trying to evade the numerous Federal occupation forces and elements of Buell's army then racing toward Nashville.

Reunited with Morgan's full command at Morgantown, Porter finally left Kentucky in a driving snowstorm by passing through Greenville and Hopkinsville, Kentucky, and proceeding to Springfield and Gallatin, Tennessee. While at Gallatin, Morgan cooperated with Major General John C. Breckinridge's division in an attack on Nashville, then held by Federal forces under the command of Brigadier General James S. Negley. The attack was broken off after it became clear to Breckinridge that the defenses of Nashville were too strong.

By the time Morgan returned to Gallatin, he learned that Buell's army was entering Nashville. Morgan moved his command to Lebanon, Tennessee, and then directed Breckinridge's Battalion to Fayetteville, Tennessee, on the Alabama state line, in order that the men might get some needed rest and refit.

We were in a dangerous situation, being on all sides surrounded by large bodies of Federal cavalry. We moved rapidly and went into camp after dark on the Kentucky River, having crossed it somewhere in the vicinity of Lawrenceburg. I can't tell where.[1]

About two o'clock in the morning, when all except the pickets were in profound sleep, the pursuing enemy began throwing shells into our camp from the hills and cliffs on the opposite side of the river. This at once aroused us, and the bugle was sounded for mounting. There was mounting in hot haste. We were roused from our rude beds by the falling and screaming shells, and, in a short time, were prepared

A company of Indiana volunteers in the Army of the Ohio in Nashville. (Library of Congress.)

either for fighting or marching. There was no time to waste in fighting; our only safety lay in our marching and evading the many enemy commands, each larger than our own, which were advancing on us from every direction with the confident expectation of hedging Morgan and forcing a surrender.[2]

The command was therefore formed in line and began a march that frosty morning before day that was one of the most rapid and remarkable on record. We were pressed on our rear by eight thousand well-mounted men. Large bodies were also coming towards us from both sides, while another large force was endeavoring to intercept our march and delay us till all their forces should unite.

Colonel Morgan comprehended everything in a moment and marched his command forward to evade and escape the avalanche prepared for him. For hour after hour the line moved on at "Double quick," and still the danger was imminent. Clouds of dust in our rear, on both sides, told that the army was making a desperate effort. Hour after hour we rode, men and horses exhausted. As soon as a horse gave out another was procured and the ride continued through all that day and all that night. We kept in our saddles till daylight.

At daylight no signs of the enemy were seen. They had faltered during the night and got some distance in the rear. The fatigue had been too severe for them, and they had fallen by the wayside, while we were expecting to ride through another day and night. When it was discovered that they were not near us, we halted for a few hours' rest and to procure something to eat. Then again we went forward.

During the night's march we had encountered a large wagon train and captured it, paroled the men and burned the wagons. Also, in trying to avoid Bardstown where there was a large force of the enemy, we ran into a host of wagons, barricades in the streets, and our company even getting up and among the Yankees who mistook us for their own men in the darkness. Through their mistake, we made our way back without being detected.

Some of the boys gave the Yankees strict orders to be on the lookout for "John Morgan," and not permit themselves to be surprised. They little dreamed that Morgan was in shooting distance of their barricades.

Reaching Elizabethtown, we captured the force there and took possession of the Louisville and Nashville Railroad at that place and Muldraugh's Hill, which we, to some extent, destroyed, and camped for the night. Leaving there, our march was unmolested to Leitchfield in Grayson County, where we again halted. By this time we had left the enemy entirely behind us and were free to march more at our leisure and ease.[3]

At Leitchfield, Captain Thomas Hines was ordered by Colonel Morgan to proceed directly to Woodbury and occupy that point for thirty-six hours, and, if at the expiration of that time he did not come up with the command, we were to proceed rapidly to Hartford, by way of Morgantown and Woodbury, or go by way of Hartford and cross the river at Paradise.[4]

Our company came directly on to Woodbury, where we forded the river below the dam and rode into town before any one knew who or what we were. Our friends were glad to see us. We took possession of the place and put our pickets out to prevent any one going out without a pass.

After remaining in town for a few hours the company moved out to a little muddy bottom and camped for the night. I went home and spent the night with home-ones whom I had not seen since Andy Kuykendall and I had left Butler County to go to Clark County in the May or June before. In the morning of the next day, the company moved to a point immediately on Little Muddy Creek between the John Kuykendall farm and the Matt Kuykendall farm, only about four hundred yards from the Morgantown Road. The day was spent in this camp. The neighbors with Southern proclivities brought in provisions and forage. In the evening, mother, Aunt Betsey and Sister Jennie journeyed to our camp. They remained a short time and then returned home.[5]

We had remained the length of time we were ordered to stay, and, hearing nothing from Colonel Morgan, we prepared for marching to Hartford in obedience to orders from Morgan, given when we left Leitchfield. Accordingly about dark we set out with the intention of marching to Hartford that night by way of Morgantown and Borah's Ferry. However, when we reached Mr. William West's house near Morgantown, we came upon some pickets who proved to be some of our men, Colonel Morgan having reached the town and put out pickets in the direction of Bowling Green. We then waited there till Captain Hines went to town to receive further orders. We were ordered to return to our camp on the creek which we had left, and remain during the night, and then, in the morning, proceed by Sugar Grove to South Union, then to Russellville, while the main body of the command proceeded by the main road to Russellville. I went to William Beard's and stayed the remainder of the night, it being perhaps 12 or 1 o'clock when I got there. So in this case our plans were very suddenly and unexpectedly foiled.[6]

Early the next morning our pickets, who had been placed at the bridge on the Bowling Green Road, a short distance from our camp, were fired on and driven in by the Yankee cavalry, which had come during the night from Bowling Green. We forthwith moved rapidly across the farms and got into the road leading to Morgantown. There was our command. I went forward alone and reached Morgantown to find the command already on the march. I informed Colonel Morgan, who with Colonel Duke and other officers had stopped at Skeltern's Tavern, that the enemy was approaching in considerable force from the direction of our previous camp. He immediately ordered me to ride to the front of the column, which had already moved out on the Russellville Road, take charge of the advance guard, turn it onto the Rochester Road, and proceed about four miles and halt for further orders. I did so and, after waiting some time, was ordered by a courier from Morgan to proceed with dispatch to Rochester and secure the flats and ferry boats at that place for the purpose of constructing a pontoon bridge over Mud River.[7]

In the meantime, the enemy came on slowly towards Morgantown, but failed to come to an engagement, although the main body of our men were awaiting their approach in line of battle. Their coming, however, had the effect of changing our entire plan and caused us to abandon going by way of South Union and Russellville, and instead, to go by way of Rochester and Greenville.

There were many incidents that occurred that day. Some of our boys had scattered around to see their friends and were thus separated from us. Each one had sundry adventures before he got with us again. Bailey, Kuykendall and others were of this number. All of them, however, came up with us at Hopkinsville about one week afterwards. The citizens of our old neighborhood about Little Muddy were very much alarmed and distressed, thinking that we would surely be caught. Such was not the case, however. Indeed, our home friends were in the most danger, for several of them were arrested and taken to Bowling Green. Among these were David M. Beard, Thomas E. Puckett, Thomas P. Ward, James M. Cook, Captain John V. Sproule and perhaps some others.[8]

The enemy was far more *valorous* in trying to arrest citizens than in attempting to capture us, or even to fight us. Such was not their wish at that time. It was perhaps fortunate for us, for we had only a few rounds of ammunition to each man, which would soon have been exhausted. If we had been well supplied with cartridges, we would have forced a contest.

During the day and night we reached Rochester and crossed the Mud River, camping about two miles beyond on the Greenville Road. The next day we marched through a driving snow to Greenville, passed out on the Hopkinsville Road a short distance, and camped for the night. No enemy was nearer than Russellville, about thirty or more miles away.[9]

This, as has been intimated in the foregoing pages, was in October, about the twenty-fourth, I think. The night was extremely disagreeable for the reason that there was a sudden and severe cold spell. Whiskey was obtained in considerable quantity in town and given out to the men. As a consequence many were intoxicated. Morning came and whiskey was still abundant. I was ordered to take charge of the rear guard for the day, it being my duty to arrest all stragglers and take them along with my command. Many were drunk and fell out of ranks. It was my duty to arrest all of them, which I did, and, when I reached Hopkinsville, which was at about midnight, I had about seventy-five men in arrest, whom I gave over to the charge of the officer of the day. Some of them were boisterous and troublesome.

Once at Hopkinsville we had a pleasant time for some days, the weather having cleared away, and becoming beautiful and fine. While there, those of our men who had gotten separated from us near Morgantown again overtook us.[10]

From this place, we moved out and spent a day or so in the vicinity of Trenton. I visited and spent a night with my kinsman, Dr. N. L. Porter of Pembroke, whose family and himself were intensely Southern in feelings. We then moved on to Springfield, Tennessee, spending a night at that place. We had encountered no enemy since leaving Morgantown. From Springfield we moved by way of Cross Plains to Gallatin and again occupied that place, in and around which we had had such stirring scenes a short time before. There, we were again joyously received and kindly cared for. We almost felt as if each one of us was at home. We viewed the spots of interest where we had met the enemy and beaten them. It was at Gallatin where the enemy had surrendered their arms without a contest. They had fought us long and hard, but finally were whipped. To here we remained a few days.[11]

I have now traced our line of march from Gum Springs in the mountains of Kentucky, down through the Blue Grass region by way of Lexington, on to Bardstown and Elizabethtown, to the Green River country, across that river, around by Hopkinsville and then across the waters of the Cumberland River. The two armies which had fought at Perryville were at this time far separated. The Confederates under General

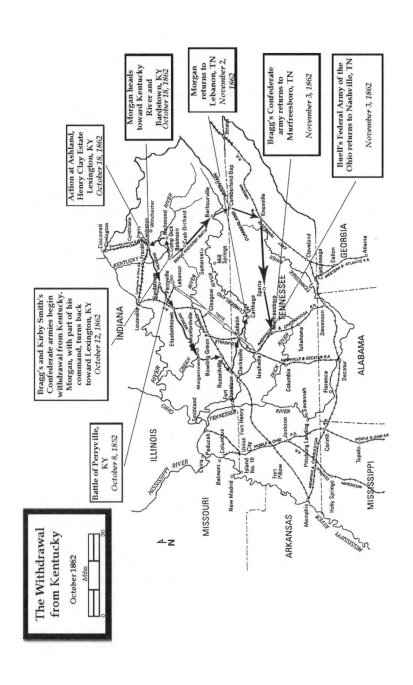

The Withdrawal from Kentucky

October 1862

Miles

0   30

Battle of Perryville, KY
October 8, 1852

Bragg's and Kirby Smith's Confederate armies begin withdrawal from Kentucky. Morgan, with part of his command, turns back toward Lexington, KY
October 12, 1862

Action at Ashland, Henry Clay Estate Lexington, KY
October 18, 1862

Morgan heads toward Kentucky River and Bardstown, KY
October 18, 1862

Morgan returns to Lebanon, TN
November 2, 1862

Bragg's Confederate army returns to Murfreesboro, TN
November 3, 1862

Buell's Federal Army of the Ohio returns to Nashville, TN
November 3, 1862

Bragg had gone to Knoxville and, by this time, were being transported to Murfreesboro. The Federal army under General Buell had withdrawn from pursuing Bragg and were marching toward Nashville again by the Louisville and Nashville Turnpike. Soon they would again confront each other.[12]

While we were at Gallatin, we had scouting parties out in every direction and kept a very vigilant watch for the enemy. I distinctly recall a scout which I made with a few picked men in the direction of Nashville. We proceeded late in the afternoon to within a few miles of the city and captured two Federal soldiers whom we safely brought into camp.

We had quite an adventure in ascertaining the cause of a great fire which we discovered some distance from us, and, after proceeding some miles very cautiously, found that the fire was caused by someone firing a bridge and trestle on the Edgefield and Kentucky Railroad. When we had ascertained this, we returned to camp at Gallatin the same night, having been in the immediate vicinity of the enemy for several hours during the darkness.[13]

While at Gallatin, Colonel Morgan determined to advance on Edgefield, and, if possible, capture the pontoons over the Cumberland River at Nashville. By previous arrangement, Major General John C. Breckinridge, who was south of the city with his Kentucky infantry, was to advance on Nashville from that side, while we would approach from the north. This was done with the hope that the eight thousand or ten thousand troops under Federal General James Negley, occupying it, might be forced to surrender.[14]

Accordingly, a night's march from Gallatin brought us at day-light in view of the city. At the same time, the distant guns to the south of it told us that Breckinridge was already at his post. An attack was made on the Federal troops on our side of the river and they fled in great confusion over to the city. The fight was quite lively for some time, but our force

Major General John C.
Breckinridge. (Library
of Congress.)

was inadequate to cross over. Very soon the enemy came in
a solid column, pouring over their bridges and forcing us
to retire after a hotly contested fight for some half hour or
more in the streets and suburbs of Edgefield and in view of
the dome of the Capitol of Tennessee.

During this fight we lost some gallant men, among whom
I particularly remember James Crabb of Warren County, by
whose side I had ridden several hours during the previous
night, and little thought of how soon he would be shot down.
Or if we even thought of the possibility of being shot, the
thought was soon banished from our minds.[15]

We returned that day to Gallatin and found that Buell's
forces were, by this time, approaching on their way to Nashville. About this time, Buell was removed from command,
and Major General William S. Rosecrans succeeded him.[16]

Major General William S. Rosecrans, who replaced General Buell as commander of the Army of the Ohio. Rosecrans's army would soon be renamed the Army of the Cumberland. (Library of Congress.)

The enemy was known to be moving toward us by way of Tyree Springs, but it was not known that they were also coming down the Scottsville Pike until they were upon us. There was mounting in hot haste, and, after a skirmish, we moved rapidly towards Lebanon, closely followed by a large force of the enemy's cavalry. The Cumberland was soon crossed and we were free from their annoyance. Leisurely, we pursued our way to Lebanon.

Bragg, in the meanwhile, had arrived at Murfreesboro and all of the Federal forces had arrived at Nashville. Lebanon thus was a place of importance to both sides; each was anxious to hold it as a flank position. Our command was placed in suitable encampments in the vicinity of the town, for its protection. A portion of our command was also sent to

Bairs's Mill on the Murfreesboro Pike, a few miles from Lebanon. That part of the command which was near the town had busy work in scouting in the direction of the enemy at Nashville and in preventing them from entering the town. At one time, a few of us went as far as in the vicinity of "the Hermitage," in the direction of the city. The enemy came to Lebanon finally and occupied the place for a short time, but very soon left, not remaining more than an hour or so. Our company was sent to reconnoiter and frightened them away. We finally left and moved to Black's Shop within a few miles of Murfreesboro where we remained for a few days. The duty upon us had been onerous and extremely severe, therefore, Colonel Morgan obtained permission to send us to the rear for a time in order to rest and recuperate ourselves and horses.[17]

Fayetteville in Lincoln County near the Alabama line was selected as the place for rest and we moved to that town by easy marches. We found plenty of forage and provisions and a good camping ground which we enjoyed for about two weeks or more. There, we had time to recover from the long and arduous duties required of us during the Summer and Fall. We had time to recount the marches from Gallatin into Kentucky in August, the marches and counter-marches throughout the almost entire length and breadth of that great State, from her mountains to her lowlands, around again to Gallatin, and thence to the borders of Alabama with scarcely any respite from our work. Two short weeks passed thus during which we had only to attend to our own wants and to those of our horses, giving, it is true, an hour or so each day to drilling and so forth.[18]

8

THE FAME AND GLORY OF MORGAN'S COMMAND

General Buell was removed from command of the Federal Army of the Ohio in Nashville on October 30, 1862. In Buell's place, the Lincoln administration named Major General William S. Rosecrans. The army would soon be renamed the "Army of the Cumberland," a name it would proudly carry through the rest of the war. General Bragg had returned to central Tennessee; his army, soon to be renamed the "Army of Tennessee," occupied positions near Murfreesboro, about twenty miles southeast of Nashville.

Although few men had flocked to the ranks of Bragg's army during the invasion of Kentucky, that was not true of Morgan's command. He had entered Kentucky with a cavalry regiment and two cavalry battalions, along with a section of artillery; he returned with six full Kentucky cavalry regiments, a Tennessee cavalry regiment, and two batteries of artillery, although some of those regiments would be assigned elsewhere. By December 1862 John Hunt Morgan was commissioned a brigadier general and commanded a division of cavalry composed of two brigades, one brigade consisting of four regiments and the other consisting of three regiments. To each brigade was assigned an artillery battery.

On Sunday, December 14, Morgan married Martha "Mattie" Ready at her home in Murfreesboro. It was a splendid occasion attended by virtually all of the prominent commanders of the Army of Tennessee.

It did not take long for Bragg to discover Rosecrans's intentions; Federal probes out the Murfreesboro Pike were frequent. Rosecrans's army was being continually augmented with additional troops and supplies by means of the Louisville and Nashville Railroad from its supply base at Louisville. If Rosecrans was to be defeated, or even slowed, that supply line had to be put out of service. Morgan and his command were given that critically important mission.

Morgan put his division in motion toward Kentucky on December 22, while Rosecrans was preparing his army for an offensive against Bragg that would erupt near Murfreesboro on December 31. Morgan's destination was the trestles of the L&N between Lebanon Junction and Elizabethtown, Kentucky. In that region the construction of the L&N, completed in 1859, ran into difficulty getting the tracks through the Muldraugh escarpment, a range of rough hills or knobs that extend from West Point, Kentucky, on the Ohio River to the Tennessee border that define the bluegrass region of Kentucky to the east and the higher western plains of Kentucky to the west. To negotiate the tracks through the Muldraugh—and to keep the roadbed at the proper grade—the L&N built a series of trestles, sixty feet high and generally between 300 and 350 feet long. The trestles were protected by log stockades manned by Federal troops. The destruction of those trestles would shut down the L&N for months.

Morgan marched his division to Tompkinsville, Glasgow, Cave City, Munfordville, and Elizabethtown, damaging the L&N tracks and bridges at Bacon Creek (now Bonnieville) and Nolin. He fought his way through the streets of Elizabethtown. Then, between Elizabethtown and Lebanon Junction, Morgan torched the trestles of the L&N, doing tremendous damage, and forced the capitulation of hundreds of Federal troops.

Returning to Tennessee was more difficult than entering Kentucky. Chased by a brigade of Federal infantry, cavalry, and artillery under the command of Colonel John M. Harlan, Morgan fought a rear guard action at Rolling Fork (near present-day Boston, Kentucky), where Colonel Duke was badly wounded. With sleet falling and the temperature below freezing, Morgan then withdrew by way of Bardstown to Springfield and to the Muldraugh by a route west of Lebanon, Kentucky. Passing through Campbells-

ville, Morgan's columns rode to Columbia, Kentucky, and finally returned to Smithville, Tennessee, on January 5, 1863, with at least three different Federal columns trying to catch up with them.

Time again arrived for action. The great historic fight of Murfreesboro was imminent and we had daring, dangerous and wild work to perform. We moved again to the front and met our newly commissioned Brigadier General John H. Morgan at Murfreesboro. He had a few days before married Miss Martha Ready of that place.[1]

The regiment to which I belonged was filled to its proper size about this time by the addition of Major Robert G. Stoner's Battalion, all Kentuckians. Stoner had just been commissioned a lieutenant colonel. We moved to the vicinity of Alexandria, Tennessee, and camped for a few days, preparatory to the famous Christmas Raid into Kentucky.[2]

Several regiments of cavalry which had been organized while our army was in Kentucky joined us, they having gone out of the State with Bragg's army, and come around to Murfreesboro. One of these regiments was commanded by Colonel David Waller Chenault. Colonel Richard M. Gano also had an addition to his battalion, and was in command of a fine regiment. Colonel Adam R. Johnson came to us with a full regiment of gallant men, mostly from the southern part of the State. Colonel James D. Bennett of Tennessee came also with a regiment. Added to all these regiments was the veteran Second Kentucky Cavalry (C.S.A.) under Colonel Duke and the Ninth Kentucky Cavalry (C.S.A.), our own, under newly commissioned Colonel William Campbell Preston Breckinridge. These men all united made a corps of cavalry, numbering about 4,500 effective men. All were camped around the little village of Alexandria among the hills and valleys of middle Tennessee. The Regiments were divided into two brigades; Colo-

Brigadier General John Hunt Morgan and Martha "Mattie" Ready at the time of their marriage in Murfreesboro, Tennessee, December 14, 1862. (Hunt-Morgan House Deposit Collection, University of Kentucky Special Collections.)

nel Duke commanding the first and Colonel Breckinridge commanding the second.[3]

The evening previous to our departure for Kentucky, a review was held and, on dress parade, a general order was read which acknowledged the arduous and dangerous expedition upon which, on the morrow, we were to start. It was a finely written order and, among other things, it said that some who were then listening as it was being read, would find a grave before the expedition was over. This produced a profound impression because no one could say he would surely live to return from Kentucky.

The night was spent in busy preparations for the morning. The morning came as brilliant and glorious as could have been desired. The bugles sounded and each regiment was formed and the march began. Regiment after regiment moved out until the line stretched out for a great distance. The appearance was a fine one. The men, arms and horses were in the finest condition; the rising sun glistening from the polished guns. Everything combined to render it the most imposing scene I had perhaps ever witnessed. Then, it made me proud to see them. There were those present who had already helped to form the fame and glory of Morgan's command.

The entire command embraced the flower of the youth of Kentucky and Tennessee, as noble a body of men as ever marched to the sound of music. The officers were all young men; none of the field officers were scarcely more than thirty years old, and the line officers, in almost every instance, were still younger. General Morgan exercised great care and judgment in the selecting of his officers, and though it was hardly possible to err materially when he had so fine a body from which to select, all being competent, or nearly all, still, it shows his fine judgment to see how finely his regiments were officered, nearly all being his appointees.

The first day's march on the famous Christmas Raid into Kentucky brought the command to the Cumberland River at Sand Shoals, near Carthage, Tennessee. The First Brigade crossed the river and camped; the Second Brigade camped on the south side of the same stream. The march was begun on the twenty-second day of December 1862. The second day we came to the edge of Kentucky and camped in the vicinity, I think, of Tompkinsville, Monroe County, Kentucky. We met no enemy.[4]

On the evening of the twenty-fourth of December, *Christmas Eve*, we arrived in the vicinity of Glasgow, Barren County, and a detachment of our regiment—the Ninth Kentucky—consisting of Company A under Captain W. E. Jones, was sent forth about dark into the town to see if the enemy was in possession of it. That detachment encountered a small body of the enemy in the center of town. A skirmish ensued which resulted in the driving of the enemy in the direction of Cave City, not without loss, however, on both sides. Captain Jones himself was killed, as well as W. R. "Will" Webb, an accomplished and gallant gentleman. Lieutenant Sam O. Peyton was quite seriously wounded and left in the care of friends in Glasgow.[5]

On the morning of the twenty-fifth, we moved forward on the pike towards Bear Wallow and encountered a small force of the enemy's cavalry at Green's Chapel in Hart County, but they fled to Munfordville after exchanging a few shots. Our company formed the rear during this day's march. I was in command of a small body of men who marched in the immediate rear of the rear guard for the better protection from surprise. This formation was always adopted in moving through a country in possession of the enemy, a precaution which was very necessary.[6]

When I reached the residence of Uncle Jordan Owen, immediately on the pike we were traveling, I called a few minutes to see him and to leave some messages to be sent to friends at home. About two hundred yards from his house the roads cross, one going in the direction of and leading to Munfordville. The enemy was making some demonstration on this road, and Colonel Breckinridge halted our company at this point and also unlimbered a piece of artillery for the purpose of fighting the enemy and holding them in check until the main body of the command should cross the Green River about six miles further on. The Yankees, however, did not come, and, after waiting till some time after dark, we moved on in the rear of the command at a rapid rate.[7]

We soon came up with an immense Sutler's wagon, the largest I ever saw. Who of that command does not remember that wagon? It was full of everything, although we were in the extreme rear and four thousand men had "gone for it." We had an abundance of everything left for us to eat and to smoke and drink. This wagon was captured in front of the residence of G. W. Blakey with whom I afterwards, in 1866, boarded, in sight of Gilead Church in Hart County, a spot sacred to me, as in its churchyard lies the body of my darling wife, the mother of my dear daughter. I little thought then what a sacred spot that would someday be to me.[8]

We passed on to where John Adair lived on the pike about a mile further, and here I halted with three or four men to picket till the rear guard could ford the river at Brickey's Ford, the bridge over Green River having been burned. The road diverged to the left and led on to the Green River through the hollows.[9]

When I had waited in the pike sufficiently long to give time for the company to cross the river, I went forward, rapidly, and, not knowing the road turned to the left, kept on the pike to the bridge. Here I found I could not cross and retraced my steps, expecting at every moment to meet the enemy. By hard work I found the right road and soon caught up with the company.

The night was extremely dark and the position was calculated to make one feel as if lost. No danger, however, befell us and about midnight we found the entire command encamped at the little village of Hammondville in the corner of Hart and LaRue Counties. The remainder of night was the rainiest I believe I ever witnessed. We were completely drenched. Morning came and the rain still fell in torrents.

Forward went the command in the direction of the Louisville and Nashville Railroad which we struck between Bacon Creek and Upton's Station. At Bacon Creek bridge was a small body of Federals which, after a brisk skirmish, surrendered. While this fight was going on, the remainder of the command was engaged in destroying the railroad track by tearing up the rails and heating and bending them. Nolin was the next station which we captured. The officer in command of the enemy at that place agreed to surrender if we could satisfy him that we had artillery with us. This was soon done by taking him a short distance and showing him some fine guns. At once he surrendered his men without a contest. This work being finished, the day was coming to a close. It was a fearful, rainy day. We were wet as water could make us.[10]

We moved on in the direction of Elizabethtown where we knew there was a considerable force of the enemy. We camped about dark at the Red Mills, a few miles from town, and remained unmolested during the night. I well remember how our company looked that night. The night before we were later getting into camp than any of the command, being, as has been stated, the rear guard. On the side of the hill, to the left of this turnpike, a mile from Red Mills, in the edge of a woods, back of a farm which extended down to the pike, we pitched our camp, wet, tired, hungry and muddy.[11]

Some of us went a half mile for forage for our horses; others set about building fires to warm and cook with. This was a serious undertaking as nothing dry could be found;

Bacon Creek Bridge as it looked after Morgan's command destroyed it on the Christmas Raid. (From a woodcut in *Frank Leslie's Pictorial History of the War of 1861*, Martin F. Schmidt Collection of Kentucky Views, 2004.41, Kentucky Historical Society, Frankfort, Kentucky.)

everything was wet and soggy. By an old log, which I think I at this time would still recognize, we finally got a fire and proceeded to warm, dry and cook. Then we lay down, four or five together on the wet ground, and slept softly and sweetly till the bugle roused us in the morning. This was only one incident among hundreds in the life of every soldier.

Morning came and we moved on toward the town. The advance was met by an officer from the enemy under a flag of truce who impudently demanded the surrender of General Morgan and his command "to avoid useless effusion of blood," saying we were already totally surrounded and could not possibly escape. To this amusing demand, General Morgan made reply that he proposed having them to surrender to him in a few hours. Safe escort was given the officer back to his lines, and we at once advanced and opened fire on their works and the town.

The enemy withdrew to the center of the town and took refuge in brick buildings from which they poured a terrible fire upon us as we advanced. Our Ninth Kentucky Cavalry Regiment dismounted west of the Louisville and Nashville Railroad tracks, and advanced on foot across an open field, across a creek waist deep, into town and filed up an open street, under a heavy fire, which fortunately did no serious harm.

Other portions of the command, by this time, had gained other portions of the town, and, when we advanced to fire the buildings, the enemy threw out white flags and surrendered. Three of us entered the basement of a large brick building and brought out about nineteen live, armed soldiers, who had taken refuge there. They fully expected to be killed. They were certainly the worst frightened men I ever saw.[12]

The fight was a severe one and many daring, gallant deeds were performed by our men. John Dunn, a gallant Irishman in our company, made his way to the large brick hotel, full of the enemy, entered it and proceeded to the top of the house. He tore down a Yankee flag which was flying from a pole, and, wrapping the flag around his body, made his way down. He came out of the building and crossed to the opposite side of the street, while yet the inmates of the house had not surrendered. For such daring deeds as this and others, a sword was presented to the company for gallantry. It is the sword I have at this time at Sugar Grove. There is a history connected with the sword which I will relate, by and by, at the proper time in this narrative. The gallant Dunn was killed during the Indiana-Ohio Raid.[13]

The entire Yankee command surrendered. It was the second time in a few months they had done the same. Major Gen-

Woodcut of a Federal stockade protecting the Louisville and Nashville Railroad near Elizabethtown, Kentucky. (Editor's collection.)

eral Edmund Kirby Smith had captured and paroled them in the previous August, and they had just been exchanged, re-equipped and sent to duty. It was an Illinois command, and the men were greatly chagrined at their calamity. The rail-road was torn up at this place also; indeed, from Bacon Creek to Muldraugh's Hill, it was pretty completely demolished.

From town we proceeded to a stockade on Muldraugh's Hill on the railroad, and, after a bout, forced the surrender of a considerable force of the enemy. We encamped near there on the road leading to Bardstown. By this time our presence, force and purposes were pretty well known to the Yankees, who were gathering large bodies of troops for the purpose of our capture. Coming into Kentucky and capturing places was comparatively easy. Going out safely was far more difficult.[14]

Leaving our encampment, we moved on the Bardstown Road and reached Rolling Fork river, which, from the recent heavy rains, was past fording at the usual crossing. While a party was finding a more shallow ford and leveling the banks to enable the artillery to cross, our rear guard was attacked by a large force of Yankees under Colonel John M. Harlan, who pursued us from Elizabethtown, having come from Louisville by railroad as far as they could, and then on horseback.[15]

This was the most critical position, perhaps, our command ever was in, except possibly when in Indiana and Ohio in 1863. It was absolutely necessary to find a passage across the angry little stream, and how to prevent the Yankees from pressing us was the question. A vigorous charge would have been serious to us.

It was determined to present a bold front and, by sheer boldness, awe them and prevent a charge. General Morgan, in person, directed the crossing of the main body of the command, while Colonels Duke and Breckinridge, *with only four companies—ours one of the four—*held at bay the large body of cavalry under Colonel Harlan for several hours until the entire command was safe over the river.

The four companies were at the mercy of the Yankees, and they had only to rush on us and destroy or capture us. For some reason they did not charge, though a hot fire was kept on *us* all the time, and their artillery was tremendous. The four companies, stretched in a weak line in front of them, bore all this and returned a vigorous and destructive fire. Our horses were a half mile in our rear on the bank of the river and the shells from the Yankee cannon burst in our company's line, killing five horses outright and knocking half the line down. E. P. Roane, a horse-holder, was seriously wounded.[16]

About the same instant, a fragment of a shell struck Colonel Duke in the head and he fell senseless from his horse. Colonel Breckinridge, who was at his side, assumed command, and directed the movements of the four companies,

Colonel Basil W. Duke.
(Hunt-Morgan House
Deposit Photographic
Collection, University
of Kentucky Special
Collections.)

while Colonel Duke was borne bleeding from the field across the river. This was a critical moment. All that could be done had been nobly performed. The entire army was in safety, and to our firmness they owed the same. And now how were we to withdraw to safety?[17]

Finally the four companies gradually began to withdraw, keeping up a constant fire all the time, and retreating *backward*. We finally reached our horses only to find many of them killed, wounded and scattered. Fortunately, and for some strange and unaccountable reason, the enemy did not pursue us, and we gathered up our wounded, mounted our dismounted men behind us and went safely over the stream. I carried over behind me James H. Holland of our company whose horse was lost.[18]

When we had reached the open field beyond the river, the enemy advanced and poured a desperate fire upon us with shell and solid shot till we passed beyond their range.

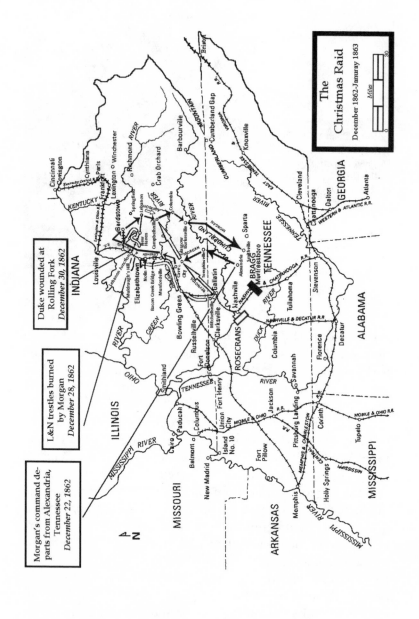

The Christmas Raid
December 1862–Januray 1863

Duke wounded at
Rolling Fork
December 30, 1862

L&N trestles burned
by Morgan
December 28, 1862

Morgan's command de-
parts from Alexandria,
Tennessee
December 22, 1862

They dared not cross the stream that night, and hence we were not molested, but proceeded on to Bardstown where we camped.

Colonel Duke was seriously, and, it was thought at the time, fatally wounded. But it turned out that he was able to be carried out with us, which was done by obtaining a carriage and bed for his use. Before the nature of his wound was ascertained, and when all of us thought he was killed, I never saw as much sorrow among the men. Colonel Breckinridge, as gallant a man as lived, moved over the field with tears streaming down his manly cheeks, and urged the four companies to hold their ground till Colonel Duke could be safely carried over the river. His appeal was complied with, and not till everything was done that could be done did he order us to our horses. I have always thought, and yet think, that the four companies saved the entire command. I do not think those four companies received the consideration they deserved, though they were flatteringly mentioned by the superior officers, and Colonel Duke in his history of the command speaks in the highest terms of them. Such a degree of heroism was rarely witnessed during the war.

I write facts, not for the purpose of lauding my own company, though it stood, as Brigadier General Bernard Bee said of General Thomas J. Jackson's brigade at Manassas, "like a stonewall." I love to think of our company, of its members, of Bailey, Gray, Kuykendall, Holland, Dulaney, Hines, Thurman, Hughes, Kennedy, Duvall, Crutcher, Morris, Grett, Plummer and hosts of others who were true as an arrow to its mark. Company E, Ninth Kentucky Cavalry, Provisional Army of the Confederate States of America; it was a glorious organization and won fame. The entire command camped at Bardstown the night after the action at Rolling Fork. The Yankees had by this time several large bodies on the move to intercept our progress. A large force was at Lebanon, almost directly in our line of march, we having turned our course towards Tennessee again. Another large body of cavalry was moving from Glasgow in the direction of Burkesville to cut off our retreat, and still another large force was approaching in our rear. Prompt and energetic action was demanded to extricate the command from the avalanche threatening to fall upon us.

We moved from Bardstown to Springfield in Washington County. Here we went to camp in order to induce the belief we were going to remain all night. The Yankees were in a large force at Lebanon, almost immediately on our line of march, and, in order to avoid them, it was necessary to make a detour around the town and get beyond it by daylight the following morning. For this purpose soon after dark we moved. Hundreds of fires were built and left burning to induce the belief that we were not marching. We knew the fires could be seen by the enemy.[19]

Then began one of the most remarkable night marches perhaps that we ever made. The weather was cold and the night dark. The ground was hard frozen and the roads full of ice, which rendered it dangerous to ride. For hour after hour, in darkness and cold, we moved on as fast as possible, but, being encumbered with artillery, our progress was greatly retarded. We passed in sight of Lebanon which was full of Yankees ready to capture us on the morrow, and at daylight had emerged from the trap prepared for us and passed on our way towards Campbellsville in Taylor County, which we reached at dark and found rest during the night.[20]

During the day, we crossed the Green River at the point where Colonel David Waller Chenault and Major Thomas Y. Brent were subsequently killed on the fourth of July 1863. The stockade at that place was built at that time, but no Yankees were found there. Here we burned a large quantity of corn which the enemy had collected and abandoned. The bridge across the river we also burned after passing over it.[21]

The enemy was pursuing us, but, during the day and night did not come up with us. It is a remarkable fact that the enemy never did come up with us when we were leaving the State. It seemed as though they were anxious to overtake us. From Campbellsville, we passed through Columbia and on to Burkesville, where we again foiled a large body of enemy cavalry sent from Glasgow to intercept us. In Cumberland County, about daylight one morning on Marrowbone Creek, I called at the gate of a farmhouse and found that some relatives of sister Mary T. Porter lived there. I did not have time to stay long, but moved on with the command. The previous night was bitter cold. Ice was on all the roads. In fact, it was very dangerous riding.[22]

Our march, from this time on, was not marked by any exciting scenes and we pursued our course leisurely till we came to the vicinity of Livingston in Tennessee, where we rested a few days. Then we passed on by way of Clarksville to Sparta, and from there to the vicinity of Rocky River, between Sparta and McMinnville. Here our regiment was in camp a few days, till ordered to Liberty to repel an attack on that place by a Federal force from Murfreesboro.[23]

The Battle of Stones River, or Murfreesboro, had been fought while we were in Kentucky, and the Confederate Army under General Bragg had retreated to Tullahoma, the enemy at the same time occupying Murfreesboro. At the time when we went first to Liberty, we little thought we would see much hard service in and around that town. This was about January 10, 1863, I think. I cannot say certainly about the day of the month. I write the main facts and cannot at this date (1872) call to mind the exact dates of the different movements. It resulted, however, that we were in and about Liberty, Alexandria, Lebanon and Woodbury until some time in May following, except at short intervals when we made sudden dashes in the line of the enemy.[24]

9

This Was a Hard-Fought Field

Probably none of John Hunt Morgan's operations are more obscure than those that occurred during the winter of 1863. Basil W. Duke writes of those operations only in generalities in his History of Morgan's Cavalry, *as he was personally absent at times. Without a doubt, those operations represent some of Morgan's most notable military achievements. John M. Porter remembered them, although they appear in his memoirs as one continuous fight, which in large measure they were.*

When General Bragg withdrew the Army of Tennessee to the Highland Rim after the Battle of Murfreesboro, Morgan's division was given the task of screening the right flank of the army. Rosecrans's Federal Army of the Cumberland occupied Nashville and Murfreesboro. Selecting a sector that included Liberty and Woodbury, Tennessee, both on direct routes to Murfreesboro, Morgan kept his command in the foothills and brought elements of it forward to attack outlying Federal positions in the darkness. Multiple times, between January 22 and the end of April 1863, Morgan seized Federal wagon trains and large numbers of officers and enlisted men and killed, wounded, or captured hundreds of other Federal troops.

Each time Morgan struck a Federal position, Rosecrans ordered a retaliatory strike. At times, elements of Morgan's command would be chased by two to three brigades of Federal infantry, cavalry, and artillery. Fighting occurred along the Murfreesboro Pike, between Milton, Tennessee, and Liberty, and along the Woodbury Pike between Murfreesboro and Woodbury.

John M. Porter recounts the savagery of the fighting in January and March 1863 along the Murfreesboro Pike from Milton to Auburn to Prosperity, and along the Lebanon Pike to Liberty and Snow Hill. The actual details of each engagement are almost impossible to recount. Porter was detached on a special scouting mission between February 7 and February 28, 1863, the narrative of which is found in chapters 10 and 11. For the rest of the winter and spring of 1863, Porter presents the fighting in central Tennessee as one continuous stream of memory.

Vividly do I call to mind the country in which we spent the Winter and Spring of 1863 in the most exciting and arduous duties. Every day was one of excitement and more or less danger. To write all that we did or all we saw of army life during this time would be merely a repetition of many things already written. It is enough to say that it was hard service, and I will only give the main items of interest, including an account of the most severe fights with the enemy.

When we first came to Liberty, Tennessee, it was to drive from the vicinity a body of Federal cavalry, which we did after a skirmish. Liberty is situated about half a mile from the intersection of the turnpike from Murfreesboro and the turnpike from Lebanon. We moved out of Liberty to meet the enemy and had a brisk fight. The object of the enemy was to gain our rear. When we withdrew to Liberty, we took up positions just beyond the town, across the creek. Here, they again advanced upon us and we had a severe battle in which we were forced to fall still farther back in the direction of Snow Hill.[1]

During this retreat, for half a mile, we were terribly shelled by the artillery of the enemy. They had a raking fire at us. We formed a line at the base of Snow Hill and again waited their approach. Our company was dismounted and sent to the left of the road from Liberty to Snow Hill. From our position we had a fine fire at the enemy as they advanced up the valley, and we held our position, driving them from our immediate front till finally it became evident that they could not advance and drive us from our position.

They made preparations to send a large force around us, one or two miles, and obtain possession of the road in our rear, and thus force us out in the hill country towards Carthage. To avoid this, we withdrew to the summit of Snow Hill just in time to engage the enemy and drive them from the road in great confusion. This repulse caused them to waver in their entire line, and soon they were in full retreat towards Murfreesboro. By this time darkness came on and we camped on the field. Our loss was considerable in wounded and several killed. The enemy lost, but how heavily we could not learn.[2]

This single narrative of an action at Snow Hill will serve for a dozen similar ones at the same place during the Winter and Spring of 1863. Every inch of the ground was fought over. Some times they came in the darkness, some times during the day time. They never found us unprepared. It may be well supposed then that our duty was onerous in the extreme, as well as dangerous.

While here we drew from the quartermaster's stores new uniforms, which were needed and gladly received by the men, and also our men were paid a paltry sum in money for their services. Of course, it was gladly received. Those who think the Southern soldier fought for *pay* does not know of what he speaks. The *pay* was the least motive; indeed, it was *no* motive at all. That was generally true of all branches of the service.

The arm to which we belonged, the cavalry, perhaps paid less attention to pay, and cared less for *pay*, than any other branch of the army. A good horse was the only thing desired, and a good horse was generally possessed by each one. He had no need of money, like a poor infantry soldier who was confined to his camp and obliged to eat what was in hand. He could use money in buying things from sutlers and others. A horseman could gallop around till he found a place where he could get a "square meal" as we called it. There were many advantages which the cavalry had over the infantry arm of the service, not the least of which was that, while the infantry for weeks and months were often confined to camp—by reason of which diseases were contracted—the cavalry were almost continually on the wing, so to speak, and, owing to their activity and exercise, they were generally more healthy, even if their service was harder.

The hardest and most severe fight we had with the enemy during the time we were at Liberty occurred at a little village called Milton on the Murfreesboro Road, some ten miles or more from our encampment, about last of March or first of April 1863. The enemy advanced from Murfreesboro in a large force of infantry, cavalry and artillery, and an engagement took place in and about Liberty. The enemy were somewhat worsted, and at nightfall began their retreat back towards Murfreesboro.[3]

During the night the remainder of our division came up with General Morgan, in person, who ordered an advance for the purpose of overtaking the enemy and making battle. The pursuit was vigorous and spirited, and early in the forenoon we came up with the rear of the enemy and at once the fight began. The enemy formed their line on the crest of a gentle hill, thickly studded with cedar and made rugged by projecting limestone rock which rose in crags all over the ground. A battery of artillery they planted immediately on the left side of the pike in a position to rake our line as it advanced.

The Tenth Kentucky Cavalry and the Ninth Tennessee Cavalry regiments (C.S.A.) were ordered to charge on horseback and capture the artillery if possible, while, at the same

Idealized portrait of Brigadier General John Hunt Morgan. (Hunt-Morgan House Deposit Photographic Collection, University of Kentucky Special Collections.)

Morgan's men ride toward the enemy. (Editor's collection.)

time, the Ninth Kentucky Cavalry, our regiment, was ordered to dismount and advance on foot on the right of the road through the open fields and drive the enemy from their position on the crest of the hill in the cedars. This was a difficult and serious undertaking, for the enemy had great protection, while we were exposed to their destructive fire.[4]

During the day, Captain Hines was in command of the regiment, which left the command of the company to me. The regiment, as ordered, charged across the open space and entered the cedar woods only to find the enemy concealed thick as Autumn leaves in the brake. We were met with a terrible fire, and a short, hotly waged contest for half an hour took place, during which time our line steadily advanced, driving them before us and capturing those who could not get away.

During this time the action waxed warm all along our lines and resulted in the enemy being driven from their positions. Just at the time when victory was in our grasp, a large

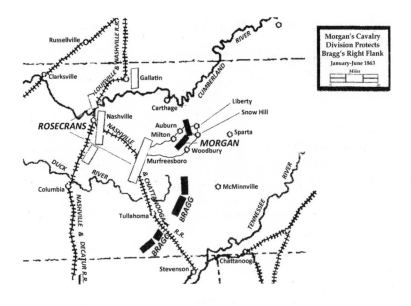

enemy reinforcement came up and the retreating Federals were rallied and we in turn were driven slowly back. Our ammunition at this time failing, we were withdrawn, and the enemy also at the same time withdrew and retired to Murfreesboro. After gathering up the dead and wounded, we went back to Liberty.[5]

This was a hard-fought field, and I dare say every man of Morgan's command who took part in that battle at Milton will remember it as long as he lives. Our loss as well as that of the enemy was severe. Several valuable officers were killed. Captain R. T. Riggen of our regiment was killed as we entered the cedar brake, and several others here fell to rise no more. It is astonishing that more were not killed when I consider the disadvantages under which we labored.[6]

Just as our company was ordered into line preparatory to

dismounting, a cannon shot from the enemy's line whizzed through the line, but fortunately did no harm. I distinctly saw it as it was coming, strange as it may seem, and before I had time to speak it struck a stump at my horse's neck and shivered it into a thousand pieces. It could not have missed my horse more than a foot. This was a narrow escape from immediate injury.

Many incidents connected with this battle will have to remain untold in these pages. The men fought gallantly and received praise from our general, who was everywhere on the field. This day's doings taught the enemy that they could not venture out from Murfreesboro without having to encounter Morgan. After this, they always came in large bodies and cautiously felt their way. Indeed, after a time, they became afraid to venture far from the main body of their army. This one single account will suffice, for all our operations were of a similar nature to the foregoing, and it is of no use to relate them all.

Many scouting parties, of from fifteen to a hundred men, were sent out into the enemy's lines, and they were always successful. One of these parties, numbering some fifty men or more, advanced to the turnpike leading from Nashville to Murfreesboro, inside the enemy's line, and, securing a position in close proximity to the road, remained for several hours and succeeded in capturing a considerable number of the enemy who were traveling along the pike. As they were captured, they would be sent off to the spot where the horses and guards were, and there kept till the party was ready to move away.

Among the number thus made a prisoner was Vincent S. Hay, Esq., whom I knew well before the war, and in whose office I had read law. He had espoused the side of the Union, as it was called, and was at the time of his capture acting as division quartermaster for some division of Rosecrans's army.

Brigadier General John Hunt Morgan, from a photograph taken in late 1863 or 1864 and showing the wear of more than two years of war. (Library of Congress.)

Being placed in my care, I treated him with all the kindness I could and loaned him some two or three hundred dollars, Confederate money, which at that time was worth about eighty cents, perhaps, to the dollar. He was sent on to Chattanooga and finally to Atlanta, Georgia, where he took sick and died, I have no doubt, from exposure. He was of delicate frame and not enured to hardships. He was a good man, but, in my opinion, controlled and guided too much by other persons. I pay this tribute to him, that he was sincere in his convictions and a man of the very highest honesty and integrity, and whole he was, sternly and unalterably, for the Union. I give him credit for his pure motives and aims. In this connection I will add that his administrator paid the amount due me for money loaned him. He was born and raised in Butler County, only two or three miles from where my father lived, and I had known him from my infancy. He was about fifty years old, I presume, at his death. After the war, his remains were removed to Butler County and re-interred in his family burying ground on the old Hay place, now known as the Bumpas farm, which belonged to my father at his day of death.[7]

Upon another occasion Colonel Breckinridge selected about one hundred men from his brigade—he was in command of a brigade—for the purpose of penetrating the lines of the enemy and capturing some couriers from Nashville to Murfreesboro with important dispatches. Most of the one hundred were chosen from our regiment, and some ten or more from our company, Captain Hines and myself and Lieutenant Edward L. Hines also being in the party.[8]

We proceeded by way of Lebanon and on in the direction of Laverne. In order to reach the pike leading from Nashville to Murfreesboro, at the point which we wished to strike, it was necessary to cross Stone's River, which was much swollen, owing to late rains, and was still rising. After nightfall, we crossed and were then in the enemy's lines. I was put at the head of the advance guard, a very dangerous and responsible position on such an occasion. I was furnished with a guide who was familiar with the country, and, after moving cautiously for some two or three hours with frequent halts and reconnaissances, we came to the pike on which the enemy was almost continually passing.

The night was dark and the roads muddy. There was a house about four hundred yards up the pike which was used as a picket stand and as a relay place for couriers. Other stands were scattered at intervals of a mile in both directions.

I was ordered to make a rapid circuit with the advance guard and take a position three hundred or four hundred yards south of the house, so as to intercept the Yankees if they should attempt to escape by flight. I had scarcely reached my position and formed in line before our men on the other side of the house began the attack. As was expected, one or two mounted their horses and attempted to escape, but ran into our arms before they knew what had been done. After a brisk skirmish we captured the entire party, and, as a matter of course, had to move rapidly to avoid being captured ourselves.

The firing had alarmed a regiment or two of cavalry in close proximity, and they were soon in close pursuit. I was not in the rear with my men, and I would think it anything but pleasant under the circumstances. The night was dark, a turbid and angry river must be crossed, and the enemy was close on us. Our march was very rapid, and fortunately we succeeded in crossing the river safely and reached the other side as the enemy came to the river bank. By this time it was near daylight, and we traveled an hour or so and camped for the purpose of getting something to eat. The enemy did not pursue us further. I do not think there had ever been any published account of this scout, but it was nevertheless one of those most daring and successful ones of the war.

10

OUR MARCH WAS CAUTIOUS

Lieutenant John M. Porter's most notable achievement as a soldier was a scout that he, Captain Thomas H. Hines, and a select group of twelve other men from Company E, Ninth Kentucky Cavalry (C.S.A.), made in February 1863. Most of them were from Butler County, Kentucky, so chosen because they were intimately familiar with the area of operations.

Apart from the official report of Captain Thomas H. Hines prepared at Liberty, Tennessee, on March 3, 1863, which singles out Porter for conspicuous praise, Porter's own account in this and the succeeding chapter is the only one known to exist of the famed operation.

The scouting party departed from Liberty, Tennessee, on February 7, 1863. The object of the scout was to proceed to the Barren River, not far from Bowling Green, Kentucky, to destroy Federal transport vessels that were plying the rivers between Bowling Green and the Ohio River at Evansville, Indiana. Because Morgan had so thoroughly destroyed the trestles of the Louisville and Nashville Railroad in December 1862, Rosecrans's Federal army in Nashville and Murfreesboro was relying on transport vessels that operated from Louisville down the Ohio River to the Green River and up the Green River to the Barren River to Bowling Green, Kentucky, for supplies. The L&N would bring the supplies to Nashville from Bowling Green. Morgan determined that a select body of men, operating under cover, could destroy those vessels and interrupt Rosecrans's desperately needed shipments of stores.

141

Porter and his men crossed the Cumberland River at Granville, Tennessee, and reached the vicinity of Bowling Green, Kentucky, on February 11. Their presence given away by a deserter, the men disbanded on the night of February 20. They first returned to Tennessee and then reentered Kentucky. An attempt to seize a transport vessel on the Barren River was foiled by the presence of Federal cavalry. Porter and his men headed for Butler County. What followed were scenes reminiscent of those recounted by members of the Virginia battalion of partisan rangers commanded by Colonel John Singleton Mosby: movements at night, hiding in the woods or outbuildings of friends and sympathizers, and avoiding enemy patrols in an effort to complete the mission.

There is one more scout, the particulars of which I will give. The party consisted of about fourteen men; among the number were Andy Kuykendall, Ayres Curtis, William Shephard McKinney, James K. Clark, James H. Holland, Joseph S. Gray, Edgar L. Mitchell, William White, Thomas Hines and myself, perhaps one or two others. It was in February 1863. Our command was in camp at Liberty. Permission was obtained to make a scout into Kentucky and injure the enemy as much as possible.[1]

Accordingly we made a detail as above and started; the first day's march was free of any incident worth relating for we were yet in our line. The second day, however, we reached and crossed the Cumberland River at the little town of Granville, some distance above Carthage. The boats were rickety and dangerous; finally, however, all were safely over, and we found ourselves in the enemy's country where we were likely, at any moment, to meet with a body of the enemy's cavalry.

Our march was cautious and at the same time as rapid as possible under the circumstances. Fortunately for us, we came through the entire route and saw no enemy. We came to the Louisville and Nashville Railroad near Woodburn in Warren County one evening some time before night. Our

Cavalrymen departing camp on a scout. (From *Harper's Weekly* newspaper, April 1, 1865, editor's collection.)

dress consisted of a Federal uniform over our Confederate uniforms, and we were very easily passed among the citizens as Yankees. By this means, we passed through a section where we were known.[2]

The day of which I speak, we came on by the Pleasant Grove Academy in Simpson County and reached the vicinity of South Union about dark. After crossing the railroad there, we went directly to Clear Fork Church and remained till about daylight, when we moved on the creek back of William H. Duncan's farm. Here we were well fed and cared for by the neighbors until evening when we heard that our presence in the country had been made known by the capture of a deserter by the name of Dr. Samuel Garvin the day previous. We heard the enemy was a short distance away and advancing for the purpose of capturing our entire party. Thinking it prudent not to be caught napping, and in order to relieve our friends of any danger which our presence might bring upon them, we prepared our horses and set out about 3 o'clock in the afternoon through a country and district with which we were all well acquainted and strange to say we were not recognized by any one except our friends. We passed the

Edmond Duncan Farm, saw Tom Duncan, passed near Proctor's Mill near Richlieu, by Captain Ben Davis's farm in open day. We managed to escape, returning to Tennessee by re-crossing the Cumberland River.[3]

The river crossing was not accomplished without difficulty. One boatload of horses and men came near being swamped. By the presence of mind and heroic effort of those in it, it was safely landed. Andy Kuykendall was in the boat at the time, and the danger of being lost was so great at one time that one of the party began to pray, when Andy called for every man to do his duty towards checking the boat—that then was no time for praying, action was what was needed—and by great exertion her course down the river was checked. Afterwards when we were all safe over, we had many laughs about the scenes and adventures of that truly fearful night.

We felt, after having crossed the river, that we were pretty safe from the attack of any cavalry that might be pursuing us, and we accordingly marched only a short distance and stopped, tied our horses and built fires. Day was about at hand and our purpose was to remain secluded during the day and travel again the succeeding night. We fortunately found Southern sympathizers who kindly furnished us, at our camp in the "deep tangled wild wood," with food for both men and horses.

The day was spent in sleeping as well as we could while a pelting rain in the forenoon and a gentle snow in the afternoon fell in our faces. Our clothing and blankets were wet and had been since the preceding night, and it was impossible to dry them while it continued to rain and snow.

This was soldiering and serving one's cause and country under decided difficulties, and yet, strange to say, there was to us then a peculiar fascination for it, and is looked back to now as an event of pleasure and almost hilarity. The trials and fatigues were severe, yet they were interspersed with episodes and occurrences which divested the hardships of their rougher points and rendered them entirely agreeable. To account for this singular fact is not difficult when we consider that, when the die is cast, or, in other words, when we set our hearts upon anything and fearlessly embark upon our undertaking, whatever it may be, we do it with the intention of being satisfied and contented with whatever we have to undergo in order to secure the prize after which we seek. So it was in an eminent degree with the gallant soldier who fought for the independence and liberties of the South. If dangers beset his pathway and hardships were to be endured, he confronted the one and encountered the other with a degree of fortitude and cheerfulness that have been the honor and glory of his desolated country.

During the night succeeding the rainy and snowy day of which I have spoken, we moved on in the direction of South Carrollton and Paradise. Our object was to intercept and capture a steamer, as a number were employed in transporting army supplies to Bowling Green, then by railroad to Nashville, for benefit of the Federal army. Procuring a guide who was familiar with the country, we compelled him to conduct us to a secluded and dense bottom on the Green River, about a mile above Paradise. Here, about sunrise, we dismounted and prepared to await the coming of a steamboat and capture her.[4]

The hours passed slowly by and twelve o'clock came but no boat was in hearing. At length, about three or four o'clock in the afternoon, we heard a boat signal for Paradise, and at once we proceeded nearer the river to take our positions behind trees on the bank and be prepared to call her to shore when she came in hailing distance.

We discovered, as soon as we took position on the river, a large body of Federal cavalry immediately in front of us on the opposite side of the river and only a short distance from the bank. This of course was a surprise to us, for we had no idea the enemy was in the vicinity, and seeing them so near us, we at once concluded that it was the party that left Bowling Green in pursuit of us. We also thought that, in all probability, there was a force in our rear on our side of the river, and, thinking thus, it was determined to forthwith withdraw from our position and make our way out of the dense bottom and swamps we were in and regain a more open country.

Accordingly, we withdrew and reached the open country in safety. We afterwards concluded that the enemy being on the other side of the river was only an accident, they having come from Hartford or some other point, and that they did not know we were there at all. At all events, we failed to get the boat as we fondly anticipated.[5]

After traveling for about an hour we met some Federal soldiers who were at home on furlough. After passing ourselves as Federal cavalry, we asked them to go to their homes and prepare supper for us, promising to be back by dark. They willingly agreed to do so, and we doubt not they had a fine and elegant supper for us, but we had gone in another direction and were miles away. This was a game we frequently played while on this expedition.

Our course was partly in the direction of Greenville until we came near the town, when we went in the direction of Russellville, for some twelve miles perhaps, to the residence of a Methodist Minister named DeWitt, an ardent Southern sympathizer who had one or two sons in our army. It was late in the night when we reached his house and convinced him we were Confederate soldiers. His good wife and his daughters fixed an excellent supper about two o'clock in the morning, which we dispatched as only hungry soldiers can do.[6]

We then, for security, repaired to a secluded spot in the wood about a mile distant and remained during the day. We found it much to our advantage to move only at night, for there were few of us, and if we moved in daylight our course could easily have been traced by the numerous scouting parties of the enemy, while, by swift and rapid night marches, we could travel fifty miles during the darkness and completely confound any parties who might pursue us. During the day that we remained in the woods near Reverend DeWitt, we were bountifully supplied with necessaries for ourselves and our horses. We were expecting the enemy to find out our location and pounce upon us, but we spent the day free from their presence.

After dark, we began our march. It was on a Saturday night, dark, muddy and rainy. Our destination was the Little Muddy neighborhood in Butler County, and the distance, by the route we were to travel, was certainly not less than thirty-five or forty miles. We marched on in the darkness and through the mud. Crossing Mud River, if I remember rightly not far from "Graveltown" or Harreldsville, we met with nothing worthy of note till we came to the vicinity of Forgyville. Here a part of our men, about four in number, remained in the neighborhood, going to Mrs. Polly Holland's, one of whose sons was of the number.[7]

The rest of us kept on. One of the party with us was sadly in need of a horse; and in this condition it was, according to usage on both sides during the war in such emergencies, certainly permissible to obtain a horse from any one and at any place when opportunity presented. Accordingly, as we passed the residence of James D. Porter, a Union man, but of no kin to me, a horse was obtained from his stable and we proceeded on our way by Stokes Factory, and passed by Sugar Grove without stopping.[8]

We found ourselves at daylight near the Buck Carson farm in the hills and hollows just beyond the residence of D. O. Helm. When we passed between his farm and Mrs. Sterritt's, I went down to the house, for the mother Helm was at the

Five officers from Morgan's command. The center figure is Captain Leland Hathaway of Clark County, Kentucky. Note the broad-brimmed hats, enormous boots, and assorted uniforms. This photograph, probably more than any other, provides the best glimpse into what Morgan's officers looked like in the field. (Hunt-Morgan House Deposit Photographic Collection, University of Kentucky Special Collections.)

time very sick, and I found my mother and sister, Mary Beard and William Beard, and perhaps others there. Of course, my going in was a very great surprise to all of them, and while they were no doubt glad to see me, at the same time their uneasiness and solicitude for my safety greatly marred the pleasure of seeing me.[9]

I remained a short time only for I was anxious to leave before the servants should be up in order to prevent their seeing me. After a few hasty words, I got a torch of fire, and started to find the balance of the party who had gone before. After winding about in the darkness for some time,

I found them near the "Dabidon" or Carson farm, and we started fires. By daylight, we were as comfortable as could be expected under the circumstances. We had made a remarkable march during the night and of course were, to some extent, tired and wearied down. During the day, it was Sunday, a good many of our friends came to see us, among the number I remember Mr. Frank Bailey, "Mitch" Sterritt, Uncle Owen Helm, William Beard and, I think, Hick Gray and Calvin Kuykendall also.[10]

The time was pleasantly spent in the forenoon, but in the afternoon an incident occurred that had something unpleasant about it. The owner of the horse which we had taken the night before, Mr. Porter, as soon as he found that his horse was gone, determined to pursue and if possible recover him. The pursuit could be and was easily made for it was very muddy and a dozen or more tracks could be easily traced. He obtained the services of some of his neighbors to accompany him, and among the number was Mr. Chesterfield Mason, a strong friend of ours at whose house we had called as we went down into Muhlenburgh County. Though he did not know of our return, still, as soon as he was informed by Mr. Porter that he had lost a horse and in what direction the tracks proceeded, he was satisfied that we were the party. He at once started with Mr. Porter and traced us very accurately till we passed Sugar Grove, some half mile, where we turned to the left, leaving the main public road. When they reached that and saw our tracks going off from the road, his knowledge of the country at once told him where we were and his surmise was correct. He then told Porter and the others that he would pursue the tracks and recover his horse if he could and directed them to go on down the road to the vicinity of Little Muddy Church and await his coming.[11]

They did so, and Mason, following our tracks, was soon in our camp and told us the situation. We were not compelled to give up the horse, but did so in order to save our friends from harm and persecution. Mason, after remaining a short time, took the horse and went on to join Porter and his party, telling them that he found the horse tied to a tree with other horses near, and that he cautiously slipped up and cut him loose and brought him away, seeing no one about. The story was satisfactory to Porter and his party who returned home in good humor and fine spirits.

About the time this incident had fully developed itself and we had been freed from any tangling circumstances connected with it, we were somewhat surprised that the enemy had come out from Woodbury that evening and arrested two or three citizens not more than a mile from where we were. Woodbury was about four miles distant. We were thus in rather close proximity to the Yankees and some movement was necessary on our part.

About dark we moved down to the back side of the farm which then was owned by Calvin Kuykendall, and stopped near the old house he formerly lived in. We did this under directions from him, he telling us we would find someone there with provisions for us. It so happened that he could not get away from the house without exciting suspicion among the negroes, and his estimable wife carried us a basket of provisions fully a half mile in the darkness for our benefit. After eating it and giving Mrs. Kuykendall time to get to her house, we moved around the farm and passed by the house.

We went by Cousin James D. Carson's residence, and I remember distinctly now of seeing Cousin Paulina, his wife, sitting by a table with a light on it, no doubt reading the Bible, for she held a book in her hand. I saw this through a window as we rode by. It was calculated in a high degree to make one long for peace, and the end of War, this seeing of family and home peacefulness.

We went directly to old Sandy Creek Church near the

residence of D. R. McKinney, whose son, William Shepard McKinney, was with us. Here we built a fire and Mrs. McKinney made some hot coffee and sent it over to the church to us, which we enjoyed very much.[12]

It was then determined to disband our men for one week, at the end of which time all were to meet at Clear Fork Church in Warren County. The men were directed to go in squads of about two or three and secure themselves from the enemy during the week as well as they could, and, in the event any of them should be captured, they were charged not to divulge anything in regard to the whereabouts of the others, nor where and when we were to meet again. The men were all true and tried, and there was no fear of any improper disclosure in case of capture, and, indeed, it would have required nice work to have captured any of them, for they were all good scouts and used to foiling the enemy in diverse ways. I venture the assertion that fourteen better, truer, braver men never made a scout.

11

THE SCENE WAS LUDICROUS
AND PITIFUL

After days and nights hiding from Federal cavalry patrols, Captain Thomas H. Hines and his men determined to strike. Led by Hines, the command proceeded to South Union and then to the Barren River, where, on February 25, 1863, the small force captured and destroyed the steamboat Hettie Gilmore *and all of the heavy stores it was carrying to Bowling Green to supply General Rosecrans's Federal army. While Hines and his men struck the river transport, John M. Porter, sick with what was probably dysentery, remained behind at the home of Coleman Covington, a friend and Southern sympathizer in Warren County. Desperately ill, he left Covington's home when Federal patrols were spotted nearby. After a harrowing few days, Porter was reunited with Hines and the scouting party after they had journeyed over forty miles. At Woodburn, in Warren County, Porter and the men captured a Louisville and Nashville Railroad freight train and set it on fire. The train was hauling, among other things, a large number of mules bound for Rosecrans's army. With the cars ablaze, Porter filled the engine's firebox and sent it under full steam down the tracks until it wrecked.*

All told, the scouting mission destroyed nearly half a million dollars in Federal government stores. The command spent twenty-one days on its mission and moved 150 miles within the Federal lines. The men traveled one hundred miles in thirty-six hours between the destruction of the Hettie

Gilmore *and the destruction of the train at Woodburn. Pursued by Federal cavalry, the men swam the angry Drake's Creek, where one trooper drowned, then made their way across the swollen Cumberland River and, finally, entered Liberty, Tennessee, on February 28, 1863.*

The members of this little squad on that dark and dreary Sunday night at Sandy Creek Church separated, some going one direction and some another. Captain Hines and myself rode that night on the old Hopkinsville Road from Sandy Creek to Berry's Lick, and from there to Mrs. Polly Holland's, where we found the three or four who had stopped there Saturday night. We went to the woods about day and remained till the succeeding night.[1]

I wish to say here what I should have said some pages back, that after leaving Mason's near Berry's Lick, we passed the residence of Ephraim Bailey. I had a sword which was presented to our company for gallantry at Elizabethtown. It was much in my way and made a good deal of noise by rattling, so I determined to leave it with Mr. Bailey for safe keeping, until such time as I should call for it. He received the sword and safely kept it during the war, and in 1871, I called at his house, got it and took it to Sugar Grove, where it is at this time.[2]

At dark on Monday night, after remaining during the day near Mrs. Holland's, Captain Hines and myself, after giving directions to the men who had stopped there on Saturday night, made a short, profitable scout towards Rochester, and returned by Mrs. Holland's, at whose house we called for a few moments. We tied our horses in a branch which ran through her lane and thus we were enabled to conceal the fact of having stopped, for our horses' tracks went into the water and came out again, and no sign was left of our halt.[3]

We soon mounted and proceeded on by Berry's Lick and about daylight reached Fidella Helm's house, who then lived on the "Bumpus" place near Sugar Grove, only about a mile distant. We did not go to Sugar Grove for the reason it was a public place and it would have been practically impossible to have kept our presence and our horses concealed from the negroes. Fidella Helm was an ardent sympathizer with our cause, and afterwards was a faithful soldier in the Confederate army. After carefully concealing our horses in a dense thicket in his field near a branch, we went to the house and got breakfast, went to bed for some rest and sent him over to let Pa and Mother know that I was there, in order that they might visit us during the day. They soon came and the day was spent as pleasantly as possible under the circumstances. Sister Cullie also came in the afternoon and remained till we had gone. By this means I was enabled to see the home ones and they permitted to see me.[4]

At dark we got our horses in trim, and bidding them "Goodbye," we started in the rain and darkness. Captain Hines was to go in the direction of Woodbury to see some of his friends, while I turned my course to go to Eldon Sloss's near South Union. Thus Captain Hines and I separated after going about half a mile, each to go his own way solitary and alone. As I have said, the night was dark and a drizzling rain was falling, and it was rendered doubly gloomy under the circumstances of leaving home ones without even daring to go home.[5]

With thoughts gloomy and sad, I rode on and met no mishap till after crossing Gasper River, when I was suddenly startled by being accosted by someone on the roadside who I supposed was drunk. But the first impulse was that it was a Yankee picket. After hearing him speak a few words incoherently, I concluded it was some poor unfortunate who had been to Richlieu and imbibed too freely and had probably fallen off his horse at that point. I rode on, but this little incident served to keep my imagination at work and made me also more cautious in my movements.[6]

I had not gone possibly more than two or three miles until an object which I then took for a man came meeting me in the road, and, failing to halt at my command, I fired at him. During the confusion and noise made by my horse, the object—whatever it was—disappeared. I did not know whether my shot had been fatal or not.[7]

I gathered myself up as well as I could from this second scare and rode forward in the darkness not knowing what might occur next. I concluded it must have been a negro belonging to William Barnett, Esq., near whose farm it happened. I heard nothing of it afterwards and, of course, nobody was killed by the shot. I soon reached my brother-in-law's house, Eldon Sloss, and aroused him. I was soon in his house and snug in bed for some rest. He took my horse to George Price's in order to better conceal him and returned home before day.[8]

I remained at Mr. Sloss's during the day, closely concealed in his parlor to which no one had ingress but himself and my sister, Jennie. The night following, it was thought advisable that I remove from Mr. Sloss's and, accordingly, I went after dark to Mr. George Price's, to whose keeping my horse had been given the night before. Here I remained during the next day. Mr. Sloss and sister Jennie came to see me during the day. About three o'clock in the afternoon I concluded to travel again as that night we thought perhaps I had better be at some other place. Indeed, we were to meet each other at Clear Fork Church and once more begin our work of annoying the enemy all we could.[9]

I left Price's and came out by the Sloss farm, saw him and his negroes at work in a field as I rode yonder; the negroes did not recognize me, and I passed making merely a formal bow as I rode past. I rode on into the Morgantown and Franklin Road and proceeded up towards South Union a few hundred yards, then turned to the left and went to old man

Bowles's who had two sons in General Morgan's command. At his house I remained till after dark, when, supper being furnished, I started in company with Mr. A. Clinton Reeves as a guide to go to the Clear Fork Church, the place of rendezvous. I was almost entirely unacquainted with the country and secured his services to pilot me to the place.[10]

When I reached the Clear Fork Church I found some of our party already there and in a short time all of us who a week previously had parted at Old Sandy Creek Church were again together, except one of our party, William M. White, who had gone to Allen County to visit his friends. He, however, soon after our return to Tennessee, rejoined our company.

While at the church I was taken quite sick with something like *cholera morbus* and was unable to continue with the party. The design was already formed to destroy the depot at South Union and, if possible, destroy a train of cars if one could be captured. Being unable to ride, I made my way to Coleman Covington's nearby and was furnished with everything I needed. The others, towards day, proceeded to South Union and effected their object by proceeding to Hadley, and, from there, destroying a steamboat loaded with government supplies. I remained at Mr. Covington's in an upper room quite sick in bed during the day.[11]

In the afternoon, it was told me that a party of cavalry was coming down the road towards the house. I arose from my bed and upon looking from a window saw about fifty Federal soldiers within fifty yards of the house.

Thinking perhaps they would search the house and seeing no chance to escape without being discovered by them, I began casting about as to what I should do to avoid detection and arrest. Spying a small aperture in the ceiling, I went up into the garret and proceeded to the side of the house nearest the front gate. By this time the party had reached

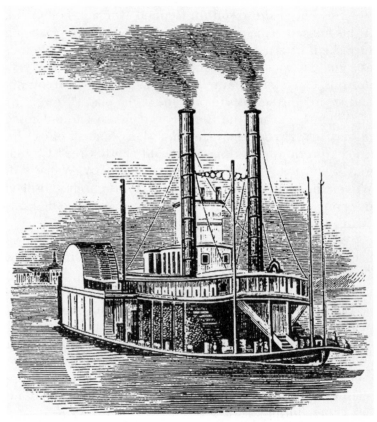

A packet steamboat similar to the *Hettie Gilmore*, which was sunk by Captain Thomas Henry Hines and his scouting party in February 1863. (Editor's collection.)

the yard gate and begun a conversation with Mr. Covington, most of which I heard in my snug retreat. They asked if any "Rebel" soldiers were there. "No" was the response. "Have you seen any Rebels today?" was another question. Covington said he had seen some soldiers riding around his farm early that morning, but he did not know whether they were

"Rebels" or not; that they were dressed in Federal uniforms and were about fifteen in number. This was really our party who, upon returning from South Union, came in sight of Covington's farm. After making some other inquiries, among others asking whose gray horse that was with his head out at a stable door close by, and receiving the reply that it was his, the entire party rode away.

My horse with my saddle and bridle was in the stable, and, being used to a crowd of horses, when he saw the party approaching, he was foolish enough to make some demonstrations of joy and stuck his head out of the door, nothing being across it but rails. This came near betraying me and would have done so if they had been careful enough to have gone in the stable and discovered my saddle and bridle, they being cavalry style.

As soon as they were gone in pursuit of our men, I concluded that it was best to change my locality, and I rode about a mile with very great difficulty to Thomas Covington's, Coleman's brother. Here I was in a more retired place, and, after remaining some day or so perhaps, I concluded to go out into the Pleasant Grove neighborhood in Simpson County.[12]

Late one evening I started from Mr. Covington's and went in the direction of South Union. About dusk I called at James Milligan's, whose wife was Southern, he himself was in the Confederate army and was soon afterwards killed. She told me the Yankees had just been there and were gone and she did not know how soon they might return. I, however, dismounted and went into the house and remained till I got supper. Fortunately they did not come, though I was hazarding too much on the uncertainty of it. I did not think so much of it then as I have done since and do now.[13]

After supper I started to go to Mr. Dudley Turner's in Simpson County. The only difficulty I was apprehensive of was in getting beyond South Union and the railroad. The

Shaker community main residence building, South Union, Logan County, Kentucky. (J. Winston Coleman, Jr. Photographic Collection, Transylvania University Library.)

burning at the depot a few days before had put the enemy on their guard and they were thick through the country. I went up the creek directly towards the Shaker village till I came to a fence. I pulled it down and rode on. Suddenly, I found myself just in the rear of one of their large houses and all mixed up in the left, and, after knocking something like twenty fences it seemed to me, I reached the railroad north of the town and crossed it, not, however, till I had gone down some distance seeking a place where I could cross.[14]

So it was I found no Yankees that night but proceeded without delay to Mr. Turner's. My object in getting in this locality was to be in position to join the party again as I knew their design was, after the capture of the boat, to attempt an interruption of the trains at Woodburn on the Louisville and

Nashville Railroad, and I was satisfied they would pass near me and enable me to rejoin them. When I arrived at Turner's late at night I had my horse put in as secure a place as I thought, and I then went to Sara Sloss's, half a mile distant, to remain during the remainder of the night and the following day.[15]

During the day, however, my horse was unexpectedly discovered by a negro, and, of course, suspicion was at once aroused that a Rebel was somewhere in the vicinity. I was on notification of this discovery and at once determined to move from that place. Accordingly, I went to M. E. Morris's about two or three miles away and remained about twenty-four hours when, sure enough, the rest of our men came along and I joined them again.[16]

In an hour from that time, we captured a train of cars at Woodburn which we destroyed by fire after attempting to drive out the mules with which the cars were filled. Many of them could not be driven out, and, in consequence, were burned. The scene was at once ludicrous and pitiful, the poor brutes neighing and plunging about, blazes streaming from their back and tips of their ears, as occasionally they sprang from the cars and ran off through a grove of Black Jacks near at hand.[17]

Filling the fire box of the engine full, steam was put on, and it went down the road like a streak of light. It kept its onward course till it finally jumped the track about twenty miles below and was shivered into a thousand pieces. This was, I confess, somewhat reckless, but the times were reckless, we must remember, and soldiers were careless of consequences.[18]

Time was precious. We hoped to capture a passenger train with Governor Andrew Johnson, afterwards President, aboard, but in this we failed. As we afterwards heard, it having halted at Franklin, a few miles south of us.

George Bernard photograph of locomotives in the railroad yards in Nashville, Tennessee. All of the locomotives pictured are emblazoned with "U.S. Military Railroad," noting their use supporting the Federal war effort. Note the damaged locomotive, possibly struck by a Confederate raiding party and brought back to Nashville to be rebuilt. (Library of Congress.)

We soon were in the saddle, and, after a rapid ride of less than an hour, came to Drake's Creek, swelled by rains to a rapid and wide stream, deep and dangerous. There was no chance to get over the creek other than by swimming, and no time for deliberation, the enemy being in the rear. One after another, in we went, horse and rider, head and ears, and after hard efforts, all succeeded in safely crossing, except Shepard McKinney who was drowned in the muddy waters. He was a gallant soldier from Butler County and was sadly missed by his comrades. We left directions with citizens to recover his body and give it a decent interment. This was a sad duty; a good boy was gone from us, buried in the muddy waters rolling at our feet. Who was the next of our little band who would be called on to God? The question was pertinent, yet it was banished from our minds, and wet, cold and gloomy, we took up our solemn march southward.[19]

[See map of Butler, Logan, and Simpson Counties on page 18.]

Very soon we had a diversion. Captain William Jennings with his Company of Second Kentucky Cavalry (C.S.A.) had started to Kentucky, and we came in sight of them. His men and ours were all finely dressed in Federal uniforms, and each mistook the other for the enemy and for some time were in great danger, but by great prudence and caution we found out each other before any firing was done and thus, fortunately, no harm was done. Quite a laugh washed over the scene, and, after hearing all the news from the command, from which we had been absent about two weeks, and giving Jones all the news we had concerning the enemy in Kentucky, we separated, his company going on to Warren County and our squad proceeding towards Lafayette in Macon County, Tennessee.[20]

By rapid and forced marches we reached Cumberland River without encountering the enemy, except one night scaring their pickets nearly to death on the Lafayette and Gallatin Road. This was effectually done by one or two shots from our men, which acted like a charm, and a pathway was soon open for us to get along. I do not think I ever heard pickets gallop as fast in my life as they did that night. They rode like wind, and we were glad to be aware that they had running ideas. It saved us a deal of trouble.

When we reached and crossed Cumberland River we were safe from attacks, the first time we had felt secure since we touched its northern bank two weeks before. Finding a good locality we halted for a few days for rest, then leisurely proceeded to the command at Liberty, Tennessee.[21]

Thus was ended a daring adventurous scout, the particulars of which, if every incident were narrated, would fill a volume with items worth reading. The foregoing, however, will have to suffice as a sufficient description of it, and, therefore, I will continue the main thread of this narration, and turn again to Tennessee.

12

I WAS CAPTURED
FOR THE LAST TIME

*As John Hunt Morgan was preparing his division to reenter Kentucky and,
possibly, cross the Ohio River into Indiana, he sent Captain Thomas H.
Hines and Lieutenant John M. Porter and eighty men from the Ninth Kentucky Cavalry (C.S.A.) into that area of Kentucky between Covington and
Brandenburg where a crossing of the Ohio River would have to be accomplished if such a venture were to be undertaken. Hines and Porter's mission
was to scout the concentrations of Federal occupation forces and select a
river crossing site most suitable for Morgan's purposes.*

*Porter believed the river crossing at Brandenburg in Meade County was
the best. Overruled by Hines and others, who favored a river crossing closer
to Cincinnati, the advance command got as far as Boston, Kentucky, west
of Bardstown, when they ran into trouble. Federal mounted forces closed in
on Porter's men; some were killed, but most were chased down and captured.
Porter was captured along the Louisville and Nashville Turnpike just south
of New Haven, Kentucky.*

*Hines not only escaped capture, he wound up crossing the Ohio River
and operating in southern Indiana, identifying Southern sympathizers—
"Copperheads"—to provide assistance to Morgan's command once it entered
Indiana. It seems one aspect of Hines and Porter's mission was to do just
that.*

Morgan's full division of cavalry—six regiments, and artillery (two batteries of four guns each)—followed Hines's advance command. Fighting engagements at Marrowbone Creek on July 2, Tebb's Bend (Green River Bridge) on July 4, Lebanon on July 5, Morgan ultimately settled upon Brandenburg as the site for his command to cross the Ohio River. The crossing was effected there on July 8. Once on Indiana soil, Morgan conferred at length with Captain Hines, who had been operating in Indiana for days. Crossing Indiana and southern Ohio, Morgan and his division were finally scattered and captured at Buffington Island and points as far north as East Liverpool, Ohio, by the last week in July 1863.

In May 1863 General Bragg's Confederate army was stationed at and in the vicinity of Tullahoma, Tennessee, while the Federal army under Rosecrans was confronting him with his forces at and in the vicinity of Murfreesboro. The Ninth Kentucky Cavalry to which I belonged was some time in May sent to the vicinity of Readyville for the purpose of guarding a very important position in the direction of McMinnville. We were required to picket a continuous line for about fourteen miles, which formed what is called in military parlance a chain picket.[1]

Our men and horses, after having gone through the arduous duties from December 1862 up to that time with scarcely an interval of rest, were, of course, to a great extent worn down. Not withstanding this, we kept up this picket line, by detailing about sixty men every twenty-four hours, who bravely sat in the face of the enemy and kept them at bay. It was a trying time, and none but the best of soldiers would have kept up under the circumstances. Forage was scarce and our horses almost starving. Rations were small and of an inferior sort of food. Our men were sadly in need of clothing too, but all these things were counted as nothing if we could only do our duty and keep the enemy. Men who at home were never seen in rags and tatters, and who had never known what it was to be deprived of all the comforts of life, were here to be seen day by day in their worn out clothing, poorly fed, going to their dangerous posts without a murmur. It was of such stuff as this that the Confederate soldier was made of.

This regular routine of arduous and laboring duty continued till about the first of June 1863, when Captain Hines and myself were directed to proceed from that place to Albany, Clinton County, Kentucky, in order to take charge of the convalescent and worn out men and horses which had been forwarded there. We proceeded with a few men to Albany, going over the mountains and dangerous country by way of McMinnville, Sparta and Livingston, Tennessee. We found collected here some two hundred to three hundred men of different regiments of General Morgan's command. Forage was abundant and pasturing was plenty, and soon the men and horses were in good condition.[2]

Indeed we remained but a short time, for Captain Hines selected about eighty men from the whole number, and, leaving the remainder in charge of some other officer, we started on a scout further into Kentucky, with the design of crossing the Ohio and raising a row in Indiana. The row was *raised, and most of us were raised also.* Joseph Haycraft and I were the officers who accompanied Hines with the scout numbering eighty men. The men were divided into two companies, one of which Haycraft commanded, and the other was in my charge.[3]

We set out, I confess, with some misgivings in my mind as to the result. We came by way of Tompkinsville in Monroe County, passing through that place about dark and giving an unsuccessful chase to some Federal soldiers whom we saw. The night was the darkest and rainiest nearly ever seen, but we kept on our way in order that daylight might find us as far from there as possible. The next point was New Roe, or Scottsville, I forget which, in Allen County, possibly we passed both places. We determined to approach as near to Bowling Green as possible and came within about four miles of the town, crossing the Barren River about four miles above it about dark, having that evening over-hauled the U.S. Mail going to Scottsville and obtained late papers.[4]

After crossing the river we struck for the railroad just above Bristow and lay for some hours in a few feet of the track while one or two trains passed which we did not molest, though they were at our mercy. After daylight we mounted our horses and rode out on the railroad bed and went down towards Bowling Green for some distance without seeing any enemy. I remember how brightly the sun shone while we rode down the road-bed between the iron track over which so many of our enemies were continually passing to and fro. We did not tear up the track.[5]

After we had gone some mile perhaps, we left the railroad and went across to the pike and traveled up the pike for a time, then diverged to the left and took the dirt road to Brownsville in Edmonson County. We passed the residence of the Reverend Jesse S. Grider, whom we met in his lane going to Bowling Green. We told him to report us to the commandant when he got to town, as we knew it was better for our friends to do so, and we were not caring as we were not afraid of being caught by the Yankees there. We passed Chamelion Springs in Edmonson County where I called and left some message with the wife of Jo Mitchell for the home ones.[6]

At Brownsville we waited long enough for the boys to get such things as they needed when we again put forward for Leitchfield in Grayson County. Here we found many things not found in Brownsville, and, although it was dark, the boys seemed to have found a heap, judging from the bundles they had when they were formed in line for a night march.[7]

We halted about midway between Leitchfield and Eliza-

Lebanon Junction, Kentucky, where the Louisville and Nashville Railroad spurline through Boston and New Haven, Kentucky, to Lebanon left the main stem of the railroad between Louisville and Elizabethtown. (Woodcut from *Harper's Weekly*, October 19, 1861, Martin F. Schmidt Collection of Kentucky Views, 2004.41, Kentucky Historical Society, Frankfort, Kentucky.)

bethtown and slept till daylight, when we again moved on to reach Elizabethtown and capture a train of cars. We found in it a variety of things, among others, about two hundred good horses on their way for the use of the Yankee army in Tennessee. Our men mounted themselves on the horses, and what were left, together with our own, were given away or turned loose at the depot. After occupying that town for some two hours or more, we evacuated it and went on our way towards Bardstown or rather Boston on the Lebanon branch of the Louisville and Nashville Railroad.[8]

Elizabethtown was not a new place to us; we had been there and captured it before when it was well garrisoned by the enemy, but this time there were no soldiers there and we were masters of the situation. I had charge of the town with my company, while the rest were attending to matters at the depot. Take it all in all, we had a very pleasant time in the place, as we had previously had, but we could not stay long, so on we went.

As I have said, the design of the raid was to go up on the enemy's own soil and cause them to feel some of the hardships of war. My own idea, and an idea which I urged upon the other officers in charge, was to march directly from Leitchfield to some point on the Ohio, such as Brandenburg, and cross over and return either by the same route or some other route and recross the Ohio below the City of Louisville. The enemy would be totally ignorant as to our designs, and the boldness of the march would have so paralyzed them that they could not have prevented our return. The other officers, however, thought it best to strike across the Louisville and Nashville Railroad, the Lebanon branch of the L&N, and the Louisville and Frankfort Railroad, and reach the Ohio River between Cincinnati and Louisville, and recross it into Kentucky at Brandenburg, where I proposed entering the State of Indiana. This to my mind was a hazardous undertaking and one likely to result in the capture of the entire party. It was ultimately determined to try and reach the river and make it by the route to which, I confess, I was opposed.

Accordingly, after destroying what we could at Elizabethtown belonging to the U.S. Government we took up our march towards the Lebanon Branch road which we reached at or near the village and station called Boston, and, after crossing the road within half a mile of a stockade garrisoned by a portion of an infantry regiment, we turned to the left and moved on toward the Bardstown Branch. After proceeding for a few miles, we halted on Wilson's Creek to feed our horses.[9]

After feeding, the day being very warm and the creek at hand, most of the command went in bathing, and, while thus in the water, the enemy, numbering about one hundred and fifty men, charged our pickets and drove them rapidly in, and before we were aware of their approach were within one hundred yards of us and firing upon us. The confusion for a moment was very great and there was every prospect of a regular stampede, but a few words of command brought most of them to their senses and a volley or two from our men stopped the enemy. Others were bridling the horses, and, in a few moments, all were mounted, many of us, however, with no other clothing than pants and jacket, not having time to dress. I well remember that I had on only a pair of pants, a jacket and a hat which was my entire dress, the rest of my clothing I left on the bank of Wilson's Creek.

As soon as the men mounted their horses, the enemy again advanced and we were under the necessity of retreating, and, accordingly, we began to give way before the enemy, expecting to make a stand on a hill some half-mile or more from us. But the enemy pressed us so closely and fired so heavily that the advance of our men became "stampeded" and fled in great confusion, only a few being kept behind and firing on the advancing soldiers.

Here began a disorderly race which was kept up for three or four miles at the best speed our horses could run. About twenty-five of us halted on the hill spoken of and fired a few volleys which were unable, however, to stop the advance, and we gave way and began our run after the rest of the command which, by this time, was in disastrous retreat. While making the stand on the hill, my horse became unmanageable; it was afterwards fatal to him. The chase was continued through lanes and farms and woodland, the enemy in our midst. Of us who were in the rear, some four or five of our men were killed and a good many dismounted by their horses being killed and wounded.

After the chase was continued for about three miles or more, my horse showed signs of giving out on account of his

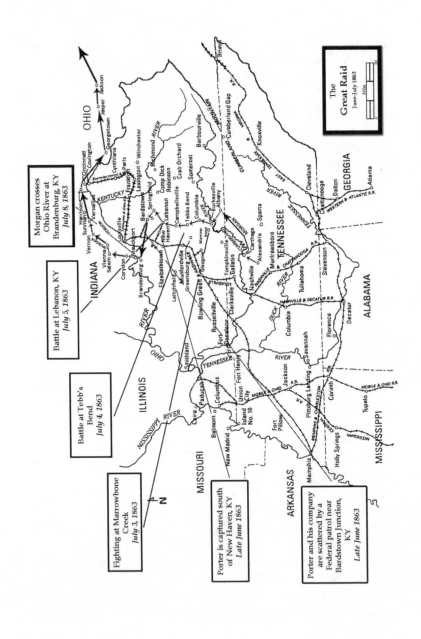

The Great Raid
June–July 1863

Miles

Morgan crosses Ohio River at Brandenburg, KY
July 8, 1863

Battle at Lebanon, KY
July 5, 1863

Battle at Tebb's Bend
July 4, 1863

Fighting at Marrowbone Creek
July 3, 1863

Porter is captured south of New Haven, KY
Late June 1863

Porter and his company are scattered by a Federal patrol near Bardstown Junction, KY
Late June 1863

wound, and, in going through a lane, he stumbled and fell with me from loss of blood. The enemy was about forty yards from me, and my only safety lay in jumping the fence, which I did. I ran across a field about one hundred yards to a woodland which I reached unhurt, though I am confident there were a score of bullets which whizzed by me. All of them continued the pursuit of our men and did not pursue me. I went a short distance into the woods and took position where I could see the road.

After they had passed, I went down to the road near where my horse had fallen to see about one of my men whom I saw fall when I fell. I found him mortally wounded. Procuring assistance from a farmer nearby, I took him to his house and did all I could for him; but poor gallant boy, his wound was fatal, having been shot through his body, and he died before a physician could reach him. I have forgotten his name. He was a member of Captain George M. Coleman's Company of our Regiment, and lived, I think, in Bath County, Kentucky.[10]

I went to look after the other killed and wounded, and had the dead buried at a church nearby. It was a sad duty, yet it was one which was incumbent on me to attend to. After this was done, I determined to make my way south. I did not know where the command was. I knew some twenty or more had been captured in the chase and some were separated from the main body, and the best I could do was to try and take care of myself. I was enraged and the citizens were in many instances traitorous. My plan was to travel on foot till I crossed the Lebanon branch and the Louisville and Nashville Railroad south of Elizabethtown. Then, I intended securing a good horse and traveling through Grayson County into Butler and reach home, and then proceed on south and rejoin the command.

I was about two days and maybe more working my way through the Muldraugh's Hill country, having to travel solely at night. Finally, I reached a point a few miles below New Haven on the Lebanon branch. I designed crossing it at night, and, after remaining all day within half a mile of a stockade, where I could see Yankees, I started out just before night to cross over at a point between the two stockades, but calling at a house for something to eat, I was *captured* by fifty Yankees who came up deployed so as to completely surround the house and cut off my escape. Someone had told the Yankees that I was there. I was thus captured for the last time during the war.[11]

At first my captors were disposed to be rough in their treatment and seemed inclined to consider me as a guerrilla and deserving a severe punishment. The entire section of the State was very much enraged at the daring and boldness of our *raid,* and for this reason we did not expect, nor did we receive, much consideration at the hands of our enemies when, by the fate of war, we fell into their hands. Our command was extremely odious to the Yankees, and when they succeeded in getting any of Morgan's men in their power, they desired in many instances to take stringent measures.

From this place I was conveyed to a point on the Lebanon branch near New Haven and placed in a strong stockade, well guarded and defended by several companies of infantry of an Indiana regiment. Here I was fed on the coarsest food and allowed no privileges, being closely guarded all the time during the few days I was kept. I was then sent to Louisville and put in prison where I met the men of our command who had been captured in the Ohio river below Louisville on their return from Indiana. Their capture took place a few days after I was captured, they having retraced their route from the Wilson's Creek route and come round by Hodgenville and on to Brandenburg and crossed over the river with the result I have indicated.

I am firmly of the opinion that if from *Leitchfield we had gone directly to Brandenburg we could and would* have made a successful trip and have gained an enduring reputation for daring and boldness. At any rate, it was acknowledged on all sides to be one of the most brilliant exploits of the war. The men were the flower of the command. I mean by this they were *of the flower of the command,* for where almost all were so gallant, it would be wrong for any particular portion to claim to be the *best.*[12]

When I arrived at Louisville I was still destitute of clothing, and my first efforts were directed towards securing some. I wrote a note to Mr. John A. Carter of the city, whom I knew, asking him to send me a few articles, among other things a pair of boots, some under-clothing, etc. He very kindly brought to the prison the things I ordered and they were delivered over to the officer in charge and by him kept for about ten days before he would even so much as tell me they were in his possession. These little exhibitions of meanness were characteristic of the Yankees.[13]

Finally, however, I succeeded in getting my clothing, which by this time I sorely needed, for I was almost absolutely without any, save a pair of army pantaloons and a gray jacket. My treatment here was by no means good and at times it was feared we might be taken out and put in irons, or sent to some penitentiary, or maybe to Tortugas.[14]

13

THE DAYS DRAGGED SLOWLY BY

John M. Porter was imprisoned at Johnson's Island Prisoner of War Depot in Sandusky Bay, Ohio. Johnson's Island was chosen for a prison site in the fall of 1861. Although it was designed to hold both officers and enlisted men, it was ultimately determined that it would house only commissioned officers. That is the reason Porter was confined there.

Johnson's Island Prisoner of War Depot was constructed on a forty-acre site on an island in Lake Erie facing Sandusky, Ohio, a railhead, two and one-half miles across the lake from the prison. Easily accessible by boat, the prison was situated on an island so as to make it difficult for prisoners to escape or for any relief expeditions to reach it. With twelve prison blocks constructed for the inmates, a prison stockade, a hospital, and a guard barracks, Johnson's Island held anywhere from 2,000 to 2,500 prisoners at a time. In January 1865 it held more than 3,200 prisoners. Stationed there was a guard garrison of more than 1,000 officers and men.

Porter was confined at Johnson's Island for more than nineteen months. He and three of his comrades tried to tunnel their way out, but the effort was foiled.

Porter's kinsman Captain Thomas H. Hines was captured with Colonels Richard Morgan and Basil W. Duke in eastern Ohio and ultimately confined with John Hunt Morgan in the Ohio State Penitentiary in Columbus, Ohio. There, Hines masterminded the construction of a tunnel through the ventilation system. Then, on November 27, 1863, Hines, Morgan, and five others escaped. Interestingly, Hines then organized a group of co-conspirators in Canada to free Confederate prisoners of war at Camp Douglas Prison and Rock Island Prison in Illinois and Camp Morton Prison in Indianapolis, Indiana. The famed "Northwest Conspiracy" failed.

The men of the command were finally sent to Camp Douglas and at least some of them to Fort Delaware. I was about the same time sent to Johnson's Island in Sandusky Bay, Lake Erie, in the extreme northern portion of the State of Ohio, together with about thirty other officers. This was in July 1863. I then began an imprisonment which for length of time, harshness of treatment and intense suffering, cannot be portrayed in these pages. No one can convey an idea of what poor, helpless Confederate soldiers saw and felt on that cold and dreary island during the long and horrid months of 1863, and the entire year of 1864, and it is well, perhaps, that I am not able to portray it, for it is enough "to move the stones of Rome to rise and mutiny."[1]

Hunger it is said will drive a man through a stone wall, yet we were, to the number of from two to four thousand, kept in this terrible place, hungry from *day to day, week to week, month to month, and I speak it, from year to year.* During the winter it was cold in the extreme, the mercury at times pointing as low as twenty-seven degrees below zero, with barely fuel enough to cook a beggar's supper. Sometimes we would have wood enough to warm us, but it was seldom, for the rest of the time we suffered and endured all for the sake of a Cause, and a nationality which was destined to be crushed.

There were gallant men held here from every State and section of the State, from every division of the great armies in the field. Lee's Army of Northern Virginia sent her representatives from the bloody fields of Gettysburg and other places which were historic. From the Army of Tennessee, under Johnston and Bragg, they came from Murfreesboro, Chickamauga and other places. From Vicksburg and Port Hudson, from Helena and the Big Black, from Missouri and Louisiana, from the Mississippi and the Gulf Coast were men, all suffering and bearing and enduring hardships the like of which they had never before experienced in battles on the hardest fought fields.

Generals talked in sad tones of the condition of the country and the prospects of success. Major General Isaac R. Trimble, who lost a leg at Gettysburg, General William N. R. Beall, captured at Port Hudson on the Mississippi River, Brigadier General James J. Archer, from Gettysburg, General John W. Frazer, captured at Cumberland Gap, Generals John S. Marmaduke and William L. Cabell, taken in Missouri, Jeff Thompson, the eccentric Missourian, General John R. Jones of Virginia, all were there.[2]

All during the entire year of 1864, the long days passed away. One day we were buoyed with the hope of an exchange and the next our hopes were dashed away from us. One day a prospect for soon being in our own South, the next mortified with the thought that we would have to remain there till the war should close. And, when would it close? This was a question none could answer, and how and on what terms would it close? This was much discussed and never answered against our success.

When General Morgan and his command were captured in Ohio soon after my capture, about fifty officers of his command were sent to Johnson's Island. I knew nearly all of them and many, indeed all of them, talked of our adventures and cheered each other in our reverses. After they had been there a few days they were sent to the Penitentiary at Columbus, Ohio, and to Allegheny, Pennsylvania. Some to both prisons. I saw them no more till the war was over, and some of them I have never seen since.

All of our old command nearly were at this time in prison

Prisoners of war at Fort Delaware, May 1864. The second standing figure from the right is Colonel Basil W. Duke. To his right are Captain Charlton H. Morgan, Colonel Richard C. Morgan, and Lieutenant Colonel Cicero Coleman. Colonel Coleman, and possibly others in this photograph, were briefly held at Johnson's Island Prisoner of War Depot with Porter. (Hunt-Morgan House Deposit Photographic Collection, University of Kentucky Special Collections.)

and the great career of Morgan's Cavalry was well nigh run. He never again had as fine a body of men as those who took part in the Ohio raid, and did the fighting in Kentucky and Tennessee in 1862 and 1863. Many died in prison. Used to active and constant exercise in the saddle, they failed and became sick when put into a filthy pen and half-starved and frozen. They *were never conquered*. In Death, their courage held up, and, if it is a virtue to be brave, they have that reward.[3]

I cannot begin to tell all that transpired in our prison worthy of record. Every day something took place. We would plan means of escape. We would arm ourselves with clubs and sticks, put them away for use at the proper time, and in fact we were constantly looking for some way to break away

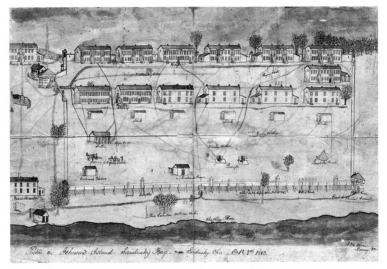

Johnson's Island Prisoner of War Depot, drawn by Joseph Mason Kern of the Thirteenth Virginia Infantry while a prisoner of war with John M. Porter, October 7, 1863. (Joseph Mason Kern Papers, Southern Historical Collection, Number 2526-Z, University of North Carolina Library.)

and escape from the place. And, yet, from what I know of other Northern prisons, Johnson's Island was perhaps the best of all. The island contained about three hundred acres, situated about three or four miles from the mainland. During the cold weather the bay was frozen over, and during the summer the island was more lovely to an outsider, but to us was anything but pleasing. The garrison was strong, assisted by a United States Revenue Cutter anchored in the bay that commanded the entire prison. The cutter, together with part of an artillery battery pointing their dark mouths in upon us, warned us to beware. This, however, and all these, would have been no fright to us if there had been any reasonable chance of succeeding.

I will give a few things of interest which occurred while in this prison. And first, I will give an account of an attempt made by myself and others to tunnel our way out of prison under-ground. And in order that the situation and position of things may be understood, I will describe the arrangement of the prison barracks or buildings. The prison enclosure embraced an area of about twelve or fifteen acres of ground, enclosed by a strong and solid fence, about seventeen feet high, made of the heaviest lumber, put endwise in the ground. Upon the top on the outside was a parapet extending entirely around the prison, upon which stood the sentinels. On the inside of the fence, and about ten steps from it, were driven in the ground white stakes about twenty feet or thirty feet apart, and we were not allowed to go nearer the fence than this row of stakes. We called this the "Dead Line," and it was properly so called, for if a prisoner chanced to cross over it, the chances were he would be instantly shot. This dead line was on our side and both ends of the prison, or, I should rather say, on three sides about as I have said, ten steps from the fence, but on the other or fourth side, bordering on the lake, the stakes or dead line was perhaps thirty yards from the fence. There were two rows of buildings. Six of each row, with a street or space of about fifty yards between them, and each building in the row was about twenty feet apart from each other.

The following will give an idea of the arrangement, roughly drawn, though it may be. The small squares numbered from one to thirteen are the buildings occupied by the prisoners. Number Six being the hospital, in which I was at one time confined sick for some days. I was put in Hock Number Two in room three, and from our room under the building on to the fence was about one hundred or perhaps one hundred fifty feet.

Hines, Markham, Duncan and myself determined to tun-

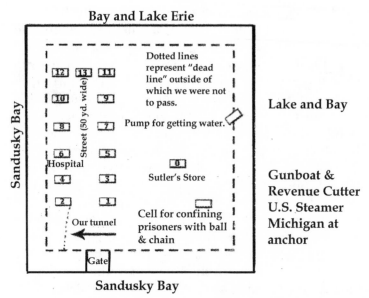

Bay and Lake Erie

Johnson's Island Prisoner of War Depot in Ohio, from a diagram drawn by John M. Porter showing his failed escape route.

nel out from beneath our room, and, if possible, to make our escape. It was necessary in order to succeed to keep the fact a secret from all save those engaged in the work, and the fewer we had engaged the better chance there was to be successful in our labor and escape. In order to begin we cut through the floor of our room in one corner by removing a bunk. We cut through two planks, and, after taking out the pieces about eighteen inches long, so fitted them that they could be replaced and removed in a short time and with so much nicety of fitness that it was hard to detect it without close examination. These examinations of our rooms were made about twice per month when every nick and corner of floor and ceiling were scrutinized.[4]

The tunnel was begun under our room and some sixty

feet we had to go before we reached the end of the building, and from there to the fence it was a distance of about forty to sixty feet. We procured a few old case knives, a piece of old iron, and made some small shovels of pieces of plank with which to prosecute our work. In order to keep the dirt which we dug out of our way, we were under the necessity of making six tunnels in which to put it, and it was carried out of our way by means of a small box which held about a peck, to each end of which we tied a string. By this means the one in the tunnel at work would, holding one string, draw the box to him, and after filling it with dirt would give a signal to him who was way back in the tunnel by a gentle pull, and he would then draw the box to him, back and forth nearly all the time when work was going on. By means of this string also, a sort of telegraphic communication was kept up between those in the tunnel and those in the room, and whenever any of the guard were skulking around, operations would instantly cease and the tunnel be vacated forthwith.

Day after day and night after night we kept on at our work, actuated by the hope of at last making our escape by means of it. We reached the corner of the building which we learned by hearing noise above us, and it then became necessary to sink our tunnel deeper into the ground in order to avoid it being crushed in and discovered, on account of so much traveling over the ground. This was very difficult to do and we labored hard to accomplish it. Hines, Markham, Duncan and myself worked long and laboriously at it and finally got it to such a depth as we thought was sufficient, when we then began to cut it in a straight line for the fence. It was necessary to have it deep enough to go under the fence, which as I have said was made by driving solid heavy plank into the ground some four feet or more. Our idea was to go completely under the fence and emerge outside some dark night and trust to fortune for the rest.

During the time we were engaged at this work our quarters were once or twice inspected, and, strange to say, our hole in the floor was not noticed. To prevent its being seen, we kept our bunk over it and then threw some old clothes, shoes and so forth under the bunk, and, by this means, covered the place so that the guards did not discover it. If it had been seen we would have been put in the cells with balls and chains on us, this being the usual punishment inflicted on all prisoners detected in any sort of attempt to escape.

To find places to secret and put away the dirt gave us much trouble, but by conveying it by means of the box to all parts of the building under the floor and piling it between the ground and the sleepers, we managed to convey it out of our way. Soon after we began to make the tunnel from the corner of the house to the fence we came on a large, hard rock directly in our pathway. We began to work around it as well as we could, but it delayed us a great deal, and, but for it, I am of opinion we would have escaped and made our way to Canada, which we designed doing. This necessary deviation from a straight line delayed us in our work and made it so much harder and so much more to do that it seemed enough to discourage us, but we persevered and steadily kept on.

No one who has not tried tunneling under such circumstances can tell the difficulties of it. We finally so far had the work done that in a very short time would entirely finish it. Suddenly it was found that somebody in prison was endeavoring to get out by this means. In fact, there were other tunnels besides ours and a general search was one day made for them by the guard, and some of them were discovered. Ours was discovered also by examining near the corner of the building, but they did not trace it up, supposing as a matter of course it was done by those who were staying in the corner room. This all at once and thoroughly put a stop to the work, which would have put us outside of the prison, and,

A sketch of Johnson's Island Prisoner of War Depot showing the USS *Michigan*. (Editor's collection.)

Providence permitting, beyond the reach of the guards. But it was not to be so. Our tunnel was abandoned and all idea of getting out through it given up.[5]

Great excitement existed one day when it was said a party of our friends in Canada were on their way over the lake to release us. They did indeed start and captured two steamers that ran between Sandusky and Buffalo and Detroit. We were expecting them and were prepared to do all in our power to aid in our escape. Every man had a club concealed in his bunk, the only weapon we could obtain, and the arrangement was to form in line of battle and make a charge at the proper time, in the event our friends came on to the attack. But they failed to come nearer than four or five miles, when they returned as we afterwards heard, leaving us all with no prospect of escape. If the attack had been made by the party outside I am of opinion we would have made our escape. The Revenue Cutter "Michigan" could have been captured by a vigorous charge, and it, once in our possession, we could have steamed over the lake with nothing to hinder us from capturing every important city and town on the lake shore. And finally, we could have landed in Canadian waters and been safe. This chance was dashed away from us as indeed every other plan for escape.[6]

The days dragged slowly by, news of battles and failures and successes of our armies reached us. How chafing it was to be confined in prison when comrades were sharing the dangers and bearing the brunt of the fight. Rumors of an exchange of prisoners barely reached our ears before another rumor denied the truth of the first. Suspense held us in a fever. There was nothing to vary the dull and awful monotony of the life. Now and then, during the heated season, we were permitted to pass out under a strong guard and bathe in the lake, but no man was allowed to swim farther than good gun shot from the guards on shore.

When a prisoner died, a detail of about eight or ten men were allowed to go out under guard to the burying ground and dig the grave and bury the dead. Upon one or two occasions, on the death of a prisoner, I was allowed to go out and give the deceased brother a Masonic burial so far as we could. Attending a Masonic burial under such circumstances is not oftentimes witnessed, and I doubt that there are many such instances on record. Our word of honor was given that we would not attempt to escape, and we were allowed to go without a guard, a non-commissioned officer being all that was with us. Of course, under such circumstances no attempt was made to get away, although it could have been easily done. We ranged around over the island considerably, and, for a short time at any rate, felt somewhat free. I remember taking a walk through the woods down to the shore and looked across wistfully three and a half miles away to the mainland, but I could not violate the promise I had given not to attempt to escape.

On the part of the island where the burying ground was, was heavy and dense timber. When I was out on the occasion alluded to, but before the winter was over, it had all been cut down for fuel for use of prisoners. The burying ground there was a sad place, low and wet and near the shore. Altogether, a dismal place and dreadful to see. The idea of a possibility of being put away in that place on that island was revolting and horrible. Providence kindly kept me alive and permitted me to see a day when I stepped away with buoyant heart for exchange.

It is unnecessary to give details of the many things which occurred during the time I was in this prison from July 1863 to February 1865, covering a period of about *nineteen months.* It was a long time to be kept in such a pen, but fortunes of war are various, and she does not always favor the same individuals. We had witnessed successes and partaken of them, and it was our fate to experience reverses. No set of men endured suffering with greater heroism and fortitude than the four thousand gallant men at Johnson's Island for a year and a half.

14

WITH THREE DAYS' RATIONS, WE STARTED HOME

John M. Porter was exchanged in February 1865. He and other prison-
ers from Johnson's Island were transported by rail from Sandusky, Ohio,
through Pittsburgh, to Baltimore, and then down the Chesapeake Bay from
Baltimore to the James River. Porter was finally set ashore at Rockets, the
location of the Confederate navy yard and a southern suburb of Richmond,
Virginia. Within days, Robert E. Lee's army evacuated the defenses of Peters-
burg and Richmond. Porter then observed, firsthand, the final collapse of the
Confederacy. He traveled west by railroad, not far behind the train carrying
President Jefferson Davis, Secretary of War John C. Breckinridge, and the rest
of Davis's cabinet officials. He entered the lines of General Joseph E. John-
ston in North Carolina, where his old regiment, the Ninth Kentucky Cavalry,
was still in the field. Porter finally reached Atlanta and then Macon, Geor-
gia, where he met his kinsman and friend, James M. Hines. From there he
traveled to Madison, Georgia, and Augusta. Returning to Madison, Porter
wound up in the home of his father's first cousin John Watson Porter. There
he met kinsmen Edward L. Hines and John H. Hines and Hugh Gwynn, all
of whom served with Morgan. By then, Lee and Johnston had surrendered
and President Davis had been captured. Searching for a way to join the fight-
ing, Porter learned that General Edmund Kirby Smith had surrendered in
the Trans-Mississippi. The Confederacy had finally collapsed.

Porter and the Hines brothers started home. When they reached Bowling Green, Kentucky, they visited the Hines brothers' mother, Ann Porter, then rode home to Sugar Grove in neighboring Butler County. Incredibly, all of his family members were still alive. He had ended an odyssey unlike anything any Americans would ever experience again. The Civil War defined Porter—and the nation. It defines the nation today.

Finally about last of January or first of February 1865, a cartel of exchange was agreed upon by the two Governments. The reason exchanging prisoners had ceased was that the United States demanded that the negro soldiers captured by the Confederate forces should be put on a footing of other prisoners and exchanged, while the Confederate Government very properly refused to do this, claiming the negro soldiers were, in truth and fact, the property of the Southern people, and, as such, when captured should be returned to their respective masters and owners. This was the barrier to an exchange; this was the reason so many men languished and died in prison. It was, however, agreed to begin the transportation of prisoners about January 1865 and about the last of that month, I think, or first of February, about three hundred of us were called out and started off for Richmond.

The bay had been frozen for weeks and we were compelled to walk over on the ice, a distance of about four miles, which was almost like killing us, because we were unused to exercise, and it was tiresome in the extreme, every rod nearly one would fall. We were sent by railroad by Pittsburgh to Baltimore. At Baltimore we were put on a steamer and sent down the Chesapeake Bay to the mouth of the James River, and up the James River to the Confederate lines. During this entire route, which consumed some week or two, perhaps, we had a hard time, yet better than in prison. Besides, we were elated at the prospect of being again in a short time among our own country-men in the South. Nothing unusual occurred on the trip from Johnson's Island to Richmond. We passed Fortress Monroe and other historic places on the bay and on the James River, the sight of which brought to mind sad thoughts.[1]

At last I stepped from a Confederate transport near the "Rockets," and was in the city of Richmond, no longer under the control nor in the power of the Yankees. I at once went to a hotel and procured something to eat and a place to sleep. For a truth, I think I had been hungry for a year. I mean by hunger this: I had not eaten at any one time enough to satisfy me. This is sounding strangely, but I have a recollection of incessant hunger.[2]

Richmond was a worn, weather-beaten place. The war had been in progress so long, and she had been so much in the center of it, that she had been particularly wrecked. The place however had about it an air and a history which commanded my respect. I always had felt a veneration for Richmond. When a boy, I had heard old men tell of rolling tobacco from Bedford, Campbell, Prince Edward, Cumberland, Halifax and other Counties to old Richmond. I had heard of the James River and the story of Captain John Smith and Pocahontas when I was older and learned enough to read. Then I had heard and read of the House of Burgesses and what was done, and by whom aforetime. I had heard of the ancient governors of the colony under the reigns of English sovereigns.

I remained in Richmond, paying board, part of the time, one hundred dollars per day at the Spottswood Hotel, since destroyed by fire, and the remainder of the time I was paying about sixty dollars per day. You must know by this time that Confederate money was not worth much and everything demanded a high price. It took a heap of money to buy the cheapest article. For instance, I paid for a pair of marina socks forty dollars, for a coat, pants and vest, uniform, *thirty-three hundred dollars*, or about that sum, I cannot say precisely. Two biscuits and a piece of meat, like the back or leg of a chicken, cost about five dollars. A meal at the hotel cost about twenty-five to one hundred dollars, according to what you ate. A set of military buttons cost five dollars each. While these prices seemed high, or seem so now, yet then money was plenty, and it was as easy to pay the prices demanded as now.[3]

From Richmond, I came to Greensboro, Guilford County, North Carolina, and remained in town a day or so sick. I then went to the country in order to find some quiet place to remain till I got well. And I was fortunate in finding a very kind family by the name of Rankin, with whom I stayed for two or three weeks, and was kindly provided for. From here as soon as I was able to travel, I went to Raleigh and on towards Goldsboro to meet General Joseph E. Johnston's army where my regiment was.

I found the regiment near Smithfield, North Carolina, and saw all the boys who had survived the preceding twenty months. I spent a few days with the Company and then returned to Raleigh. The army under General Joseph E. Johnston was slowly retreating before the army of Major General William T. Sherman who was in command of the Yankee forces. Fighting was going on daily and almost hourly.[4]

Affairs were drawing to a close with the Southern Confederacy. The gallant armies, which for four years had been the admiration of the world, were dwindling to a mere handful of men who, day after day kept back the immense armies of Grant and Sherman. The grand panorama was winding to a close. The curtain had begun to waver and ere long descended and the act was over; the last scene was ended, and in a hole of Glory, though defeated and surrendered, the armies of Generals Robert E. Lee and Johnston laid down their arms at the feet of a foe many times their own number.

The ruins of Richmond, Virginia, April 1865, showing the Capitol Building and the James River. Note the American flag flying near the capitol, evidence of the Federal occupation. (Library of Congress.)

Can the history of the world present anything to equal this? A more gallant contest had never been waged. A more noble army never enlisted and fought.[5]

From Raleigh, I came back to Greensboro and then started to Richmond, but, on arriving at Manchester on the opposite side of James River from Richmond on Sunday evening April 2, 1865, I found the utmost commotion and excitement prevailing. That day General Lee had been forced to evacuate Petersburg, which he had so long and ably defended, and this necessitated the evacuation of Richmond also and the surrender of that city to the enemy. Everybody was wild with excitement, and the only idea any one seemed to have was go get away from the city. The Government officials, heads of departments and so forth were leaving in hot haste. Members of Congress were getting their effects together and preparing to leave.[6]

Finding all things so much confused, I determined not to be caught in a trap and resolved to take care of myself. I had no idea of putting myself in the hands of the Yankees without an attempt to retrace my steps to Carolina. I knew the army of General Lee would, in all probability, retreat by way of the Southside Railroad, running from Petersburg to Lynchburg; indeed this was the only avenue of escape open to him, and this was fast being closed by twenty thousand cavalry under Major General Philip Sheridan, the best barn burner of the Yankee Army, who was advancing towards Burkeville, the junction of the Southside Railroad with the Richmond and Danville Railroad, or rather the crossing of these two roads. If he should reach there before the fugitives from Richmond and before General Lee with his army did, the result would be disastrous. This I well knew. During the night, however, the train I was on went back to Burkeville and remained till day-light. All the time the enemy was closing in. President Jefferson Davis and family went up the road to Danville the same night in a special train to which we gave way and let them pass out of danger.[7]

Morning came and we proceeded on to Danville. From Danville, I determined to make my way across to Georgia and find out what was being done there. The *check* was about over with General Lee's and General Johnston's armies. Accordingly, I proceeded by railroad by Greensboro to Charlotte via Salisbury, North Carolina. Here the road was destroyed, and for forty miles I walked across to Chester, South Carolina, and took train again and went to Newburg. And from this place made my way on foot to Washington, Georgia.[8]

All this time since I left Danville, I had heard no news from General Lee's nor Johnston's armies. Communications were so destroyed that it was impossible to obtain information. I do not remember how long a time it took me to reach Washington. From Washington I went by railroad to Barnett, on the Georgia Central Railroad. Then, from there I went to Atlanta and on to Macon.[9]

Atlanta had been burned by Sherman and presented one continual scene of ruins. At Macon I met my old friend James F. Hines of our old command, and from him soon learned that the Yankee Major General James Wilson, with a large body of cavalry, was approaching the fine city from the direction of Columbus, Selma, Montgomery, etc. It was too evident that the collapse was at hand, the entire fabric was broken. The garrison of Macon under Major General Howell Cobb was insufficient to prevent one thousand men from entering the town, and he determined to send a flag of truce to meet the Federal commander, then a short distance off, and proposed a surrender of the forces and the city.[10]

Information deemed reliable was received that Lee had surrendered and Johnston and Sherman had declared an armistice. When I found that Macon was to be surrendered I determined to try again, if possible, to keep out of the hands of enemy. A train was just starting to Atlanta, and, without any ceremony, I got aboard with an avowed purpose that General Cobb should not surrender me to the enemy.

The train went as far as Griffin, when it halted, and intelligence was given that the enemy, consisting of a portion of Wilson's command, had intercepted us and tapped the road a few miles in our front. Upon receiving this news, the train with all on board, except Frank White of Tennessee and myself, returned to Macon and gave up the effort. I left the train at once when I heard that it was going back, and struck out across the country to reach the Georgia Central Railroad, which was about forty miles at the nearest point, "Social Circle." This shows something of the situation.[11]

After about two days I reached Social Circle and remained a short time. There was now no doubt as to General Lee's surrender and the early surrender of General Johnston's army. The only chance to prolong the war and the only hope left was the army on the west of the Mississippi under General Edmund Kirby Smith. A hope still existed that I might be able to get across in that department, but two or three large States were to traverse, each of which was full of the enemy. A few days' delay would determine the chance and could not render things worse. So I went to Madison, Georgia, to remain with some relatives and wait the turn of fortune's wheel.[12]

Cousin John Porter, a first cousin of my father, lived then in Madison and I was received kindly by him and his family. In a few days I went down to Augusta and here I found Jimmie Hines whom I had left in Macon and who also refused to be surrendered by General Cobb. While here the fate of the Confederacy was heard. All hope was gone. Both armies had surrendered. General Dick Taylor had surrendered and General Kirby Smith was forced to do so also. This prevented any further efforts towards reaching the Mississippi and crossing over. Only one thing was to be done, and that was to cease all further attempts at resistance and return to our homes as best we could.

I returned to Madison and took up my quarters with my relatives and waited for a favorable time to come home. Now that the war was over I was anxious to be at home. While it lasted, the prospect of getting home was gloomy indeed, but when it ended and I found myself living and breathing, the desire was irresistible and made me impatient to start. The way was long, however, and I had no money. I was poor.

Soon after I returned from Augusta to Madison, Georgia, and took lodging with Cousin John Porter and family. I was joined by Jimmie F. Hines, Edward L. Hines and Hugh Gwynn, all of whom had gone through the war and were now only waiting an opportunity to get home. We were very kindly treated by Cousin John who was withal a devout Christian. We concluded, after having remained at his house for about two or three weeks or perhaps a month, that we would buy

Uncle John Watson
Porter of Madison,
Georgia, from
a portrait made
about 1860. (Block,
*Historical Relics of My
Porter Kin,* 17.)

horses and come through to Nashville and thence home. We
did not, however, conclude to do so until we were satisfied
from newspaper accounts that we could return to Kentucky
without being molested. In this, however, some of us afterwards found ourselves disappointed.[13]

While we were at Madison, President Jefferson Davis was
captured and brought through that town, guarded by a train
full of Federal soldiers. The car in which he was confined was
securely locked and the windows closed, so that his escape
was impossible, and his body carefully concealed from view.
Only a few weeks before, I had seen him and his family leaving Richmond for Danville, Virginia. We still had hopes that

Railroad car shed, Atlanta, Georgia, destroyed by General William T. Sherman's troops in September 1864. (Library of Congress.)

all would be well with the Confederacy. Now, all hope was gone; the armies were all surrendered and the President himself a prisoner in the hands of the enemy. He was taken on to Augusta and from there sent to Savannah and on to Fortress Monroe.[14]

198

The idea of buying horses in Madison was generally given up, and, about the twentieth of May 1865, we started for home. We came by railroad to Atlanta, and, after having obtained paroles, we hired a wagon, giving fifteen dollars in gold apiece for being conveyed to Dalton, a distance about ninety-eight miles. The railroad to Chattanooga was entirely destroyed, and we had either to walk or obtain private conveyances such as we got for the purpose.[15]

Providing ourselves with three days' rations, we *started home*. The route was directly in the path of the hostile armies a few months before, and there was not a horse, cow, hog or other animal to be seen the entire way. The houses were all burned, the towns destroyed and the people driven from their homes. There was absolutely no sign of life the greater portion of the trip. Sherman's army, like an Angel of Death, had passed that way, and left devastation in its track. It was one continual battle-field the entire way, and rude graves were on all sides which gave sad evidence of the destruction—terrible destruction—of human life. Here a row and there a row; here a long trench and there a trench, all these signs recalled bitter memories of the past. And it was almost like a dream to think that I was alive and homeward bound, while thousands, no worse than myself were covered by the sod in that dreary, gloomy region. Peach Tree Creek, Kennesaw Mountain and a hundred other places loomed before our eyes and brought recollections of a gloomy kind.[16]

We finally, on the fourth or fifth day after leaving Atlanta, reached Dalton. Here we got a new quantity of rations as our supply had failed, and were furnished transportation by railroad to Chattanooga, Tennessee. I think we remained in Chattanooga a day and night, and then to transportation to Nashville. It will be understood that at all these places there were soldiers. In fact, we could not turn around without rub-

Train leaving the Chattanooga Railroad terminal in the fall of 1865. (Library of Congress.)

bing against a dozen almost. It took some time to reach Nashville, owing to the bad condition of the railroad. We finally got there and, by using some strategy, we jumped off the train before it stopped at the depot and made our way to the City Hotel. By this means we saved ourselves from being sent to the Guard House that night, which they did to all of the soldiers. It being about dark, we, by eluding the guard, reached the hotel safely and found something to eat and good bedding. Times in Nashville were squally. After remaining there

KENTUCKY

VIRGINIA

Richmond •
Petersburg •

Danville •

•Sugar Grove
• Bowling Green

•Greensboro
•Raleigh

TENNESSEE   NORTH CAROLINA   •Goldsboro

•Nashville

•Charlotte

Chattanooga •

SOUTH CAROLINA

Washington •
• Atlanta

•Social Circle

Griffin   •
Madison   Augusta

• Macon

GEORGIA

Porter's
Travels Home
Spring 1865

a day or two, I came on the cars to Bowling Green, leaving my companions in Nashville.[17]

I arrived in Bowling Green on Saturday and went from the depot, through Main street and the public square, to Mrs. Anna Hines's, the mother of John Hines, who had shared my fate on Johnson's Island. I did not recognize a single person as I passed through the town. Everything was changed. Nothing seemed natural. I had not seen the place since January 1862, and war's wild havoc had been there.[18]

I could not get a conveyance home that evening and was forced to remain in town till Sunday morning. On the morrow, I obtained a horse and rode out the Morgantown Road in the direction of home. How strange it seemed that

I was almost home and the war over; how great the change since I had last ridden over the same road. Since then I had ridden thousands of miles through Kentucky, Tennessee, Alabama, Mississippi, Georgia, Virginia, North and South Carolina, and seen and participated in almost a hundred battles. But by a kind and merciful Providence I was spared to see the end of the struggle and, notwithstanding our cause had gone down, I had a proud satisfaction that I had discharged my duty to the Cause which I heartily espoused at the beginning.[19]

I arrived at home and found the dear ones all alive. I cannot and will not attempt to describe the meeting.

Almost four years had gone by since I joined the Confederate States Army, and during that time many and great changes had taken place. They had been years as full of great events as any like number of years since the beginning of the Christian Era. Eight million Southern people had been battling against thirty million Northern people and their foreign allies, and when I say allies I mean the partial favor shown the North by most of the nations of Europe. The struggle was the most heroic that has ever marked the course of human events. There is, in my opinion, no doubt of it.

At last, in the Spring of 1865, one hundred and twenty thousand Southern soldiers, stretched from Virginia to Texas, surrendered to one million, one hundred thousand Northern soldiers. Was there not and is this not, of itself, evidence of the heroic struggles? To have been one of the number of Confederate soldiers who remained true and steadfast to the last is, I consider, one of the brightest honors which a man can claim.

I have never regretted that I was one who supported the cause of the South. And while giving that cause my humble aid, I feel it to be a proud satisfaction at knowing I was attached to the command of Brigadier General John H. Mor-

John Marion Porter, from a photograph taken in Bowling Green, Kentucky, after the war. (Thomas Henry Hines Collections, University of Kentucky Special Collections.)

gan, the greatest cavalry leader which the world, for five hundred years, has seen. And when I think of all the gallant and glorious deeds of that command, performed by brave young Kentuckians, I am prouder than ever that I was one of them, and can claim for them and all of us, Kentucky as our home, and the South as our favorite Section.

MEMORANDUM

John M. Porter included the following note at the end of his war reminiscences.

I began practicing law, that is obtained license, in December 1868, at Morgantown, Kentucky, and remained at that place until October 1870, at which time I removed to Bowling Green, Kentucky, and engaged in practice.

J. M. Porter

NOTES

INTRODUCTION

1. John M. Porter, "Historical Sketch of the Porter Family," page 6, typescript prepared in 1872, Western Kentucky University, Kentucky Library and Museum, Manuscripts and Archives.

2. Ibid., 1–3, 5–6; J. Adger Stewart, *Descendants of Henry Hines, Sr., 1732–1810* (Louisville: Morton, 1925), 31–35.

3. Porter, "Historical Sketch of the Porter Family," 9.

4. Ibid., 6.

5. Ibid., 6–7.

6. Ibid., 7–8.

7. Census Population Schedules, Butler County, Kentucky, 1860, Sugar Grove, Reel 358, Box 6, U.S. Federal Census Records, University of Kentucky Special Collections (hereafter cited as UKSC).

8. Stewart, *Descendants of Henry Hines, Sr.,* 5, 11, 15–16.

9. Ibid., 25.

10. Edward McKenzie Coffman, "The Civil War Career of Thomas Henry Hines" (Master's thesis, University of Kentucky, 1955), 62–118, University of Kentucky Library, Thesis and Dissertation Collection.

11. Porter, "Historical Sketch of the Porter Family," 6–7.

12. Record of Burials, Fairview Cemetery, Bowling Green, Kentucky, Cemetery 1, Section C, C-225, Western Kentucky University, Kentucky Library and Museum, Manuscripts and Archives; Stewart, *Descendants of Henry Hines, Sr.,* 25.

13. Coffman, "The Civil War Career of Thomas Henry Hines," 119.

14. Record of Burials, Fairview Cemetery, Bowling Green, Kentucky, Cemetery 1, Section C, C-225, and Cemetery 1, Section E, E-10, Western Kentucky University, Kentucky Library and Museum, Manuscripts and Archives.

15. David W. Blight, *Race and Reunion: The Civil War in American Memory* (Cambridge, Mass.: Belknap Press of Harvard Univ. Press, 2001), 140–170. See also: William Blair, *Cities of the Dead: Contesting the Memory of the Civil War in the South, 1865–1974* (Chapel Hill: Univ. of North Carolina Press, 2004).

1. TO THE MILITARY I SUBMITTED MYSELF

1. In the presidential election of 1860, John Cabell Breckinridge, vice president of the United States under James Buchanan, a native of Lexington, Kentucky, and the candidate of the Southern Democrats, received 52,800 votes in Kentucky; Stephen A. Douglas of Illinois, candidate for the Democratic Party, received about 25,000 votes; and John Bell of Tennessee, the Constitutional-Union Party candidate, received some 66,000 votes. The Republican Party candidate, Abraham Lincoln, polled less than 1,400 votes in Kentucky. (E. Merton Coulter, *The Civil War and Readjustment in Kentucky* [Chapel Hill: Univ. of North Carolina Press, 1926], 24.)

2. Butler County was formed in 1810 from portions of Logan and Ohio counties in a region drained by the Green River. It is located in west central Kentucky, bounded by Grayson County on the north, Edmonson County on the east, Warren and Logan counties on the south, and Muhlenberg and Ohio counties on the west. Morgantown, a village with only 125 inhabitants at the time of the Civil War, was the county seat. (Lois Russ, ed., *Butler County, Kentucky History* [Morgantown: Butler County Historical and Genealogical Society, 1987], 18; Richard Collins, *History of Kentucky*, 2 vols. [Frankfort: Kentucky Historical Society, 1966], 2:106, 263.) To illustrate the sentiment of Butler County in 1861, the Union candidacy of James S. Jackson of Hopkinsville for Congress was overwhelmingly victorious. Jackson received 1,031 votes; his States' Rights opponent received 14 (*Louisville Daily Courier*, July 2, 1861). James S. Jackson would become a Federal brigadier general and

would be mortally wounded at the Battle of Perryville, Kentucky, on October 8, 1863.

3. Colonel Pierce B. Hawkins of Bowling Green, Kentucky, raised the Eleventh Kentucky Infantry (U.S.A.). He was enrolled at Calhoun, McLean County, Kentucky, on September 3, 1861, and would be mustered out on June 25, 1863, at Bowling Green. He would lead the regiment in the Battle of Shiloh and would command a brigade in the invasion of Kentucky and at the Battle of Stone's River. (D. W. Lindsey, *Report of the Adjutant General of the State of Kentucky [Federal]*, 2 vols. [Frankfort: Kentucky Yeoman Office, 1866], 1:824.)

4. Colonel Thomas E. Puckett was fifty-six years old in 1861 and lived at Sugar Grove, where he was a tobacco merchant. His wife, Eliza, was born in Kentucky. They had four children, ranging in age from thirty to six years. Thomas E. Puckett and his family lived on a farm near Little Muddy Cumberland Presbyterian Church; they were close neighbors and close friends of the Porters. No record exists of Thomas E. Puckett's actually serving in the Confederate Army, although he was staunchly pro-Southern politically. In fact, he was arrested by Federal occupation forces in the fall of 1862 because of his pro-Southern political activities. There were numerous Pucketts living in Butler County; most of them were natives of Virginia, like Thomas. (Census Population Schedules, Butler County, Kentucky, 1860, Sugar Grove, Reel 358, Box 6, UKSC; Porter, "Historical Sketch of the Porter Family," 4.)

5. Simon Bolivar Buckner, an 1844 graduate of the U.S. Military Academy and a veteran of the Mexican War, was given command of all troops raised and trained at Camps Boone, Burnett, and Trousdale. Located near Clarksville, in Montgomery County, Tennessee, on the Memphis, Clarksville and Louisville Railroad, just below the Kentucky border, those camps were the sites where elements of the Second, Third, Fourth, Fifth or Ninth, and Sixth Kentucky Infantry (C.S.A.), the First Kentucky Cavalry (C.S.A.), and the Third, Eighteenth, and Twenty-third Tennessee Infantry (C.S.A.), along with Edward P. Byrne's Kentucky Battery (C.S.A.) and a Tennessee artillery battery (C.S.A.), were raised and trained. (Arndt M. Stickles, *Simon Bolivar Buckner: Borderland Knight* [Cha-

pel Hill: Univ. of North Carolina Press, 1940], 92–107; War Department, *War of the Rebellion: A Compilation of the Official Records of the Union and Confederate Armies,* Series I, 128 vols. [Washington, D.C.: U.S. Government Printing Office, 1880–1901], 4:407, 484 [hereafter cited as "OR"]; Ed Porter Thompson, *History of the Orphan Brigade* [Louisville: Thompson, 1890], 44–51; Civil War Centennial Comm'n., *Tennesseans in the Civil War: A Military History of Confederate and Union Units with Available Rosters of Personnel,* 2 vols. [Nashville: Civil War Centennial Comm'n., 1964], 1:181, 212, 222.)

6. Colonel Roger Weightman Hanson's Second Kentucky Infantry (C.S.A.) and Colonel Thomas Hunt's Fifth or Ninth Kentucky Infantry (C.S.A.), along with Captain Edward P. Byrne's Kentucky Battery (C.S.A.), all of Buckner's division, occupied the southern bank of the Green River at Woodsonville, across from Munfordville, the site of the Green River bridge of the Louisville and Nashville Railroad (Thompson, *History of the Orphan Brigade,* 51–52; Basil W. Duke, *History of Morgan's Cavalry* [Cincinnati: Miami Printing and Pub. Co., 1867], 91).

"Frank Jackson's," "Lewis's" and "Captain Ben Davis's" were residences along the road from Bowling Green to Rochester in southern Butler County. "Berry's Lick" was the site of an early saltworks, where furnaces were used to boil large kettles of water from more than fifty wells in order to render salt. (Russ, ed., *Butler County, Kentucky History,* 19.) The sites mentioned by Porter may be found along present-day Ky. 626 in southern Butler County. "Davis Crossroads" is the site of Captain Ben Davis's residence. General Buckner followed what is now Ky. 626 to present-day Ky. 1153 and Ky. 1187 in Butler County to reach Rochester, a town of 151 people then. (Collins, *History of Kentucky,* 2:263.)

7. General Buckner destroyed the lock on the Green River at the mouth of the Mud River at Rochester, Kentucky, in order to deny navigation of the Green River to the Federal troops. Buckner removed all Federal troops from the Rochester area, as it was behind the newly established Confederate lines along the Green River. His troops foraged for subsistence and quartermaster stores throughout the operation. Buckner seized the saltworks at Berry's

Lick, too, as his division remained there for several days. Food for the soldiers and forage for the horses and mules in the army were always in short supply, as was salt, a necessary preservative for foods. Buckner ultimately moved his division to Hopkinsville, the county seat of Christian County, which borders Montgomery County, Tennessee. (OR, 4:201.)

8. Captain James W. Johnson was a native of Shelby County, Kentucky. He first enrolled in the Sixth Kentucky Infantry (C.S.A.) and became first lieutenant of Company K. He resigned from the Sixth Kentucky and enlisted in Company E, First Kentucky Calvary (C.S.A.), and was elected captain. (Thompson, *History of the Orphan Brigade*, 805, 1033.) Because Kentucky and Tennessee contributed troops to both sides during the Civil War, the initials "U.S.A." or "C.S.A." have been added to Porter's text after the name of each regiment, battalion, and artillery battery from those states to denote whether it is Federal or Confederate.

"Underwood Grove" was a property along the bank of the Barren River northwest of Bowling Green owned by the family of Joseph Underwood, a former congressman, senator, judge of the Kentucky Court of Appeals, and an opponent of secession. It was a favorite picnic ground for the town residents of Bowling Green before and after the Civil War. (Nancy D. Baird, Carol Crowe-Carraco, and Michael L. Morse, *Bowling Green: A Pictorial History* [Norfolk: Donning, 1983], 18, 25, 26.)

9. Captain Alonzo Ridley was an officer in a California militia company at the outbreak of the war. Although of northern birth, he armed a group of Southern sympathizers with rifles requisitioned from state armories and led them across the mountains, deserts, and plains to the Confederacy. Joining Ridley's group was Albert Sidney Johnston, who had been stationed at Los Angeles with the U.S. Army, but had resigned his commission to join the Confederacy. Ridley was named captain of "Buckner's Guides" when it was formed in October 1861. (William Preston Johnston, *The Life of General Albert Sidney Johnston* [New York: Appleton, 1878], 277–291; Charles P. Roland, *Albert Sidney Johnston: Soldier of Three Republics* [Austin: Univ. of Texas Press, 1964], 252–257; J. Tandy Ellis and W. J. Stone, *Report of the Adjutant General of the State of Kentucky, Confed-*

erate Kentucky Volunteers, War 1861–65, 2 vols. [Frankfort: Kentucky State Legislature, 1913 and 1918], 2:411.)

10. "Buckner's Guides" was formed in October 1861 while General Buckner's division occupied Bowling Green, Kentucky. The command was made up of about fifty men selected from various mounted units in the division and from newly arrived recruits who were intimately familiar with the Green River and Barren River country. (Ellis and Stone, *Report of the Adjutant General of the State of Kentucky*, 2:411–412.) Those members of Buckner's Guides who hailed from Butler County and who would serve with Porter throughout the war were Andrew Kuykendall, Joseph Gray, Hezekiah I. Kuykendall, Reuben M. Johnson, and Dempsey Burton Bailey. All of them enlisted in Buckner's Guides at Bowling Green, Kentucky, in October 1861. (Ibid.) Andrew Kuykendall was twenty-one years old and had been born in Illinois. Raised at Sugar Grove, he was the son of Magdaline Kuykendall, a fifty-eight-year-old widow. The Kuykendalls were Virginians and close neighbors of the Porters. Andrew would serve with Porter as sergeant of Company E, Ninth Kentucky Cavalry (C.S.A.), and would be captured on June 19, 1863, in Ohio during General John Hunt Morgan's Indiana-Ohio raid. Hezekiah I. Kuykendall was a cousin to Andrew. He was twenty-five years old and married to Eamdy E. Kuykendall, twenty years of age. They had a two-year-old daughter and lived in Woodbury. Hezekiah fails to appear in any other Kentucky Confederate unit after his service with Buckner's Guides. Dempsey Burton Bailey was born in North Carolina, like virtually all the Baileys of Butler County. He lived in Sugar Grove not far from Porter. Twenty-two years old, Bailey would later serve with Porter in Company E, Ninth Kentucky Cavalry. He would be captured on June 19, 1863, in Ohio. Reuben M. Johnson was a forty-year-old native of Sugar Grove. He was married to Margaret Johnson, age thirty-six. They had no children. (Census Population Schedules, Butler County, Kentucky, 1860, Sugar Grove, Reel 358, Box 6, UKSC.)

11. William J. Hardee was elevated to the rank of major general on October 7, 1861 (Ezra J. Warner, *Generals in Gray: Lives of the Confederate Commanders* [Baton Rouge: Louisiana State Univ. Press, 1959], 124).

2. You Have Crowned Yourselves with Glory

1. Russellville, Kentucky, is the county seat of Logan County. It was the site of the convention that formed the government of Confederate Kentucky in November 1861. To the north of Logan is Butler County. On Logan County's southern border is Robertson County, Tennessee.

Brigadier General Thomas L. Crittenden, a native of Russellville, Kentucky, and the son of U.S. Senator John J. Crittenden of Kentucky, commanded a division of two brigades in the Federal Army of the Ohio that was situated along the north bank of the Green River. (OR, 7:460–467, 447, 449–450, 543–544; Ezra J. Warner, *Generals in Blue: Lives of the Union Commanders* [Baton Rouge: Louisiana State Univ. Press, 1959], 100.)

2. Calhoun, the county seat of McLean County, is on the north bank of the Green River; South Carrollton, in Muhlenberg County, is on the west bank of the meandering Green River.

"Buckner's Guides" remained as scouts with General Johnston's army when Porter and his five companions were detached to accompany General Buckner to Fort Donelson. Confederate operations were designed to keep the area south of the Green River clear of Federal forces.

3. General Grant's ground forces arrayed against Fort Donelson consisted of three divisions, with three brigades each, totaling, in all, in excess of 30,000 officers and men (OR, 7:167–253).

4. "*Abatis*" is a French military term describing obstructions, then mostly wooden spikes and felled trees, placed in front of defense lines to slow an enemy advance.

5. Although the weather was relatively warm when General Grant's army began its overland march to Fort Donelson, it quickly deteriorated. By the time the fighting began, the temperature had plummeted to below freezing, and snow and sleet had begun to fall. (OR, 7:174; Thompson, *History of the Orphan Brigade,* 65–66.)

6. Captain Rice E. Graves commanded Graves's Kentucky Battery (C.S.A.) at Fort Donelson, a unit formed in November 1861 at Bowling Green. A native of Rockbridge County, Virginia, Graves grew up in Daviess County, Kentucky, and attended the U.S. Mili-

tary Academy. Graves would be mortally wounded at the Battle of Chickamauga on September 20, 1863. (Thompson, *History of the Orphan Brigade*, 455–458.)

Captain Thomas K. Porter, a native of Paris, Tennessee, graduate of the U.S. Naval Academy, and former U.S. Navy officer, commanded Porter's Tennessee Battery, Light Artillery (C.S.A.), at Fort Donelson. After the Battle of Chickamauga, Porter would resign from the Confederate army and enter the Confederate naval service. (James D. Porter, *Tennessee*, vol. 10 in *Confederate Military History*, ed. Clement Evans [Atlanta: Confederate Pub. Co., 1898], 260–263.) Captain Thomas K. Porter was not related to John Marion Porter.

7. On February 14, Flag Officer Andrew H. Foote attacked Fort Donelson with four "city class" ironclad gunboats, the *St. Louis, Carondelet, Louisville*, and *Pittsburgh*, and two timberclad gunboats, the *Tyler* and *Conestoga*. After a severe fight, the defenders of Fort Donelson turned back the naval attack, severely crippling two of the ironclads and both timberclads. (OR, 7:166–167.)

8. General Gideon J. Pillow recalled his troops after they had actually attacked and broken through the center of General Grant's lines on February 15 (OR, 7:278–285, 332–333).

9. Colonel Roger Weightman Hanson was born in Winchester, Kentucky, in 1827 and practiced law in Lexington before the war. A local political figure, Hanson raised the Second Kentucky Infantry Regiment (C.S.A.) and commanded it at the siege of Fort Donelson, where he was forced to surrender. Upon his release from prison, Hanson would become commander of the Orphan Brigade, with the rank of brigadier general. He would be mortally wounded at the Battle of Stone's River on January 2, 1863. (Thompson. *History of the Orphan Brigade*, 375–380.)

10. Major Samuel K. Hays was a native of Kenton County, Kentucky. He enlisted in Company H, Second Kentucky Infantry (C.S.A.), but was appointed major and assistant quartermaster on the staff of General Buckner while at Bowling Green in the fall of 1861. (Ibid., 604.)

11. General Buckner's headquarters was in the Dover Tavern, Dover, Stewart County, Tennessee, which still stands today.

12. The Forty-fourth Indiana Infantry was the first Federal regiment to enter Dover, Tennessee, as the surrender conference was taking place. Hugh B. Reed was the colonel commanding the Forty-fourth Indiana at the siege of Fort Donelson. (OR, 7:249.)

13. Dr. Frank Porter was actually Dr. Francis D. Porter, John M. Porter's uncle, and is referenced in the rosters of the Sixth Kentucky Infantry (C.S.A.). He enlisted at Bowling Green, Kentucky, on October 29, 1861, and was transferred from Company F to Company I on April 26, 1862. Although of advanced age, he volunteered to accompany those Kentucky troops who defended Fort Donelson. He was captured at Fort Donelson and then released. Porter was discharged from service in November 1862 due to his age. Returning to his home in Butler County, Dr. Porter was later arrested by Federal occupation troops and imprisoned at Bowling Green, Kentucky, where he died in captivity. John M. Porter believed Dr. Porter had been "murdered." Dr. Porter was married to the former Mary Carson. They raised a large family, mostly daughters. He was known by the men in the army as "Uncle Frank," and was, recalled John M. Porter, "a brave and gallant old gentleman." (Porter, "Historical Sketch of the Porter Family," 2; Ellis and Stone, *Report of the Adjutant General of the State of Kentucky*, 1:314, 326.)

3. It Was Literally a Leap in the Dark

1. The individual named Spurrier referenced by Porter was fifty-three-year-old E. Spurrier. He operated a hotel in Clarksville with his wife, M. E. Spurrier, and their five children. (Census Population Schedules, Montgomery County, Tennessee, 1860, Clarksville, M653, No. 1266, Reel 102, UKSC.)

The Federal troops in Clarksville, Tennessee, consisted of Brigadier General Charles F. Smith's division of Grant's Army of the Tennessee, summoned there after Flag Officer Foote had brought his fleet up the Cumberland River and received the town's surrender. (OR, 7:423–424.)

2. Camp Boone was located in Montgomery County, Tennessee, along present-day Tenn. 13 (US 79), northeast of Clarksville.

The camp was on the north side of the road; the Memphis, Clarksville and Louisville Railroad (MC&L) was on the south side.

The old typescript of the Porter manuscript referred to the "Mime" family. The family referred to was actually that of forty-two-year-old George D. Mimms, his thirty-three-year-old wife, Sarah, and their three children. George D. Mimms was one of Montgomery County's largest slaveowners. Their Greek revival home was known as "Idlewild." Ardent Southern sympathizers, the Mimms opened their farm up to be used for Confederate military recruiting and instruction. The camp was named "Camp Boone" by the Kentuckians who established it. (Byron Sistler and Barbara Sistler, *1850 Census, Tennessee*, 4 vols. [Evanston: Sistler, 1975], 4:275; Census Population Schedules, Montgomery County, Tennessee, 1860, Clarksville, M653, No. 1266, Reel 102, UKSC; Rootsweb .com/~orphanhm; 1860 U.S. Federal Census—Slave Schedules Record for G. D. Mimms, Montgomery County, Tennessee, ancestry .com.)

3. Jane Porter lived near Elkton, the county seat of Todd County. Her husband was E. T. Porter, a farmer, who was an uncle of John M. Porter. Todd County borders Logan County on the west. Montgomery County, Tennessee, borders Todd County on the south. (Census Population Schedules, Todd County, Kentucky, 1860, Elkton, Reel 396, Box 44, UKSC; Porter, "Historical Sketch of the Porter Family," 1.) Porter and his comrades were traveling on present-day Tenn. 13 (US 79), northeast, from Clarksville to Russellville.

4. Porter may be referring to William Withers, a large landowner and slaveowner in Logan County (Montgomery Vanderpool, *Logan County, Kentucky Vital Statistics, Births, 1852–1859* [Russellville, Ky.: Montgomery Vanderpool, 1987], 55, 63). The Morgantown Road is now Ky. 79, the principal highway between Russellville and Morgantown.

5. To reach Pleasant Hill Church, a site in northeast Logan County, Porter left the Morgantown Road, taking what is now called the Joe Beauchamp Turner Road. It is almost impossible to identify Mr. Anderson. Anderson was, and is now, a somewhat common surname in Logan County, and neither the vital statistics nor the 1860 Census for Logan County references any Anderson oper-

ating a tanyard. (Ibid., 1, 17, 18, 26, 31, 55, 58, 64, 70, 71; Census Population Schedules, Logan County, Kentucky, 1860, Reel 383, Box 31, UKSC.) It is clear Porter was near the Butler County line, though, as his friend Eaton Davis, of Butler County, had a home "nearby." (Census Population Schedules, Butler County, Kentucky, 1860, Sugar Grove, Reel 358, Box 6, UKSC.)

6. Uncle Moody was William A. Moody, who married Martha Jane Helm, John Marion Porter's mother's sister. They lived near South Union in Logan County with their seven children—six boys and one girl. (Porter, "Historical Sketch of the Porter Family," 8; Census Population Schedules, Logan County, Kentucky, 1860, South Union, Reel 383, Box 31, UKSC.)

Sugar Grove is a small settlement located in southeast Butler County on what is now Ky. 1083, less than five miles from the Logan County border, and not more than a half-mile from the Warren County border. The Porter family cemetery is located at Sugar Grove. The cemetery includes the burial sites of Colonel John Porter and Lieutenant William Porter, both Revolutionary War veterans from Virginia and ancestors of John M. Porter. (Kentucky Records Research Committee, *Kentucky Cemetery Records*, 5 vols. [Lexington: Keystone Printery, 1960], 1:76.) Sugar Grove was formally established in 1851, although families had settled there since the Revolution. The community acquired its name from the large quantities of maple sugar and syrup made and sold there. Reverend Nathaniel Porter gave Sugar Grove its name. The Porters, Kuykendalls, Baileys, Johnsons, Grays, Helms, and Carsons were the prominent families in Sugar Grove before the Civil War. John P. Carson was the first postmaster in the community, in 1832; Nathaniel Porter, John M. Porter's father, became postmaster in 1851. (Russ, ed., *Butler County, Kentucky History*, 34.)

7. Porter is referring to T.L.S. Proctor. He and his wife, Agnes, and their seven children lived near Proctor's Mill, not far from South Union, in Logan County, about twelve miles south of Sugar Grove. T.L.S. Proctor farmed a sizable amount of land. Agnes was formerly Agnes Carson, daughter of Thomas Carson and his wife, Sarah Dinwiddie Carson. Porter referred to her as Cousin Agnes. They were staunchly pro-Southern. (Census Population Schedules,

Logan County, Kentucky, 1860, South Union, Reel 383, Box 31, UKSC; Porter, "Historical Sketch of the Porter Family," 10; Stewart, *Descendants of Henry Hines, Sr.,* 27–28.)

8. Hickman Gray, often called "Hick," was forty-two years old and married to a woman named Mary, then thirty-nine. They had three little children and lived at Berry's Lick, not far from the Porters. Jerry Bailey was John W. Bailey, fifty-nine. He and his family were close neighbors of the Porters in Sugar Grove. His wife, Lucy, was fifty-one and they had seven children. Bailey was a native of North Carolina. Frank Bailey was Jerry's brother. Calvin Kuykendall was the brother of Andrew Kuykendall. Calvin, born in Illinois, never entered the Confederate service. He was thirty-three years old and married to Magdaline Kuykendall, also thirty-three. They had three children. (Census Population Schedules, Butler County, Kentucky, 1860, Sugar Grove, Reel 358, Box 6, UKSC.)

9. South Union Depot in Logan County was a railroad station on what was then the MC&L, linking Bowling Green, Kentucky, and the Louisville and Nashville Railroad with the Memphis and Ohio Railroad to Memphis, Tennessee. The village of South Union was the site of a colony of about 350 Shakers. (Census Population Schedules, Logan County, Kentucky, 1860, Shakers, Reel 383, Box 31, UKSC.) Many of the original buildings and dormitories of the Shakers still stand there. South Union is about four miles east of Auburn, Kentucky, in eastern Logan County, at the crossroads of present-day Ky. 80 (US 68) and Ky. 73. (Edward Coffman, *The Story of Logan County* [Nashville: Parthenon, 1962], 272.)

The "Franklin Road" is now known as Ky. 73 through eastern Logan County. It is the principal road to Franklin, Kentucky, county seat of Simpson County, which borders Robertson and Sumner counties in Tennessee.

John McCutchen lived at South Union Depot with his wife, Susan, and their five children. He was a substantial farmer. (Census Population Schedules, Logan County, Kentucky, 1860, South Union, Reel 383, Box 31, UKSC.)

10. General Don Carlos Buell commanded the Federal Army of the Ohio. As General Albert Sidney Johnston's Confederate forces evacuated Kentucky, Buell's army assumed control. When John-

ston abandoned Nashville after the fall of Fort Donelson, Buell's army entered the Tennessee capital city. All of Kentucky was, by then, occupied by Federal troops. Buell was commissioned a major general of volunteers on March 21, 1862. (OR, 7:418–424, 434, 899–901.)

Dickson Beard was most likely Miles Beard, a forty-five-year-old farmer in Simpson County. Born in Tennessee, Beard was married to a wife named Elizabeth, age forty. The Beards had seven children, ranging in age from seventeen to three. There were three Beard families in Simpson County. All of them were related, and all of them were related to the Beard and Porter families in Butler County. John M. Porter's sister, Mary Thomas, married William P. Beard in 1861. (Porter, "Historical Sketch of the Porter Family," 6; Census Population Schedules, Simpson County, Kentucky, 1860, Franklin, Reel 395, Box 43, UKSC.)

The Thomas Dobbins referenced by Porter was probably Thomas C. Dobbins of Sumner County, Tennessee. With his wife, Ann, he had eight children. (Sistler and Sistler, *1850 Census, Tennessee*, 4 vols. [Evanston: Sistler, 1975], 2:158.)

11. Captain John Hunt Morgan, on September 20, 1861, took his prewar State Guard company, "The Lexington Rifles," out of Federal-occupied Lexington, Kentucky, and rode to Woodsonville, Kentucky, on the Green River. There, he and his men were sworn into Confederate service on September 30 on the steps of the Green River Baptist Church by none other than Colonel William Preston Johnston, General Albert Sidney Johnston's son. The command became known as Morgan's Squadron; Morgan was commissioned a captain in the Confederate Army. The squadron performed scouting duties and served as the rear guard of General Johnston's army as it retreated from Nashville, Tennessee. (Duke, *History of Morgan's Cavalry*, 88–94; OR, 7:433–434; James Ramage, *Rebel Raider: The Life of General John Hunt Morgan* [Lexington: Univ. Press of Kentucky, 1986], 45–56.)

12. Porter refers here to the residence of William Bibb, the son of William Wyatt Bibb, governor of the territory and state of Alabama from 1817 to 1820 (Colonel James Edmonds Saunders and Saunders Blair Stubbs, *Early Settlers of Alabama with Notes and Gene-*

alogies [New Orleans: L. Graham and Son, 1899], 435–436). General Johnston had wooden planks placed upon the Memphis and Charleston Railroad bridge over the Tennessee River so that his army could move across it.

13. Major General Leonidas Polk's command was moving from Columbus, Kentucky, to Corinth, Mississippi, by means of the Mobile and Ohio Railroad (M&O); troops were en route to Corinth from New Orleans and Memphis on the Memphis and Charleston Railroad (M&C) under Brigadier General Daniel Ruggles; Major General Braxton Bragg was bringing a division up from Pensacola, Florida, by means of the M&O; troops under Major General Earl Van Dorn were marching toward the Mississippi River from Arkansas and Missouri; and Johnston's main force was moving toward Corinth alongside the M&C from Decatur, Alabama. (OR, 7:899–924; 10:385–392.)

14. Morgan's Squadron was attached to Colonel Robert P. Trabue's brigade—known as the Orphan Brigade later in the war—in Brigadier General John Cabell Breckinridge's Reserve Division of General Johnston's Army of the Mississippi. (Duke, *History of Morgan's Cavalry*, 138–153; OR, 10:566–571.)

15. The Battle of Shiloh was fought on April 6 and 7, 1862; heavy rains had preceded the battle. On Sunday morning, April 6, General Johnston's Army of the Mississippi attacked General Grant's divisions of the Army of the Tennessee that were bivouacked around Shiloh Church and drove them almost to the Tennessee River. Johnston was mortally wounded early in the afternoon. That evening and night, elements of General Buell's Army of the Ohio, after marching from Nashville, arrived and were ferried across the Tennessee River to reinforce Grant's shattered army. On April 7, Grant's and Buell's combined forces counterattacked and drove the Confederates back. General P.G.T. Beauregard, commanding the Army of the Mississippi after the death of Johnston, withdrew the army back to Corinth. Beauregard would resign as commander after withdrawing the army farther south to Tupelo. Elevated to the rank of full general, Braxton Bragg would be named commander of the army on June 20, 1862. (Grady McWhiney, *Braxton Bragg and Confederate Defeat*, vol. 1, *Field Command* [New York: Columbia Univ.

Press, 1969], 260; OR, 10:108–111, 385–392; Warner, *Generals in Gray*, 30.)

4. WE STRUCK OUT ON OUR OWN RESPONSIBILITY

1. Jacinto was the county seat of Tishomingo County, Mississippi, when the county was created in 1836 (Dunbar Rowland, *History of Mississippi*, 2 vols. [Chicago-Jackson: Clarke, 1925], 1:589). William L. Dulaney was a member of "Buckner's Guides." He joined in February 1862 in Nashville after most of the "Guides" withdrew to the city with General Johnston's army. (Ellis and Stone, *Report of the Adjutant General of the State of Kentucky*, 2:412.)

Colonel Benjamin Franklin Terry, a native of Russellville, Kentucky, raised a regiment of Texas Rangers in September 1861 known as the Eighth Texas Cavalry. Terry was elected colonel while the command was at Bowling Green, Kentucky. Terry was killed in his first engagement leading the Rangers, at Rowlett's Station, near Woodsonville, Kentucky, on December 17, 1861. (O. M. Roberts, *Texas*, vol. 15 in *Confederate Military History*, ed. Clement Evans [Atlanta: Confederate Pub. Co., 1899], 653.)

Colonel Benjamin Hardin Helm, son of two-time Kentucky governor John L. Helm of Elizabethtown, Kentucky, and a graduate of the U.S. Military Academy, raised the First Kentucky Cavalry (C.S.A.) and commanded it during the operations leading up to the Battle of Shiloh. Helm would command the Orphan Brigade at the Battle of Baton Rouge on August 5, 1862, and at the Battle of Chickamauga, where he would be mortally wounded on September 20, 1863. He was married to Emily Todd of Lexington, Kentucky, half-sister to Mary Todd Lincoln. (Thompson, *History of the Orphan Brigade*, 383–384.)

2. Brigadier General Ormsby M. Mitchel commanded a division in General Buell's Army of the Ohio. After the Battle of Shiloh and the Federal occupation of Corinth, Mississippi, Mitchel's division was sent east toward Chattanooga, Tennessee, to repair the trackage and bridges of the Memphis and Charleston Railroad and possibly seize Chattanooga. (OR, 10:871–879.)

Andy Kuykendall's brother was Joseph C. Kuykendall, a private in Company G, Eighth Texas Cavalry. Porter and Kuykendall joined Company G of the Eighth Texas Cavalry. (Janet B. Hewett, ed., *The Roster of Confederate Soldiers, 1861–1865*, 16 vols. [Wilmington, N.C.: Broadfoot, 1996], 9:255.)

Captain Charles T. Noel, an Owensboro, Kentucky, physician in civilian life, was mortally wounded "in the side" at a place called Hewey's Bridge, Alabama, on May 9, 1862. He died on May 11. (Thompson, *History of the Orphan Brigade*, 884, 996.)

3. John Hunt Morgan and his squadron returned to central Tennessee, around Murfreesboro, after Shiloh. There he fought a near disastrous encounter with Federal forces at Lebanon, Tennessee, and then made a successful raid to Cave City, Kentucky, destroying railroad rolling stock and trackage of the Louisville and Nashville Railroad. Having been commissioned a colonel, Morgan moved his command to Chattanooga and began raising what became the Second Kentucky Cavalry Regiment (C.S.A.). (Duke, *History of Morgan's Cavalry*, 159–168; Ramage, *Rebel Raider*, 82–91.) He took that regiment to Knoxville in June, along with a squadron of Texans under Major Richard M. Gano, a native of Bourbon County, Kentucky. He later added a regiment of Georgia partisan rangers under Major F. M. Nix in central Tennessee, prior to advancing into Kentucky, and added two companies of Kentuckians to Gano's command. (OR, 16 [1]: 766–767; Warner, *Generals in Gray*, 96.)

4. Dix River Bridge, a wooden covered structure, spanned the Dix River (now Herrington Lake) at King's Mill on present-day Ky. 34 between Danville, in Boyle County, and Hoskins Crossroads (the site of Camp Dick Robinson), in Garrard County. The tavern where Porter and his friends stayed was unquestionably Old Burnt Tavern at Bryantsville, facing present-day US 27. It was a massive two-story brick building erected around 1795. It stood until 1956. (J. Winston Coleman Jr., *Historic Kentucky* [Lexington: Henry Clay Press, 1967], 31.)

5. The David Hays referenced by Porter was sixty-seven-year-old David B. Hays, who was married to Rachel (Berkley) Hays. David B. Hays was the son of the Clark County pioneer William Hays, a former state senator. The Hayses lived on the McClure Pike, present-day Ky. 3370, southwest of Winchester. (George F. Doyle,

M.D., *Clark County Tombstone Records* [Winchester: privately printed, 1935], 19–20; Census Population Schedules, Clark County, Kentucky, 1860, Reel 362, Box 10, UKSC.)

6. John Hunt Morgan was promoted to colonel of the Second Kentucky Cavalry (C.S.A.) on April 4, 1862 (Warner, *Generals in Gray*, 220–221). He entered Kentucky on the first raid by way of Tompkinsville, moved north on present-day Ky. 63, and arrived at Glasgow on July 10 (OR, 16 [1]: 767–770, 777–778).

Thomas Henry Hines was born in Butler County, Kentucky, near Woodbury, on October 9, 1838. He was the second of seven children born to Warren Walker Hines and Sarah Carson Hines. Like John M. Porter, Hines could trace his ancestry back to Virginia. His great grandfather, Henry Hines, fought in the Revolutionary War. Porter and Hines were related through marriage into the Carson family. The Hines family moved to western Kentucky in the early years of the nineteenth century; Thomas's grandfather, Henry Hines Jr., fought at the Battle of New Orleans in 1815. Young Thomas Hines grew up in Woodbury, where his father owned a general store. He attended local schools and thereafter pursued an independent course of study. He advanced himself so well that he became a mathematics and science instructor at the Masonic University in LaGrange, Kentucky, in 1859. Hines was ardently pro-Southern; so were most of his students. In May 1861, some of those students announced that they had formed a company to fight for the protection of the state against "the howling hell-hounds of Abolitionism." Hines left LaGrange and organized the company known as "Buckner's Guides" with John M. Porter in Bowling Green. Hines became first lieutenant. He remained with Buckner's Guides until they were disbanded. He then joined John B. Castleman's Company D, Second Kentucky Cavalry (C.S.A.), in Chattanooga in early June 1862. As Morgan moved his command into Kentucky, Hines was detached in order to locate John M. Porter and Andy Kuykendall, who he had heard were in central Kentucky trying to join Morgan's command. (Coffman, "The Civil War Career of Thomas Henry Hines," 1–6; Stewart, *Descendants of Henry Hines, Sr.*, 25; *Lexington Herald*, January 24, 1898; *Louisville Daily Courier*, May 6, 1861.)

7. Lexington was then occupied by a Federal force under the command of Brigadier General William T. Ward, a Virginian who had grown up and practiced law in Greensburg, Kentucky, before the war (Warner, *Generals in Blue,* 538; OR, 16 [1]: 212, 740, 742–744, 746, 759, 764, 777, 778). Lexington had ten hotels in 1862 (Lewis Collins, *Historical Sketches of Kentucky* [Cincinnati: J. A. and U. P. James, 1847], 265). Porter and Hines probably stopped at the brick, three-story Phoenix Hotel on East Main Street at the corner of Limestone Street, a hostelry noted for catering to Federal occupation soldiers and their officers. The proprietor, C. T. Worley, was the colonel of the local Federal Home Guard unit. (Frances Peter, *A Union Woman in Civil War Kentucky: The Diary of Frances Peter,* ed. John David Smith and William Cooper Jr. [Lexington: Univ. Press of Kentucky, 2000], 21, n 4.) Porter and Hines then went out to the Lexington Cemetery on West Main Street. The Lexington Cemetery was incorporated in 1848 and began operation in 1850. The ground there was rather high, offering good views of the western approaches to Lexington. (George W. Ranck, *History of Lexington, Kentucky* [Cincinnati: Robert Clarke and Co., 1872], 360.) The Winchester Road is present-day US 60.

8. Morgan and his command were then riding from Lawrenceburg, Kentucky, on present-day US 62, in order to cross the Kentucky River at Shryock's Ferry, not far from Versailles. They took the Versailles-Midway Pike, present-day US 62, from Versailles to Midway. (OR, 16 [1]: 767–770.)

9. Thirty-three-year-old Colby T. Hays was from Clark County, Kentucky, the son of David B. Hays and Rachel Hays. He enlisted at Georgetown, Kentucky, on July 15, 1862, with Porter in the Second Kentucky Cavalry (C.S.A.). He ultimately became a member of Company E, Ninth Kentucky Cavalry (C.S.A.). He would serve throughout the war, finally being paroled at Washington, Georgia, in May 1865. (Ellis and Stone, *Report of the Adjutant General of the State of Kentucky,* 2:20; Census Population Schedules, Clark County, Kentucky, 1860, Reel 362, Box 10, UKSC.)

10. Tate's Creek Pike, now Ky. 1974, enters Lexington from the south. It originates in Fayette County at the site of the Valley View Ferry, which crosses the Kentucky River to Madison County.

11. Porter is probably referring to Luther Alexander Martin and his wife, Ann M. (Barnes) Martin. Luther Martin was the son of Lewis Young Martin and his wife, Ann B. (Shreve) Martin, whose two-story brick house still stands off of the Tate's Creek Pike, present-day Ky. 1974, south of Lexington, Kentucky, in Jessamine County, about three miles from the Fayette County line. Luther Martin's brother William Upton Martin was a surgeon in the Confederate Army. (Robert Peter, *History of Fayette County, Kentucky* [Chicago: O. L. Baskin and Co., 1882], 665; "Luther Alexander Martin," www.jesshistorical.com/Jessamine%20County%20Kentucky%20Families/b231.htm#P2549.)

12. Keene, Kentucky, is located about five and one-half miles north of Nicholasville, at the intersection of the Keene Road, present-day Ky. 169, and the Keene-Troy Road, present-day Ky. 1267, in Jessamine County. There was built the Keene Springs Hotel, which in 1862 was owned by Alfred McTyre. It still stands. Keene Springs was known in the nineteenth century as having "the best medical water on the continent." People from all over the South visited there to "take the waters." (Coleman, *Historic Kentucky*, 192.) Porter followed the Union Mills Road, present-day Ky. 169, from the Tate's Creek Pike to reach Keene. Shryock's Ferry over the Kentucky River was located at the mouth of Grier's Creek, opposite Tyrone, in Woodford County. Originally Sublett's Ferry, it passed into the hands of the Shryock family before the Civil War. (W. E. Railey, *History of Woodford County* [Lexington: Woodford Improvement League, 1968], 45.) Shryock's Ferry on the Kentucky River was located near the present-day US 62 bridge.

13. Abraham, or "Abram," Buford lived at Bosque Bonita Farm on the Versailles-Midway Pike, present-day US 62, in Woodford County, Kentucky. Lane's End Farm now occupies much of the land of the former Bosque Bonita Farm. (Martha McDowell Buford, *Peach Leather and Rebel Gray: Diary and Letters of a Confederate Wife*, ed. Mary E. Wharton and Ellen F. Williams [Lexington, Ky.: Helicon, 1986], 17.) Buford was placed in command of a brigade of cavalry that was raised during the invasion of the state in 1862; it would become attached to the cavalry command of then Brigadier General Nathan Bedford Forrest. He would later com-

mand a brigade during the Vicksburg campaign and return to General Forrest's command as a brigade commander. (Railey, *History of Woodford County*, 92.) Morgan's command entered Midway, Kentucky, on Tuesday morning, July 15, 1862. The telegraph office was seized and the tracks of the Lexington and Frankfort Railroad were destroyed. (*Louisville Daily Journal*, July 26, 1862, Bill Penn Collection, Cynthiana, Kentucky.)

Porter followed the Keene-Versailles Road (present-day Ky. 169, to present-day Ky. 33) to reach Versailles.

14. Morgan's command stopped at Georgetown on July 15, 1862 (Duke, *History of Morgan's Cavalry*, 194–199). Porter followed the Versailles-Midway Pike (present-day US 62), and then the Paynes Depot Road (also present-day US 62) from just east of Midway to Georgetown.

5. A PERFECT TORNADO OF SHOTS WAS FIRED AT US

1. Captain James W. Bowles enlisted in the Confederate Army on September 9, 1861, in Richmond, Virginia, and became commander of Company C, Second Kentucky Cavalry (C.S.A.), at Chattanooga in the summer of 1862. He would be promoted to major later that year, lieutenant colonel in 1863, and colonel in 1864. John B. Castleman enlisted on June 1, 1862, in Chattanooga. He was promoted to captain of Company D, Second Kentucky Cavalry, almost immediately thereafter. Castleman was born and raised on Castleton Farm on the Ironworks Pike, north of Lexington, Kentucky. Castleman's company had been detached to position itself between Lexington and Paris to make the Federal occupation forces in Lexington believe Morgan was closer to Lexington than he actually was. Castleman's company patrolled the Ironworks Pike north of Lexington. After the war Castleman authored a memoir entitled *Active Service*. (Ellis and Stone, *Report of the Adjutant General of the State of Kentucky*, 1:552–553, 556–557; John B. Castleman, *Active Service* [Louisville: Courier-Journal Job Printing Co., 1917], 81–92.) Although Hines was a member of Company D, Second Kentucky Cavalry, he, Porter, and Kuykendall "fell in with" Company C, as Company D was on detached service

nearly ten miles distant from Georgetown, Kentucky, when they met Morgan's command.

2. Lieutenant Colonel John J. Landrum of the Eighteenth Kentucky Infantry (U.S.A.) commanded at Cynthiana about fifteen men from his own regiment and sixty Home Guards under Captain J. B. McClintock and from fifty to sixty Home Guards under Captain Lafe Wilson, all from Cynthiana and Harrison County. In addition, he had fifty Home Guards from Newport, Kentucky, under Captain John S. Arthur, forty men from Cincinnati, Ohio, under Captain J. J. Wright, thirty-five Home Guards from Bracken County under a Captain Pepper, seventy-five men from the Seventh Kentucky Cavalry (U.S.A.) under Major William O. Smith, one brass twelve-pound howitzer and a gun crew of Cincinnati policemen under Captain W. H. Glass from Cincinnati, and others, a total of over five hundred men. Landrum placed the artillery piece in the courthouse lot, and positioned his "infantry" in buildings along the Licking River as well as east and west of town. (OR, 16 [1]: 756–759.) The bridge over the Licking River, south of town, was 320 feet long and stood on two stone piers. Made of wood, it was covered with a shingle roof. It was completed in 1837 and stood until 1946. The old bridge stood just under one hundred yards west of the present concrete John Hunt Morgan Bridge that carries US 27/62 over the Licking River into Cynthiana. (Coleman, *Historic Kentucky*, 71.)

3. Morgan's command reached Cynthiana by way of present-day US 62 from Georgetown. That road entered Cynthiana by means of the covered bridge over the Licking River. Morgan detached Companies A and B of the Second Kentucky, dismounted, to the right of the bridge, Companies E and F to the left, also dismounted. Company C was held in reserve, mounted. Company A tried to wade through the Licking River to get into Cynthiana, but was driven back by heavy gunfire. Major Gano was sent to the far right and crossed Kimbrough's Bridge southeast of town, while Major Nix's Georgians approached Cynthiana from the west and north. Company C of the Second Kentucky (C.S.A.) was ordered to charge through the covered bridge into town, and it succeeded, driving before it the defenders all the way up Bridge Street to the

Kentucky Central Railroad depot, with the rest of the Second Kentucky alongside. (OR, 16 [1]: 756–759, 767–770, 771–774, 781–784; Duke, *History of Morgan's Cavalry*, 200–203; William A. Penn, *Rattling Spurs and Broad-Brimmed Hats: The Civil War in Cynthiana and Harrison County, Kentucky* [Midway, Ky.: Battle Grove Press, 1995], 73–78.)

4. Colonel George St. Leger Grenfell was an English soldier-of-fortune who met Morgan and his command at Knoxville. He had served in a French Algerian regiment and then lived in Tangier. He had even served for several years with Abd-el-Kader. From north Africa, Grenfell fought in the Crimean war, the Sepoy Rebellion, and in Garabaldi's South American service. He arrived in the Confederacy to offer his services and wound up in Knoxville. Morgan made him adjutant general of the Second Kentucky. At Cynthiana, Grenfell was noticeable by his red fez with gold tassel and French Algerian Zouave jacket. (Duke, *History of Morgan's Cavalry*, 180–181.)

5. Colonel Landrum's Federal force was finally hemmed in at the Kentucky Central Railroad depot, although Landrum himself escaped. Colonel Grenfell led the attack against the depot. (OR, 16 [1]: 769; Duke, *History of Morgan's Cavalry*, 201–202.)

6. The Federal losses at Cynthiana were ninety killed and wounded, along with 420 taken as prisoners. Morgan lost about forty men, killed and wounded, while taking the town. (Duke, *History of Morgan's Cavalry*, 202; OR, 16 [1]: 769.)

7. Captain Castleman's Company D, Second Kentucky (C.S.A.), had been detached north of Lexington to keep the Federal force in the town from moving toward Paris and Cynthiana (OR, 16 [1]: 769; Castleman, *Active Service*, 88–92).

8. Morgan's command rode to Paris and then to Winchester by means of present-day Ky. 627. From Winchester, the command rode to Boonesboro along roughly the route of present-day Ky. 627 (the modern road does not follow the old path) and on to Richmond on present-day Ky. 388. They continued on to Crab Orchard, Somerset, and Monticello before crossing back into Tennessee. (Duke, *History of Morgan's Cavalry*, 203–205.)

9. Brigadier General Green Clay Smith was sent from the south-

ern part of Kentucky to Frankfort by order of Brigadier General
Jeremiah T. Boyle, commander of the Military District of Kentucky.
Smith chased Morgan with 1,320 men from the Ninth Pennsylva-
nia Cavalry Regiment, Eighteenth Kentucky Infantry Regiment
(U.S.A.), various Home Guards, and assorted artillery, including
elements of the Thirteenth Indiana Battery. (OR, 16 [1]: 759–762.)

10. Brigadier General Felix Kirk Zollicoffer was killed while
commanding a brigade at the Battle of Fishing Creek, or Mill
Springs, on January 19, 1862. That battle was the first blow to General Johnston's Confederate defenses in Kentucky, as his eastern
flank collapsed as a result. Zollicoffer was a newspaper editor in
Nashville and a congressman before the war. (Warner, *Generals in
Gray*, 349–350.)

11. Basil W. Duke was born and raised in Scott County, Kentucky, and educated at Centre College and by the Transylvania
University law department. He married Henrietta Morgan, Colonel John Hunt Morgan's sister. Practicing law in St. Louis, Missouri,
when the war broke out, he joined Confederate forces in Missouri,
but then returned to Kentucky to join his brother-in-law, then Captain Morgan, at Woodsonville. At the time of the first Kentucky
raid, Duke was a lieutenant colonel, commanding the Second Kentucky Cavalry Regiment (C.S.A.). (Gary Robert Matthews, *Basil Wilson Duke: The Right Man in the Right Place* [Lexington: Univ. Press of
Kentucky, 2005], 7–14.)

12. James Cook enlisted in October 1861 at Bowling Green and
became a member of "Buckner's Guides." He was a native of Warren County. (Ellis and Stone, *Report of the Adjutant General of the
State of Kentucky*, 2:410–412.) He does not reappear in the rosters
of Morgan's command, but undoubtedly was with the command in
July 1862.

6. It Was a Grand and Imposing Ovation

1. John M. Porter was attached to Company D, Second Kentucky Cavalry (C.S.A.). Chestnut Mound is a hamlet south of the
Cumberland River in the highlands of Tennessee about twenty
miles east of Lebanon on present-day Tenn. 24 (US 70N). It was

deep enough in the foothills to provide sanctuary for Morgan's men while they rested. Hartsville, in Trousdale County, north of the Cumberland River, is about twenty miles northwest of Chestnut Mound, connected by present-day Tenn. 24 (US 70N) and Tenn. 25.

Virgil Gray was twenty years old and a native of Sugar Grove. He was the son of Bradford Gray, age fifty years, and Jane Gray, forty-five; both were native Kentuckians. Virgil was the oldest of six children. He eventually enlisted in Company L, Second Kentucky Cavalry, at Hartsville, Tennessee, and rose to the rank of third sergeant. (Census Population Schedules, Butler County, Kentucky, 1860, Sugar Grove, Reel 358, Box 6, UKSC; Ellis and Stone, *Report of the Adjutant General of the State of Kentucky*, 1:586.)

2. Gallatin, Tennessee, in Sumner County, north of the Cumberland River, is located on the main stem of the Louisville and Nashville Railroad. There the L&N made a sharp western bend as it led into Nashville. Between Gallatin and the Kentucky border, the L&N right-of-way passed through two tunnels in the rugged foothills.

3. Colonel William P. Boone of New Haven, Nelson County, Kentucky, was a former member of the state legislature. Enrolled in the Federal service on November 6, 1861, he was commissioned a colonel on January 7, 1862. He raised the Twenty-eighth Kentucky Infantry (U.S.A.) at New Haven, and from the time of its organization until 1863 they protected the L&N and the approaches to Nashville. (Lindsey, *Report of the Adjutant General of the State of Kentucky [Federal]*, 260–285.) Boone had been in command at Gallatin with the Twenty-eighth Kentucky since May 1, 1862. He was actually captured on August 12, 1862, by a detachment of the Second Kentucky Cavalry (C.S.A.) commanded by Captain Joseph Desha of Cynthiana. Captured with Boone were five companies of the Twenty-eighth Kentucky, about 375 men. (OR, 16 [1]: 845–857; Duke, *History of Morgan's Cavalry*, 211–212.)

4. Hiram A. Hunter was the chaplain of the Twenty-eighth Kentucky Infantry (U.S.A.). He was enrolled on January 3, 1862, in New Haven, Kentucky. (Lindsey, *Report of the Adjutant General of the State of Kentucky [Federal]*, 2:260.)

5. Brigadier General Richard W. Johnson was a native Kentuckian, having been born and raised near Smithland, a hamlet located at the confluence of the Cumberland and Ohio rivers. He was an 1849 graduate of the U.S. Military Academy. Johnson was commissioned a brigadier general of volunteers on October 11, 1861, and commanded a brigade in Major General Alexander McDowell McCook's Corps of the Army of the Ohio. He vowed to "capture [Morgan] and bring [him] back in a band-box." (Ezra J. Warner, *Generals in Blue*, 253–254.) Johnson led a special brigade against Morgan that consisted of infantry and elements from the Second Indiana Cavalry, Fourth Kentucky Cavalry (U.S.A.), Fifth Kentucky Cavalry (U.S.A.), and Seventh Pennsylvania Cavalry. Johnson was captured during the action at Gallatin on August 21, 1862. (OR, 16 [1]: 871–882.)

6. The recapture of the citizens of Gallatin was one of the actions most fondly recalled by Morgan's men. Morgan's men were virtually worshipped by the people of both Gallatin and Hartsville as a result. (Duke, *History of Morgan's Cavalry*, 217–218.)

To protect the L&N, General Buell directed the construction of log stockades near vulnerable river and creek crossings. The stockades were defended by infantry and artillery detachments.

7. Major General Edmund Kirby Smith and General Braxton Bragg met in Chattanooga to plan the invasion of Kentucky. Smith's army, soon to be known as the Provisional Army of Kentucky, left Knoxville and marched through Rogers Gap into Kentucky, arriving at Barbourville on August 17, 1862. Leaving Brigadier General Carter L. Stevenson's division at Barbourville to keep Brigadier General George W. Morgan's Federal division at Cumberland Gap from menacing Smith's rear, Smith moved the rest of his army toward Richmond, Kentucky. Big Hill is a village at the foothills of the mountains in Madison County, about sixteen miles south of Richmond. There, Kirby Smith's army opened the fighting on August 23, 1862, that concluded at Richmond, Kentucky, on August 30. Kirby Smith's army followed present-day US 421. Bragg's Army of the Mississippi marched from Chattanooga on August 28, 1862, toward Carthage, Tennessee; it crossed into Kentucky, arriving at Glasgow on September 13, 1862. (OR, 16 [1]: 2–3, 1088–1094.)

8. After wrecking the L&N at Gallatin, Morgan marched northward on August 29, 1862, ahead of Bragg's army (Duke, *History of Morgan's Cavalry,* 229).

9. General Smith virtually annihilated a Federal army of newly raised regiments assembled south of Richmond, Kentucky, by Major General William "Bull" Nelson of Kentucky. On August 30, 1862, Smith overwhelmed and crushed Nelson's force, capturing more than four thousand Federal troops. Smith marched to Lexington, along present-day US 25, entering the town on September 2, 1862. He set up his headquarters in the Phoenix Hotel. (OR, 16 [1]: 931–935; Edward O. Guerrant, *Bluegrass Confederate: The Headquarters Diary of Edward O. Guerrant,* ed. William C. Davis and Meredith L. Swentor [Baton Rouge: Louisiana State Univ. Press, 1989], 154.)

10. Morgan and his command entered Lexington on the morning of September 4, 1862, by way of the Nicholasville Road (US 27) and Limestone Street. Church bells pealed all over the city and thousands of people lined the streets as Morgan led his troopers back into his hometown. (Peter, *A Union Woman in Civil War Kentucky,* 30–31; Duke, *History of Morgan's Cavalry,* 233–234.)

11. Major William Campbell Preston Breckinridge, a young lawyer from Lexington, Kentucky, was the son of the Presbyterian cleric, Unionist, and abolitionist Reverend Robert J. Breckinridge. W.C.P. Breckinridge had been graduated from Centre College and the University of Louisville law department. He joined Morgan's command in Georgetown, Kentucky, in July 1862 during Morgan's first Kentucky raid. (Colonel J. Stoddard Johnston, *Kentucky,* vol. 11 in *Confederate Military History,* ed. Clement Evans [Atlanta: Confederate Pub. Co., 1899], 286–287.) Breckinridge's Battalion became known as the Ninth Kentucky Cavalry later in the fall of 1862.

12. General Smith directed a division of infantry under the command of Brigadier General Henry Heth northward, past Cynthiana, to near Covington, Kentucky. Brigadier General Patrick R. Cleburne's brigade was sent as far west as Shelbyville, not far from Louisville, and Brigadier General Carter L. Stevenson's division remained at Barbourville, southeast of Lexington. When Federal brigadier general George W. Morgan abandoned Cumberland

Gap and moved his division toward Greenupsburg, Morgan was ordered to follow. At that same time, Brigadier General Humphrey Marshall of Kentucky was marching his six-thousand-man Army of Southwest Virginia (C.S.A.) into Kentucky from Abington, Virginia, by way of Pound Gap. (OR, 16 [1]: 1088–1094; Guerrant, *Bluegrass Confederate*, 142–154.)

13. Morgan's command followed present-day Ky. 52 from Richmond, Kentucky, to Irvine and to Jackson; it then followed present-day Ky. 1812 and Ky. 1010 north to Hazel Green, through the mountains of Wolfe County.

14. Brigadier General Humphrey Marshall's army marched toward Mt. Sterling, Kentucky, and then to Lexington (Guerrant, *Bluegrass Confederate*, 151–154).

15. Morgan's return to Lexington was generally along present-day US 60, from Carter County through Rowan County, Bath County, Montgomery County, and Clark County, and on into Lexington.

16. Lieutenant Colonel Basil W. Duke had taken the Second Kentucky Cavalry (C.S.A.) northward to screen the movements of Brigadier General Henry Heth's division near Covington. On September 27, 1862, Duke became locked in a bloody fight with Home Guards in the streets of Augusta, Kentucky, on the Ohio River. Duke suffered the loss of twenty-one killed and eighteen wounded in his Second Kentucky Cavalry, but he captured the town and all of its defenders. (OR, 16 [1]: 1013–1014; Duke, *History of Morgan's Cavalry*, 242–257.)

17. The newly raised Eighth Kentucky Cavalry Regiment (C.S.A.) under Colonel Roy S. Cluke and the newly raised Eleventh Kentucky Cavalry Regiment (C.S.A.) under Colonel David Waller Chenault protected the rear of Bragg's and Smith's armies as they left Bryantsville, Kentucky (on present-day US 27), on October 12, 1862, until they reentered Tennessee. Morgan took the rest of his command with him back toward Lexington. (Duke, *History of Morgan's Cavalry*, 281–282.)

18. Accompanying Duke's Second Kentucky Cavalry and Gano's and Breckinridge's battalions were Captain C. C. Corbett's two mountain howitzers (ibid., 284–285).

19. Morgan surprised two battalions of Federal cavalry from the Third and Fourth Ohio Cavalry regiments behind "Ashland," the reconstructed residence of Henry Clay, on the morning of October 18, 1862. Although Morgan's losses were very small, Major George Washington Morgan, his second cousin and adjutant of the Second Kentucky Cavalry (C.S.A.), was mortally wounded. He was taken to "Hopemont," the Hunt-Morgan House on Gratz Park in Lexington, where he died on October 27, 1862. He is buried in the Morgan plot in the Lexington Cemetery alongside his cousin Captain Samuel Dold Morgan of the Second Kentucky Cavalry, who was killed at the Battle of Augusta, Kentucky, on September 27, 1862. Capturing almost 290 Federal troopers at the Clay estate and in the town, Morgan held Lexington until the afternoon. Then, he and his command departed for Versailles and Lawrenceburg, as a large Federal force under Major General Gordon Granger was moving toward Lexington from near Paris, Kentucky. (Duke, *History of Morgan's Cavalry*, 282–287; Lucien Wulsin, *The Story of the Fourth Regiment Ohio Veteran Volunteer Cavalry* [Cincinnati: N.p., 1912], 32–34; History Committee, *History of the Service of the Third Ohio Veteran Volunteer Cavalry* [Toledo: Stoneman, 1910], 46–54; *The Vidette* [transcript, after-action report of the action at "Ashland"], Hopkinsville, Ky., October 28, 1862, Dr. Dan Rush Collection, Kingsport, Tennessee.)

7. THE WHISKEY WAS STILL ABUNDANT

1. Morgan and his command crossed the Kentucky River at Shryock's Ferry, about four miles from Lawrenceburg. The command was following present-day US 62. Since the early twentieth century, a bridge has spanned the river near the site of the ferry. (Duke, *History of Morgan's Cavalry*, 287.)

2. The enemy forces consisted of the division of Brigadier General Joshua H. Sill of Major General Alexander McDowell McCook's Corps operating out of Frankfort, Kentucky. The skirmish occurred on October 19, 1862. (OR, 16 [1]:1134.) Duke claimed that the division of Brigadier General Ebenezer Dumont of McCook's Corps was present also (Duke, *History of Morgan's Cavalry*, 287–288).

3. Morgan's command continued following present-day US 62 to Bardstown, Elizabethtown, and Leitchfield, Kentucky. The command arrived at Leitchfield, Grayson County, Kentucky, on October 21, 1862. (Duke, *History of Morgan's Cavalry*, 289.)

4. Woodbury is a small hamlet in Butler County, about five miles south of Morgantown, on present-day Ky. 403. Formed in 1810, it is located near the Green River about one mile from the Warren County line. Morgan's men arrived at Woodbury on October 22, 1862. (Ibid., 289.) Thomas H. Hines was born and raised near Woodbury. The Hines, Sproules, and Carsons were prominent families in Woodbury. (Russ, ed., *Butler County, Kentucky History*, 35.)

5. Little Muddy Creek runs through southeastern Butler County. Sugar Grove is located along Little Muddy Creek.

John Kuykendall and Matthew Kuykendall were brothers living near Morgantown, Butler County, Kentucky. John was twenty years old and Matthew was sixteen. Their parents were deceased and they appear to have been living with their sister, Amanda Lee, age twenty-one, and her husband, James B. Lee, age twenty-four. With John and Matthew were two other siblings, Andrew, age twelve, and Margaret, age nine. Each of the Kuykendall children had their own farms, each valued in 1860 at $3,000.00, obviously acquired by inheritance. (Census Population Schedules, Butler County, Kentucky, 1860, Morgantown, Reel 358, Box 6, UKSC.)

Aunt Betsey was sixty-one-year-old Elizabeth Porter, who lived in Sugar Grove. She was the daughter of Francis and Sallie Porter. She never married and died in 1868. Sister Jennie was John M. Porter's sister, Nancy Virginia Porter, then nineteen years old. (Census Population Schedules, Butler County, Kentucky, 1860, Sugar Grove, Reel 358, Box 6, UKSC; Porter, "Historical Sketch of the Porter Family," 5.)

6. "Borah's Ferry" is located on the road leading from Morgantown to Hartford, present-day Ky. 403, on the Green River about nine miles downstream from Morgantown. The ferry began operation in 1828; Jacob E. Borah was the first owner and operator. By 1862, the ferry was operated by a gentleman named H. Clark. (Russ, ed., *Butler County, Kentucky History*, 26.)

John M. Porter probably followed present-day Ky. 1083 to present-day US 231 to travel from Sugar Grove to Morgantown. William E. West was a constable in Morgantown. He was thirty-two years old with a wife, Sarah, and three children. (Census Population Schedules, Butler County, Kentucky, 1860, Sugar Grove, Reel 358, Box 6, UKSC.)

William Beard, thirty-four years of age, lived in the neighborhood of Little Muddy Creek in Butler County. He was a substantial farmer and a very close neighbor of John M. Porter's family. In 1861, he married then twenty-four-year-old Mary Thomas Porter, John M. Porter's oldest sister, who had been educated at a school in Winchester, Tennessee. (Porter, "Historical Sketch of the Porter Family," 6; U.S. Federal Census Record for William Beard, Butler County, Kentucky, ancestry.com.)

7. Skeltern's Tavern was actually the old Aberdeen Hotel, a one-and-one-half-story log structure that stood in the village of Aberdeen, on the north bank of the Green River, from the early 1800s. It was built to serve the traffic on the Green River. (Russ, ed., *Butler County, Kentucky History,* 26.) The tavern stood along present-day Ky. 79, across the river from Morgantown, on the route taken by Morgan.

Instead of moving south, Morgan directed his command toward Rochester on present-day Ky. 70. That route, and present-day Ky. 176, lead to Greenville in Muhlenberg County.

8. Thomas P. Ward was the county judge of Butler County; forty years old, he and his wife, Martha, age thirty-nine, lived in Woodbury with their five children, ages twelve, ten, nine, three, and nine months, and Thomas's sister, age twenty-four. James M. Cook, age thirty-eight, lived in Morgantown with his wife, Mary, age thirty-four, and their six children, ages fourteen, eleven, nine, five, two, and three months. Captain John V. Sproule, age forty-six, lived in Woodbury with his wife, Lurila, age thirty-five, and their four children, ages sixteen to two. One of the children was eighteen-year-old Nancy Sproule. Nancy was engaged to marry Captain Thomas Henry Hines. The Sproule and Hines families lived on adjoining farms near Woodbury. Nancy Sproule and Thomas Henry Hines would be married in Covington, Kentucky,

after Hines escaped from the Ohio State Penitentiary in late 1863. David M. Beard, age forty-three, lived in Sugar Grove with his wife, Mary, age forty-one, and their seven-year-old daughter, Hester Ann. Beard was related to John M. Porter. Thomas E. Puckett is identified in chapter 1, note 4. All of those arrested were Southern sympathizers. (Census Population Schedules, Butler County, Kentucky, 1860, Woodbury, Morgantown, and Sugar Grove, Reel 358, Box 6, UKSC; "James D. Horan's interview with Ann Winn, granddaughter of Thomas and Nancy Hines," Thomas Henry Hines Papers, 1772 [1860–1869] 1954, Winn Collection, 46M97, Box 3, UKSC.) The arrests of Southern-sympathizing Kentucky citizens by the Federal occupation forces were a source of immense contention and resulted in long-lasting bitterness for many Kentuckians toward the Federal armies and the Lincoln administration (Coulter, *The Civil War and Readjustment in Kentucky*, 153–156). John M. Porter's uncle, Dr. Francis D. Porter, although feeble and advanced in age, was arrested by Federal occupation troops and imprisoned at Bowling Green, Kentucky, where he died (Porter, "Historical Sketch of the Porter Family," 2). Porter's own bitterness as a result of such occurrences is plainly evident throughout his memoir.

9. Morgan's command reached Hopkinsville, Christian County, Kentucky, on October 28, 1862, by means of present-day Ky. 189 and 107 from Greenville (Duke, *History of Morgan's Cavalry*, 292).

10. Morgan's men remained in Hopkinsville for three days. Colonel Richard M. Gano's Battalion was ordered to proceed toward Bowling Green, Kentucky, and destroy the Louisville and Nashville Railroad main stem and the Russellville branch line. The bridges over Whipporwill Creek and Elk Fork and the bridges between Russellville and Bowling Green were burned. (Ibid., 292–293.)

11. Trenton is a small town in southwestern Todd County, Kentucky, located on present-day US 41, about five miles from the Tennessee border. Morgan and his men arrived at Springfield, Tennessee, on November 1, 1862. Springfield is the county seat of Robertson County. Morgan's command followed present-day Tenn. 49 and Tenn. 25 to reach Gallatin, about twenty-five miles east of Springfield. The command reached Gallatin on November 4. (Ibid., 293.)

Dr. Nathaniel L. Porter was a Pembroke, Christian County, Kentucky, physician and kinsman to John M. Porter. Forty-nine years old, Dr. Porter was married to E. A. Porter, age forty. They had three children, a girl age fifteen, and two boys, ages twelve and two. Dr. Nathaniel L. Porter was the son of Reverend Thomas Porter, a preacher in the Cumberland Presbyterian Church and grandson of Lieutenant William Porter, the brother of John Marion Porter's grandfather, Francis Porter. Pembroke is a village in southeastern Christian County not far from the Todd County line. (Porter, "Historical Sketch of the Porter Family," 1.) G. W. Porter, a brother to Dr. Nathaniel L. Porter, was also a Hopkinsville physician (Census Population Schedules, Christian County, Kentucky, 1860, Hopkinsville, Reel 362, Box 10, UKSC).

12. General Braxton Bragg's Army of the Mississippi and Major General Edmund Kirby Smith's Army of Kentucky retreated from Kentucky by means of the Cumberland Gap. They both returned to Knoxville, Tennessee. Bragg then moved his army westward toward Murfreesboro, arriving in early November 1862. Major General Don Carlos Buell followed Bragg, but then moved off toward Nashville, which his army reoccupied. The Louisville and Nashville Turnpike is present-day US 31W and 31E. (OR, 16 [1]: 4, 1088–1094.)

13. Edgefield was actually known as Edgefield Junction in 1862. Located about ten miles north of Nashville, it was the site of the junction of the L&N and the Edgefield and Kentucky Railroad (E&K). Where the L&N proceeded east to Gallatin, the E&K proceeded northwest toward Springfield, Tennessee, connecting with the Memphis, Clarksville and Louisville Railroad at Guthrie, Kentucky. (Maury Klein, *History of the Louisville and Nashville Railroad* [New York: Macmillan, 1972], 17, 131, 134; Duke, *History of Morgan's Cavalry*, 297.)

14. Major General John C. Breckinridge had marched his division (which included the famed Kentucky Orphan Brigade) northward from near Jackson, Mississippi, in an effort to reinforce Bragg's army. As the Confederate armies in Kentucky were retreating, Breckinridge's division reached eastern Tennessee. Breckinridge was directed to move his division to Murfreesboro, where Bragg's army would join it. (OR, 20 [2]: 393, 411, 432.)

Brigadier General James S. Negley commanded the Federal defenses of Nashville while Buell's army was in Kentucky. On November 5, 1862, Negley reported defeating an "attack upon Nashville." (OR, 20 [1]: 3.)

15. James Crabb was a private in Company E, Second Kentucky Cavalry (C.S.A.). He enlisted on June 1, 1862, in Tennessee and was reported killed in action at Edgefield Junction on November 5, 1862. (Ellis and Stone, *Report of the Adjutant General of the State of Kentucky*, 1:562–563.)

16. General Buell was removed from command on October 30, 1862. (OR, 16 [1]: 4.)

17. "The Hermitage" was the home of President Andrew Jackson. It is located about ten miles northeast of Nashville, off of the road to Lebanon, present-day Tenn. 24 (US 70). Black's Shop was a small hamlet northwest of Murfreesboro, along the old Nashville Pike. Morgan patrolled the area to screen the Confederate forces congregating at Murfreesboro. (Duke, *History of Morgan's Cavalry*, 305–307.)

18. Fayetteville, Lincoln County, Tennessee, is about fifteen miles north of the Alabama state line, east of Pulaski, Tennessee, and southwest of Lynchburg, Tennessee. Because John M. Porter and the Ninth Kentucky Cavalry were sent to Fayetteville, they did not participate in the Battle of Hartsville, Tennessee, on December 7, 1862. (OR, 20 [1]: 65–72; Duke, *History of Morgan's Cavalry*, 309–316.)

8. The Fame and Glory of Morgan's Command

1. John Hunt Morgan was commissioned a brigadier general on December 11, 1862, because of his splendid service from July to December and at the Battle of Hartsville, Tennessee, on December 7. He had been an acting brigadier general ever since Bragg's army had returned to Murfreesboro from the invasion of Kentucky. (OR, 20 [1]: 62–73; Duke, *History of Morgan's Cavalry*, 321; Ramage, *Rebel Raider*, 134.) John Hunt Morgan married Martha "Mattie" Ready of Murfreesboro, Tennessee, on Sunday, December 14, 1862; they had courted off and on ever since they first met just

before Confederate forces evacuated Murfreesboro in February 1862. The wedding was a grand spectacle. It was held in the Ready home in Murfreesboro; Lieutenant General Leonidas Polk, the former Bishop of Louisiana, officiated. In attendance were most of the commanders of the Army of Tennessee, including Generals Braxton Bragg, Benjamin Cheatham, John C. Breckinridge, William J. Hardee, and others. (Duke, *History of Morgan's Cavalry*, 322; Cecil F. Holland, *Morgan and His Raiders: A Biography of the Confederate General* [New York: Macmillan, 1943], 176–177; Ramage, *Rebel Raider*, 134–135.)

2. Lieutenant Colonel Robert Gatewood Stoner was born in Bath County, Kentucky, the youngest of twelve children. Early in the war he served with Generals Felix Zollicoffer, Humphrey Marshall, and John S. Williams. He raised a battalion of mounted troops, and when Bragg's army fell back to Tennessee from Kentucky in the fall of 1862, Stoner's Battalion was consolidated with the battalion raised by Colonel W.C.P. Breckinridge to form the Ninth Kentucky Cavalry Regiment. Breckinridge became the regimental commander, Stoner the regiment's lieutenant colonel. (Johnston, *Kentucky*, vol. 11 in Evans, ed., *Confederate Military History*, 541–543.)

3. Colonel David Waller Chenault of Richmond, Madison County, Kentucky, commanded the Eleventh Kentucky Cavalry Regiment (C.S.A.). Chenault raised the regiment in Madison, Estill, and Clark counties during the invasion of Kentucky in 1862. Colonel Roy S. Cluke, a native of Clark County, Kentucky, and Lieutenant Colonel Cicero Coleman raised the Eighth Kentucky Cavalry Regiment (C.S.A.) in central Kentucky during the invasion. By the late fall of 1862, Colonel Richard M. Gano's Battalion had grown to become the Seventh Kentucky Cavalry Regiment (C.S.A.) and was commanded by Lieutenant Colonel J. M. Huffman. Gano was transferred to the Trans-Mississippi Department. Colonel Adam R. Johnson raised a regiment of partisan rangers; when it joined Morgan's command it became the Tenth Kentucky Cavalry Regiment (C.S.A.). Colonel James D. Bennett commanded the Fourteenth Tennessee Cavalry Regiment (C.S.A.) that joined Morgan's command upon Morgan's return to Tennessee from Kentucky. Colonel William Campbell Preston Breckinridge's battalion had grown to

become the Ninth Kentucky Cavalry Regiment (C.S.A.) and was commanded in December 1862 by Lieutenant Colonel Robert G. Stoner. The Ninth Kentucky Cavalry was the regiment to which John M. Porter was attached. Lieutenant Colonel John B. Hutchinson commanded the Second Kentucky Cavalry Regiment (C.S.A.). The First Brigade consisted of the Second Kentucky Cavalry, the Seventh Kentucky Cavalry, the Eighth Kentucky Cavalry, and a battery of four guns. The First Brigade was commanded by Colonel Basil W. Duke. The Second Brigade, commanded by Colonel William Campbell Preston Breckinridge, consisted of the Ninth Kentucky Cavalry, the Tenth Kentucky Cavalry, the Eleventh Kentucky Cavalry, the Fourteenth Tennessee Cavalry and a battery of artillery. (Duke, *History of Morgan's Cavalry*, 324–325.)

4. Morgan's division generally followed present-day US 31E to Glasgow, Barren County, Kentucky.

5. The skirmish at Glasgow occurred when Morgan sent two companies of the Ninth Kentucky Cavalry forward to take possession of the town on December 24, 1862. A battalion of the Second Michigan Cavalry Regiment held Glasgow. Captain William E. Jones and W. R. Webb of Company A, Ninth Kentucky Cavalry (C.S.A.), were mortally wounded in a skirmish with the Second Michigan's advance guard. Lieutenant Samuel O. Peyton of Company A, Ninth Kentucky Cavalry, was seriously wounded and left behind in Glasgow. Captain William H. Jones of Company M, Second Kentucky Cavalry, was also killed. Morgan lost six or seven other men, who were captured by the enemy. (OR, 20 [1]: 184; Ellis and Stone, *Report of the Adjutant General of the State of Kentucky*, 1:591–592; 2:4, 5, 8, 9.)

6. Bear Wallow is a small town located on present-day US 31E along the Hart County–Barren County line. The hamlet derived its name from an old salt lick where deer, buffalo, and bear "wallowed." In 1862 there stood along the turnpike several brick and frame two-story buildings that were built as a tavern and hostelry complex. It is said Morgan and some of his officers were given a meal at the tavern owned by a William Hare. (Florence Edwards Gardiner, *Cyrus Edwards's Stories of Early Days in What Is Now Barren, Hart and Metcalfe Counties* [Louisville: Standard Printing, 1940], 223–225.)

7. The Jordan Owen referenced by Porter was probably J.J.C. Owen of Hart County, Kentucky. Porter's maternal grandmother was Nancy Owen. She married Moses Helm. J.J.C. Owen was the only living brother of Porter's grandmother. (Porter, "Historical Sketch of the Porter Family," 9; Census Population Schedules, Hart County, 1860, Reel 372, Box 20, UKSC.) The action referred to by John M. Porter took place at Hardyville, in Hart County. Morgan ordered Breckinridge to send two companies toward Munfordville on present-day Ky. 88 and drive in the enemy's pickets.

Woodsonville and Munfordville were garrisoned by Federal troops commanded by Colonel Edward H. Hobson. The Federal force consisted of Hobson's own Thirteenth Kentucky Infantry (U.S.A.), the Twenty-fifth Michigan Infantry, the Thirty-sixth Indiana Infantry, the Twelfth Kentucky Cavalry (U.S.A.), elements of the Third Kentucky Cavalry (U.S.A.) and the Fourth and Fifth Indiana Cavalry, and the Sixth Michigan Battery. The Federal command was protecting the L&N bridge over the Green River. (OR, 20 [1]: 148–150.)

8. Mt. Gilead Church is located in Hart County, Kentucky, along the Louisville and Nashville Turnpike, present-day US 31E, just north of the village of Hardyville. The reference to "G. I. Blakey" in the typescript of Porter's memoir was obviously to G. W. Blakey, the only person in the 1860 Census records for Hart County, Kentucky, bearing a surname similar to what Porter recalled. Blakey lived near Mt. Gilead Church. (Census Population Schedules, Hart County, Kentucky, 1860, Reel 372, Box 20, UKSC.)

9. Porter probably refers here to John Adair. The typescript of Porter's memoirs refers to a "D. Adair," but no one with the surname "Adair" living in Hart County at the time had the initial "D" in his or her name. Porter's claim that Adair lived about a mile north of Mt. Gilead Church indicates that he meant John Adair, who lived in that area and on that road. (Census Population Schedules, Hart County, Kentucky, 1860, Reel 372, Box 20, UKSC.) Porter's wife, the former Mary Bell Burch, came from Hart County and attended Mt. Gilead Church along present-day US 31E. They were married in 1866. The couple had one child, a daughter named Minnie Bell. Porter's wife died on July 11, 1868, probably as a result of complica-

tions from childbirth, and was buried with her family members at Mt. Gilead Church. (Porter, "Historical Sketch of the Porter Family," 6.) Brickey's Ford is the ford of the Green River on the old Louisville and Nashville Turnpike (US 31E).

10. The bridge at Bacon Creek was located in the town of Bonnieville, Kentucky, about eight miles north of Munfordville on present-day US 31W. Morgan's command rode west from near Hammondville to strike the bridge that carried the L&N over Bacon Creek. On December 26, 1862, Morgan sent Hutchinson's Second Kentucky Cavalry, Huffman's Seventh Kentucky Cavalry (C.S.A.), and a section of artillery to attack the Federal troops protecting the bridge. The Federal troops occupied a log stockade near the bridge. Morgan took the rest of his force toward Upton, where they cut the telegraph line. He then moved the command to Nolin, the next station up the L&N toward Elizabethtown. Leaving some of his command, including the Ninth Kentucky Cavalry (C.S.A.), at Nolin in Hardin County, Morgan circled the rest of his force back to the Bacon Creek bridge. Morgan captured ninety-three prisoners of the Ninety-first Illinois Infantry. At Bacon Creek, the stockade and bridge were burned. At Nolin, Morgan took seventy-six more prisoners from the Ninety-first Illinois; the stockade and bridge were burned there also. Large fires were started along the railroad right-of-way for four miles in order to warp the rails and destroy the wooden ties. (OR, 20 [1]: 154–155.)

11. Red Mills was located where the Louisville and Nashville Turnpike (US 31W) crossed the Nolin River, near present-day Nolin, Kentucky, about nine miles south of Elizabethtown, Kentucky (Mary Joseph Jones, *The Civil War in Hardin County, Kentucky* [Vine Grove, Ky.: Ancestral Trails Historical Society, 1995], 11).

12. Morgan's command approached Elizabethtown, Kentucky, on December 27, 1862. The town was held by elements of the Ninety-first Illinois Infantry under Lieutenant Colonel Harry S. Smith. When Smith refused to surrender, Morgan attacked the Federal garrison in Elizabethtown by advancing Hutchinson's Second Kentucky (C.S.A.) and Stoner's Ninth Kentucky (C.S.A.), all dismounted, and an artillery piece. After a half-hour of "vigorous

shelling," the garrison surrendered. A total of 652 Illinois soldiers and their officers surrendered. (OR, 20 [1]: 156.)

13. John Dunn was a private in Company E, Ninth Kentucky Cavalry (C.S.A.), who had enlisted in the Confederate service in New Orleans, Louisiana, in December 1861. He joined Breckinridge's Battalion in the fall of 1862. The roster lists him as "killed in Indiana, July 1863." (Ellis and Stone, *Report of the Adjutant General of the State of Kentucky*, 2:20–21.)

14. Muldraugh's Hill, present-day Colesburg, Kentucky, is located approximately six miles north of Elizabethtown on the L&N. The "Muldraugh" is a range of rugged hills or knobs that begins on the Ohio River at West Point, Kentucky, and runs southeast to Tennessee. Building the L&N through the Muldraugh was difficult. To keep the track level and of the proper grade, the L&N built a series of trestles, sixty feet high and 300 to 350 yards in length. They were among the largest on the L&N. Federal troops protected those trestles by the use of log stockades. On December 28, 1862, Morgan attacked and seized the Federal troops holding the stockades, and then burned the trestles between Elizabethtown and Muldraugh's Hill. In the process, he captured seven hundred Federal soldiers and officers and shut down the L&N for months. (OR, 26 [1]: 156.)

15. Morgan withdrew out of Hardin County, Kentucky, by way of the road to Bardstown, now US 62. His command camped on the west bank of the Rolling Fork River, not far from Boston, Kentucky. Pursuing Morgan was a brigade commanded by Colonel John Marshall Harlan of Kentucky that included the Tenth Indiana Infantry, the Seventy-fourth Indiana Infantry, the Tenth Kentucky Infantry (U.S.A.), the Thirteenth Kentucky Infantry (U.S.A.), the Fourteenth Ohio Infantry, and the Fourth Kentucky Infantry (U.S.A.), along with Battery C, First Ohio Artillery. Harlan had brought his own commands north from Gallatin, Tennessee, and had assumed command of the regiments commanded by Colonel Edward Hobson. (OR, 20 [1]: 134–141.)

Colonel John Marshall Harlan was born in Boyle County, Kentucky. He was graduated from Centre College and the Transylvania University law department. He practiced law in Franklin County, Kentucky, and was elected county judge there in 1858. He was narrowly defeated in a run for Congress the next year. Harlan supported the moderate Bell-Everett ticket in the 1860 presidential election; he relocated to Louisville in 1861. There, he established a law practice. He abandoned his law practice in the summer of 1861 to make speeches with Lincoln's attorney general, James Speed, encouraging Kentuckians to stand by the Union. That fall, as a colonel, he raised the Tenth Kentucky Infantry (U.S.A.), serving at the Battle of Mill Springs in January 1862, the advance to Corinth, Mississippi, in the spring of 1862, and the Battle of Perryville in October 1862, before he became a brigade commander. Although nominated for promotion to brigadier general, it was never acted upon, as Harlan resigned from the service after the death of his father. He would be named Associate Justice of the Supreme Court of the United States in 1877 by President Rutherford B. Hayes. (John E. Kleber, ed., *The Kentucky Encyclopedia* [Lexington: Univ. Press of Kentucky, 1992], 407.)

16. The Ninth Kentucky Cavalry (C.S.A.) was eventually supported by Colonel Roy S. Cluke's Eighth Kentucky Cavalry (Duke, *History of Morgan's Cavalry*, 338–339). E. P. Roane was a private in Company E, Ninth Kentucky Cavalry. He enlisted in Lexington, Kentucky, on August 1, 1862. His wound at Rolling Fork disabled him from further service. (Ellis and Stone, *Report of the Adjutant General of the State of Kentucky*, 2:20–21.)

17. At the time that Harlan's artillery began to fire, Colonels Duke, Breckinridge, Cluke, Hutchinson, and Stoner were concluding a court-martial of Colonel Huffman for alleged mistreatment of prisoners at Bacon Creek. Huffman was acquitted. Duke rushed to the Rolling Fork River. He concluded that he would have to hold the western riverbank, as the Eighth Kentucky Cavalry (C.S.A.) under Major Robert S. Bullock had not returned from burning one of the trestles. Bullock and the Eighth Kentucky finally arrived, but Duke had to extricate his men from Harlan's attack. Shelled by rifled guns and assaulted by the better part of nearly three thousand Federal troops, Duke decided a counterattack would stun the attackers enough to allow his men to get across the river and out of range. As he ordered the counterattack, Duke was struck in the head by a fragment from an exploding shell. Captain Tom Quirk

rushed to Duke and carried him to safety. Breckinridge assumed command of the operation. Morgan's command moved to Bardstown, where Duke's wounds were examined. To the relief of all, they were deemed nonfatal. Duke returned to Tennessee in Quirk's wagon. (Bennett H. Young, *Confederate Wizards of the Saddle* [Boston: Chapple, 1912], 437–438; John Allen Wyeth, *With Saber and Scalpel: The Autobiography of a Soldier and Surgeon* [New York: Harper, 1914], 186–186; Matthews, *Basil Wilson Duke*, 118–120.)

18. James H. Holland was a second lieutenant in Company E, Seventh Kentucky Cavalry (C.S.A.). He enlisted in Rochester, Kentucky, on October 15, 1861. (Ellis and Stone, *Report of the Adjutant General of the State of Kentucky*, 1:698–699.) He was the son of Polly A. Holland, a widow, forty-nine, of Quality Valley in Butler County. At twenty-four years of age, James was the oldest of eight children. (Census Population Schedules, Butler County, Kentucky, 1860, Quality Valley, Reel 358, Box 6, UKSC.)

19. The turnpike from Bardstown to Springfield, Kentucky, is now US 150.

20. To get around the Federal troops gathering in Lebanon, Morgan pulled off the Bardstown-Springfield Turnpike onto a narrow country road that ran through St. Mary's. Morgan's column likely followed present-day Ky. 152 to Loretto, then Ky. 49 to Ky. 327 to St. Mary's, and Ky. 412 to the Lebanon-Columbia turnpike, present-day US 68 and Ky. 55. (Duke, *History of Morgan's Cavalry*, 340–341.)

21. Porter refers to the bridge over the Green River at Tebbs Bend. The bridge was a wooden, covered structure and was protected by a wooden stockade constructed on the bluff along the south bank. Colonel Chenault, commander of the Eleventh Kentucky Cavalry (C.S.A.), and Major Brent, adjutant of the Fifth Kentucky Cavalry (C.S.A.), were killed there during Morgan's attacks against the Twenty-fifth Michigan Infantry on July 4, 1863, at the outset of the Great Indiana-Ohio Raid.

22. Federal commands under Colonel William A. Hoskins and Brigadier General Joseph J. Reynolds, with a full division of five thousand troops, including six hundred cavalry and two batteries of artillery, in addition to Colonel Harlan's brigade, attempted to

close in on Morgan's division. (OR, 20 [1]: 142, 145–47; OR, 20 [2]: 174, 188, 225, 236, 251, 284, 291.)
Mary T. Porter was the sister of John M. Porter and wife of William P. Beard, a native of Butler County. Mary was twenty-six. They lived at Sugar Grove. (Porter, "Historical Sketch of the Porter Family," 6; Census Population Schedules, Butler County, Kentucky, 1860, Sugar Grove, Reel 358, Box 6, UKSC; 1870 U.S. Federal Census Record for Mary T. Porter, Butler County, Kentucky, ancestry .com.) It is not known who John M. Porter visited in Cumberland County. Presumably, they were kin of Mary T. Porter's husband, most likely his mother's close relatives.

23. Morgan summed up the successes of the "Christmas Raid." He destroyed "the L&N Railroad from Munfordville to Shepherdsville, within 18 miles of Louisville, rendering it impassable for at least two months; [captured] 1,877 prisoners, including 62 commissioned officers; [destroyed] over $2,000,000 of United States property, and a large loss to the enemy in killed and wounded." The loss in Morgan's division was two killed, twenty-four wounded, and sixty-four missing. (OR, 20 [1]: 158.)

24. The Battle of Murfreesboro, or Stone's River, was fought on December 29, 30, and 31, 1862, and January 2, 1863. Major General William S. Rosecrans's Army of the Cumberland moved out of Nashville to attack General Braxton Bragg's Army of Tennessee, then holding positions west of Murfreesboro, Tennessee, along Stone's River. On January 2, Bragg hurled Major General John C. Breckinridge's division (including the Kentucky Orphan Brigade, which was decimated in the attack) against Rosecrans's left flank, but it was repulsed. The casualties were heavy on both sides. Bragg withdrew to the Highland Rim at Tullahoma, Tennessee, southeast of Nashville, in the mountains between Nashville and Chattanooga.

9. This Was a Hard-Fought Field

1. Liberty is a small village in DeKalb County, Tennessee, about twenty-five miles northeast of Murfreesboro. It is located on present-day Tenn. 26 (US 70), the Lebanon Pike. The area around Liberty is drained by a creek known as Smith Fork, a tributary of the

Caney Fork River. Tenn. 26 (US 70) intersects Tenn. 96, the Murfreesboro Pike, about one mile west of Liberty. The countryside around Liberty is very rough and mountainous. Just south of Liberty the land flattens in a geographic feature of Tennessee known as "the Barrens." Snow Hill is a village along present-day Tenn. 26 (US 70), about five miles southeast of Liberty, and two miles from "the Barrens." While General Bragg's army occupied the Highland Rim, Morgan protected the right flank of the army. Morgan's command operated along present-day Tenn. 96 in the vicinity of Auburn, Prosperity, and Milton, Tennessee. Elements of Morgan's command also patrolled the Woodbury Pike, eight miles south of Auburn, near the town of Woodbury. The Woodbury Pike, present-day Tenn. 1 (US 70S), connects Woodbury with Murfreesboro. Morgan's command patrolled a front of nearly thirty miles, from Liberty to well below Woodbury. Throughout the winter of 1863 Morgan sent detachments of his command back into Kentucky to disrupt Federal logistical support systems, scout, and recruit, all the while maintaining active operations with the command remaining in Tennessee against the Federal forces in and around Murfreesboro. John M. Porter left Liberty, Tennessee, on a scouting mission into Kentucky on February 7, 1863. That mission is described in great detail in chapters 10 and 11. He returned to Liberty on February 28, 1863. (Duke, *History of Morgan's Cavalry*, 357–358.) The sentence in the second paragraph beginning with "We moved out" is a transition sentence used by the editor to join the manuscript where a page was missing.

2. On January 22, 1863, Lieutenant Colonel John B. Hutchinson and his Second Kentucky Cavalry (C.S.A.) struck a camp of Federal troops near Murfreesboro, capturing and taking back to the foothills near Woodbury thirty wagons and 150 prisoners. In response, elements of the Fourth U.S. Cavalry, commanded by Captain Elmer Otis, along with the First Middle Tennessee Cavalry (U.S.A.) and the Second East Tennessee Cavalry (U.S.A.), were ordered to chase the Confederate raiders. The Federal force proceeded toward Liberty, where it encountered Breckinridge's Ninth Kentucky Cavalry (C.S.A.). The fighting was intense, but it was broken off at dark. (OR, 23 [1]: 12–18.) Two days later, another Federal

advance toward Woodbury by a brigade commanded by Colonel William Grose, consisting of the Sixth Ohio Infantry, Twenty-third Kentucky Infantry (U.S.A.), Eighty-fourth Illinois Infantry, Twenty-fourth Ohio Infantry, and elements of Captain Charles Parsons's U.S. Battery advanced toward Woodbury. In a brief encounter on January 24, Lieutenant Colonel Hutchinson was killed in action. (Ibid., 18–19; Ellis and Stone, *Report of Adjutant General of the State of Kentucky*, 540–541.)

3. The fighting Porter recounts began on March 20, 1863, when a Federal brigade from the Fifth Division, Fourteenth Army Corps, commanded by Colonel Albert S. Hall, began to push elements of Morgan's command up the Murfreesboro Pike (Tenn. 26 [US 70]) from Prosperity across Smith Fork to Liberty. In the Federal brigade were the One hundred and twenty-third Illinois Infantry, the Eightieth Illinois Infantry, the One hundred and first Indiana Infantry, the One hundred and fifth Ohio Infantry, one section of Captain Samuel J. Harris's Nineteenth Indiana Battery (two guns), and Company A of the First Middle Tennessee Cavalry (U.S.A.), altogether more than 1,300 officers and men. (OR, 23 [1]: 155–158.)

4. Morgan brought the Second Kentucky Cavalry (C.S.A.), the Tenth Kentucky Cavalry (C.S.A.), and the Seventh Kentucky Cavalry (C.S.A.) to the assistance of the Ninth Kentucky Cavalry (C.S.A.). In addition, two other regiments, the Fourteenth Alabama Cavalry and the Ninth Tennessee Cavalry (C.S.A.), joined Morgan. Morgan's artillery consisted of two brass guns (one rifle and one howitzer) and two twelve-pound mountain howitzers. Altogether, Morgan was able to bring into the engagement nearly 2,750 officers and men. (OR, 23 [1]: 160.)

5. The fighting lasted six hours. The Federal brigade was reinforced by two brigades of cavalry under Colonel Robert H. G. Minty. Minty advanced the Third Ohio Cavalry toward Liberty. There it ran into the Ninth Kentucky Cavalry (C.S.A.), left behind by Morgan as an "outlying picket" after the rest of Morgan's command fell back to Snow Hill. (OR, 23 [1]: 159.)

It appears from Federal after-action reports that the Fifth Kentucky Cavalry (C.S.A.) and the Sixth Kentucky Cavalry (C.S.A.) may have been engaged. It was during Porter's absence on the scouting mission described in chapters 10 and 11 that the Fifth Kentucky Cavalry, commanded by Colonel Dabney Howard Smith, and the Sixth Kentucky Cavalry, commanded by Colonel J. Warren Grigsby, joined Morgan's command. Colonel Smith hailed from Georgetown, Kentucky, and Colonel Grigsby hailed from Danville, Kentucky, although he was a native of Rockbridge County, Virginia. Both regiments were raised during the invasion of Kentucky in the fall of 1862, but were initially assigned to Brigadier General Nathan Bedford Forrest's command. When they joined Morgan's division, they raised it to eight cavalry regiments. (Duke, *History of Morgan's Cavalry,* 358–359.)

6. Captain R. T. Riggen hailed from Mason County, Kentucky. He enlisted on September 15, 1862, in Bath County, Kentucky, and rose to command Company H of the Ninth Kentucky Cavalry (C.S.A.). He was reported mortally wounded in action at Milton, Tennessee, dying on April 29, 1863. (Ellis and Stone, *Report of the Adjutant General of the State of Kentucky,* 2:28–29.)

7. Vincent S. Hay was the quartermaster of the Eleventh Kentucky Infantry (U.S.A.), the regiment raised by Colonel Pierce B. Hawkins of Bowling Green, Kentucky. Hay was mustered into service in Calhoun, Kentucky, on December 9, 1861; he was a native of Morgantown, Butler County, Kentucky. (Lindsey, *Report of the Adjutant General of the State of Kentucky [Federal],* 1:824, 2:925.)

8. Edward Ludlow Hines, the twenty-four-year-old son of Ann E. Hines of Bowling Green, Kentucky, enlisted in Colonel Roger Weightman Hanson's Second Kentucky Infantry (C.S.A.) at Camp Boone, Tennessee, in June 1861. Hines subsequently was transferred to "Buckner's Guides," serving through the Battle of Shiloh. He became a first lieutenant in Company E, Ninth Kentucky Cavalry (C.S.A.), with John M. Porter, serving throughout the war, and finally surrendered at Washington, Georgia, on May 6, 1865. Edward L. Hines was the brother of James Fayette Hines, also of the Ninth Kentucky Cavalry, and of John Henry Hines of the Second Kentucky Cavalry (C.S.A.). The Hines brothers were cousins of Captain Thomas H. Hines. (1860 U.S. Federal Census Record for Edward L. Hines, Warren County, Kentucky, ancestry.com; Edward

Ludlow Hines, "The Hines Family," undated typescript, 9–14, Cora
Jane Spiller Collection, Bowling Green, Kentucky.)

10. OUR MARCH WAS CAUTIOUS

1. Ayres Curtis enlisted in Company F, Ninth Kentucky Cavalry
(C.S.A.), in Bath County, Kentucky, on September 15, 1862. He
eventually deserted, leaving no other record. All the remaining soldiers referenced enlisted in Company E, Ninth Kentucky Cavalry.
William Shepard McKinney was the twenty-six-year-old son of D.
R. and Elizabeth McKinney, of Berry's Lick in Butler County, Kentucky. He enlisted at Bowling Green, Kentucky, in September 1861
and rose to become third corporal. He would drown in Drake's
Creek, Simpson County, Kentucky, at the conclusion of this operation. James K. Clark enlisted in Bowling Green, Kentucky, on September 1, 1861. He would be captured in June 1863 in Ohio during
Morgan's Indiana-Ohio raid. James H. Holland was the twenty-
three-year-old son of Polly A. Holland, a widow, of Sugar Grove in
Butler County, Kentucky. He enlisted in Rochester, Kentucky, on
October 15, 1862, and became commissary sergeant. He would be
captured in Ohio in June 1863 during the operation conducted in
advance of Morgan's Great Indiana-Ohio Raid recounted in chapter 12. Joseph S. Gray, a native of Hardin County, Kentucky, enlisted
in Elizabethtown, Kentucky, on October 15, 1862. He would be
captured in Ohio in June 1863. Edgar L. Mitchell enlisted in Hartsville, Tennessee, on August 15, 1862. He would be captured on
June 19, 1863, in Ohio. William White was a twenty-year-old native
of Tennessee who grew up in Berry's Lick in Butler County, Kentucky. He was the son of Willis M. and Rhoda White. He enlisted
in September 1861 in Bowling Green, Kentucky, and rose to the
rank of second corporal. He would fight all the way to the end of
the war, surrendering at Washington, Georgia, in May 1865. (Census Population Schedules, Butler County, Kentucky, 1860, Sugar
Grove, Berry's Lick, Reel 358, Box 6, UKSC; Ellis and Stone, *Report
of the Adjutant General of the State of Kentucky*, 2:18–22.)

At the same time as Captain Hines was leading his command
into Kentucky, Morgan was preparing to send another—and

larger—command into Kentucky. Colonel Roy S. Cluke, a native of
Clark County, Kentucky, who was raised on a farm that was partly
in Clark, Bourbon, and Montgomery counties, was directed to pro-
ceed to Richmond, Winchester, and Mt. Sterling, Kentucky, and
damage Federal logistical support systems there. With his own
Eighth Kentucky Cavalry (C.S.A.), commanded by Major Robert
S. Bullock, two companies each from the Ninth Kentucky Cavalry
(C.S.A.), the Seventh Kentucky Cavalry (C.S.A.), and the Eleventh
Kentucky Cavalry (C.S.A.), a company from the Second Kentucky
Cavalry (C.S.A.), and two mountain howitzers, altogether 750 officers and men, Cluke left McMinnville, Tennessee, on February 14,
1863, and reached Mt. Sterling on February 24. Cluke and his men
were selected for the mission because all of them hailed from the
Richmond, Lexington, Winchester, and Mt. Sterling area. Cluke's
force destroyed more than $1 million worth of Federal property
and captured and paroled hundreds of Federal officers and men
before returning to McMinnville in March. (Young, *Confederate Wizards of the Saddle*, 171–194.)

2. Porter and his comrades were riding along the Louisville
and Nashville Turnpike, present-day US 31W, through Simpson
County and its county seat of Franklin. Woodburn is the first village in southern Warren County, just above the Simpson County
line and east of the turnpike. The Louisville and Nashville Railroad
right-of-way followed the turnpike to the east, through Woodburn.
Porter and his comrades rode off of the turnpike at Woodburn and
headed northwest on present-day Ky. 240 to South Union Depot in
Logan County.

3. Pleasant Grove is near present-day Turnerstown in Simpson
County. Clear Fork Church is located along Clear Fork Creek in
Warren County, just northeast of South Union Depot, not far from
present-day Ky. 1466, and off of Clear Fork Church Road.

William H. Duncan was a farmer in the Gordonsville District of
Logan County (Census Population Schedules, Logan County, Kentucky, 1860, Gordonsville, Reel 383, Box 31, UKSC).

Dr. Samuel Garvin had actually volunteered to accompany
Captain Hines and his command. He was probably "planted" by
Federal authorities to join one of Morgan's contingents, desert,

and then report the intentions of the raiders to the nearest Federal command. (Duke, *History of Morgan's Command*, 358.) Garvin was a twenty-three-year-old recent graduate from medical school in Louisville. He was the only son of forty-nine-year-old John Garvin and his forty-nine-year-old wife, Elga. (1860 U.S. Federal Census Record for Samuel Garvin, Jefferson County, Kentucky, ancestry. com.) He was the only physician in Kentucky in 1863 by that name. The Federal military department of Kentucky was headquartered in Louisville, and any such intelligence operations had to be conducted by some individual youthful enough to withstand its rigors and mirror in age most Confederate cavalrymen. Young Dr. Samuel Garvin absolutely fits the mold.

Thomas Duncan was the youngest son of Gillard Duncan, age sixty-seven, and his wife, Elizabeth, age sixty-two. He farmed in Rabbittsville, Logan County, Kentucky. Thomas was twenty-three. He had a brother, William, age thirty, and a sister, Elizabeth, age twenty-seven. There were actually three Duncan families living next to one another in Rabbittsville. Two of them were the families of brothers Gillard Duncan and Henry Duncan, age fifty-four. (Census Population Schedules, Logan County, Kentucky, 1860, Rabbittsville, Reel 383, Box 31, UKSC.) At the end of the sentence beginning with "We passed the Edmond Duncan farm," Porter's manuscript contained a gap, although the page numbers do not lead one to believe a page was missing. The editor inserted two sentences as a transition to fill that gap.

4. This time Porter and his comrades headed toward South Carrollton and Paradise, two towns in Muhlenburg County on the Green River. Paradise, in eastern Muhlenburg County, is on present-day Ky. 176, while South Carrollton is located in northern Muhlenburg County on present-day US 431. The Federal occupation troops were using the Green River and the Barren River to transport supplies from Louisville to Bowling Green and, from there, by rail to Nashville on the L&N. This process was necessary because of the tremendous damage done to the L&N by Morgan during the Christmas Raid. The L&N was shut down from Bacon Creek to Louisville. Porter and the command were located in a bend of the Green River near where Jacobs Creek enters the Green River.

5. Hartford is the county seat of Ohio County. Ohio County forms the northern bank of the Green River, across from Muhlenburg County, and Hartford is on present-day Ky. 69, northeast of South Carrollton.

6. Greenville is the county seat of Muhlenberg County and is located in the center of the county. From Paradise, Porter and his comrades followed present-day Ky. 176 to Greenville and then used the Old Russellville Road, present-day Ky. 181 and 1163, to Logan County. They then followed present-day US 431.

The name of the Methodist minister of whom Porter wrote was Alanson C. DeWitt. He was sixty-one years old; his wife, Julia, was fifty-seven, and they lived in the Gordonsville area in Logan County, along present-day Ky. 1151. They had six children and probably moved to the Gordonsville area during the war, as they do not appear in the 1860 census and their children had been born in Texas and Missouri. DeWitt was a native of Virginia. (Census Population Schedules, Logan County, Kentucky, 1860, Gordonsville, Reel 383, Box 31, UKSC.)

7. Porter and his comrades turned north toward Lewisburg in Logan County and entered Butler County on present-day Ky. 1153 through Harreldsville to present-day Quality, Kentucky, in southwest Butler County. Forgyville is present-day Forgy's Mill, named for a mill on the Mud River owned by the Forgy family of Butler County.

Porter refers to Polly A. Holland, a widow, and the mother of Lieutenant James H. Holland. Polly was fifty-two years old and a native of Tennessee, as were all of the Hollands who were then living in Butler County. (Census Population Schedules, Butler County, Kentucky, 1860, Quality Valley, Reel 358, Box 6, UKSC.) The Hollands lived near the present town of Quality in Butler County on present-day Ky. 1153.

8. James D. Porter, forty-four years old, and his wife, Sarah, forty-one, were neighbors of the Hollands in Quality Valley. He was a newcomer to Butler County, as three of his seven children had been born in Arkansas. Being an "outsider" may have contributed to his being viewed as "a Union man," as many of his Quality Valley neighbors were pro-Confederate. (Census Population Sched-

ules, Butler County, Kentucky, 1860, Quality Valley, Reel 358, Box 6, UKSC.)

9. Porter and his party had ridden east on present-day Ky. 626, then north on present-day Ky. 1083 to near Sugar Grove. Buck Carson was related to John M. Porter. His full name was James D. Carson. A native of Virginia, he was fifty-nine years old; his wife, Paulina or "Pollie," was fifty-four. They had four children, and farmed in Sugar Grove. Buck Carson was also related to Thomas H. Hines. (Census Population Schedules, Butler County, Kentucky, 1860, Sugar Grove, Reel 358, Box 6, UKSC.)

D. O. Helm was actually David O. Helm, thirty-five years old, and an uncle to John M. Porter. He lived in Sugar Grove with his wife, Lydia, their three children, and his seventy-year-old mother, Nancy Helm of Virginia. It was Nancy Helm who Porter referred to as "mother Helm" who was "very sick." Nancy was the wife of Moses Helm, John M. Porter's maternal grandfather. Nancy, formerly Nancy Owen, was Porter's maternal grandmother. (Ibid.; Porter, "Historical Sketch of the Porter Family," 9.)

Porter's reference to the Sterritts was in actuality a reference to the family of Jane Sterritt, a sixty-two-year-old widow. She had five children, one of whom was Stanford M. Sterritt, twenty-seven, and probably the one who was a friend of Porter's. William P. Beard, thirty-five, and his wife, Mary, were close neighbors and kin of the Porters at Sugar Grove. Beard was originally from Pennsylvania. (Ibid.)

10. Mitch Sterritt was probably Stanford M. Sterritt, the son of Jane Sterritt. Uncle Owen Helm was David O. Helm, and Hick Gray was Hickman Gray, who, along with Calvin Kuykendall and Frank Bailey, are identified in chapter 3, note 8. (Census Population Schedules, Butler County, Kentucky, 1860, Sugar Grove, Reel 358, Box 6, UKSC.)

11. The Porter mentioned is James D. Porter, referred to in chapter 10, note 8. Chesterfield Mason was a farmer in Berry's Lick, Butler County, Kentucky. Mason, age thirty-nine, was married to Mary S. Mason, age thirty-eight. They had five children, ages fourteen through six. They were substantial property owners in Butler County. (Census Population Schedules, Butler County, Kentucky, 1860, Berry's Lick, Reel 358, Box 6, UKSC.)

Porter and his comrades were heading north from near Sugar Grove to Little Muddy Church on present-day US 231. Little Muddy Cumberland Presbyterian Church is located near the village of Needmore in east central Butler County, just north of Sugar Grove. It was built of brick on land given by Thomas Carson. The early members were the Porter, Carson, Helm, Kuykendall, and Puckett families. John M. Porter's father, Nathaniel Porter, was the minister at Little Muddy Cumberland Presbyterian Church. (Russ, ed., *Butler County, Kentucky History*, 40–41.)

12. D. R. McKinney was a fifty-two-year-old native Kentuckian. A substantial farmer, he was married to a woman named Elizabeth who was fifty-three. They had five children, including William Shepard McKinney, twenty-six. (Census Population Schedules, Butler County, Kentucky, 1860, Berry's Lick, Reel 358, Box 6, UKSC.) Sandy Creek Church is located along present-day Ky. 1153 near the hamlet of Leetown in south central Butler County.

11. THE SCENE WAS LUDICROUS AND PITIFUL

1. Porter and the squad of men rode down present-day Ky. 79 to Ky. 626. Turning west on Ky. 626, they passed Berry's Lick in southern Butler County.

2. Ephraim Bailey was a forty-five-year-old farmer living in Berry's Lick, in southern Butler County, with his wife, Prixilla, age forty-four, and their children, ages twenty-two to two years (Census Population Schedules, Butler County, Kentucky, 1860, Berry's Lick, Reel 358, Box 6, UKSC).

3. Rochester is located in western Butler County on the Green River. Porter and Hines would have gotten there from Berry's Lick by way of present-day Ky. 106 from present-day Ky. 626.

4. Alanson Fidella Helm, thirty-five years old, was born in Tennessee, but grew up in Sugar Grove in Butler County, Kentucky, near the Porters. He was a cousin of John M. Porter. His father was James Helm, a native Virginian, who was Porter's mother's eldest brother. Helm enlisted in Company H, Seventh Kentucky Cavalry (C.S.A.), in Morgan's command, and served through the end of the war. (1860 U.S. Federal Census Record for Alanson Fidella Helm,

Butler County, Kentucky, ancestry.com; Ellis and Stone, *Report of the Adjutant General of the State of Kentucky*, 1:708–709; Porter, "Historical Sketch of the Porter Family," 8.)

To get to the Helm house, Porter and Hines would have taken present-day Ky. 1083 north from Ky. 626. Sugar Grove is in far southeastern Butler County.

Sister Cullie was John M. Porter's younger sister, Martha Cullie Porter, born 1848. She married a Felix G. McKay in 1872 and lived at Sugar Grove. Porter commented in 1872 that "When I left home for the army she was a little girl, when I came back in 1865 she was grown." (Porter, "Historical Sketch of the Porter Family," 6–7.)

5. Hines rode north on present-day Ky. 1083 to the old Woodbury Road. Woodbury is located in east central Butler County on the Green River, upstream from Morgantown about six to eight miles. At Woodbury were not only Hines's own family, but Nancy Sproule, his fiancée, who lived on the neighboring farm. Porter rode south on present-day Ky. 1083 and Ky. 1038 to Ky. 73 to South Union in northeastern Logan County.

6. Richlieu is a town in northeastern Logan County near the Butler County line. Present-day Ky. 1038 passes through Richlieu. Present-day Ky. 73 crosses the Gasper River in northeastern Logan County about two miles from the Butler County line.

7. This event took place on present-day Ky. 73, near Cave Spring Church in Logan County.

8. William Barnett was the thirty-four-year-old son of Frances Barnett, fifty, of near Morgantown. His father was deceased and he farmed the family's modest land holdings. (1860 U.S. Federal Census Record for William R. Barnett, Butler County, Kentucky, ancestry.com.)

Eldon H. Sloss, age thirty, was Porter's brother-in-law. He was married to Porter's sister, Nancy Virginia Porter, age twenty. They lived at Black Lick, near the present town of Auburn, in Logan County, Kentucky, with their one child, Mary, age one. (1860 U.S. Federal Census Record for Eldon Sloss, Logan County, Kentucky, ancestry.com; Porter, "Historical Sketch of the Porter Family," 7.)

George Price was a twenty-two-year-old son of Lemuel Price, age fifty-four, and Amanda Price, fifty, who were farmers in Rabbittsville, Logan County, Kentucky, not far from South Union (Census Population Schedules, Logan County, Kentucky, 1860, Rabbittsville, Reel 383, Box 31, UKSC).

9. Clear Fork Baptist Church was organized in Warren County in 1832. The church, made entirely of logs, was built in 1834. (Kenneth C. Thompson Jr. and Nancy D. Baird, *Warren County, Kentucky Families* [Paducah: Turner, 1991], 19.)

10. Porter refers to Stephen P. Bowles, age sixty-two. Bowles and his wife, Mary, age fifty-two, lived on a large farm in South Union, Logan County, Kentucky. The Bowles had six children; two of them, Thomas, age twenty-one, and Henry, age seventeen, were privates in Company L, Second Kentucky Cavalry (C.S.A.). Henry would die at Alexandria, Tennessee, on July 23, 1863. (Census Population Schedules, Logan County, Kentucky, 1860, South Union, Reel 383, Box 31, UKSC; Ellis and Stone, *Report of the Adjutant General of the State of Kentucky*, 1:586–587.)

11. *Cholera morbus* is an acute gastroenteritis occurring in the summer and autumn marked by severe cramps, diarrhea, and vomiting.

Coleman Covington was a thirty-six-year-old farmer who lived in Woodburn, Warren County, Kentucky, near the main stem of the Louisville and Nashville Railroad, about nine miles south of Bowling Green and six miles southeast of Clear Fork Church. Covington probably lived along present-day Ky. 240. (1860 U.S. Federal Census Record for Coleman Covington, Warren County, Kentucky, ancestry.com.)

Captain Hines and his command proceeded to Hadley, Kentucky, a village located at the intersection of present-day US 231 and Ky. 626 in western Warren County. They then rode just over two miles north to the Barren River, where they destroyed the steamboat *Hettie Gilmore*, which was "heavily laden with stores for the Army of the Cumberland, all of which [was] destroyed," on February 25, 1863, at midnight. (Duke, *History of Morgan's Cavalry*, 358.)

12. Simpson County borders Warren County on the south and Logan County on the east. The Pleasant Grove neighborhood was probably present-day Turnertown.

13. James Milligan, forty-two years old, lived on a farm west of Bowling Green, Kentucky. His wife, Nancy, forty years old, lived with him and their seven children, ages nineteen through six. James Milligan's brother, William Milligan, age forty-five, lived nearby with his wife, Eliza, and their four children. (Census Population Schedules, Warren County, Kentucky, 1860, Bowling Green, Kentucky, Reel 397, Box 45, UKSC.) James Milligan joined Company D, Second Kentucky Cavalry, on September 2, 1862, when it entered Lexington (Ellis and Stone, *Report of the Adjutant General of the State of Kentucky*, 1:502–503).

14. The railroad through South Union was the Memphis, Clarksville and Louisville Railroad (MC&L), which ran from Clarksville, Tennessee, to Memphis Junction, three miles south of Bowling Green. At Clarksville, the MC&L connected with the Memphis and Ohio Railroad, which ran to Memphis.

15. Sarah Sloss was the wife of Malin Sloss and the mother of Eldon H. Sloss, Porter's brother-in-law who lived in Logan County, Kentucky, near the town of Auburn (1860 U.S. Federal Census Record for Sarah Sloss, Logan County, Kentucky, ancestry.com).

16. M. E. Morris was a fifty-eight-year-old farm laborer who lived with his two young children, Rebecca, age thirteen, and Thomas, age eleven, in South Union, Logan County, Kentucky. It appears Morris's wife had died before 1860. (Census Population Schedules, Logan County, Kentucky, 1860, South Union, Reel 383, Box 31, UKSC.)

17. Woodburn is located on the main stem of the L&N in Warren County, about one mile from the Simpson County line.

18. The train would have gone off the tracks somewhere near the town of Franklin, Kentucky.

19. Drake's Creek is a tributary of the Barren River, draining much of Warren County east and south of Bowling Green, Kentucky, and much of northern Simpson County. Captain Hines reported that Corporal W. S. McKinney was "washed from his horse and drowned." Drake's Creek was swollen due to winter snow and rain and was fast-moving. Hines described the stream as "angry." (Duke, *History of Morgan's Cavalry*, 358.) McKinney probably would have drowned in northern Simpson County.

20. Captain William Jennings, a thirty-six-year-old physician from Madison County, commanded Company K, Second Kentucky Cavalry (C.S.A.). He enlisted on July 25, 1862, at Livingston, Tennessee. Jennings had a wife, twenty-nine, and two infant children. (1860 U.S. Federal Census record for William Jennings, Madison County, Kentucky, ancestry.com.) Porter referred to a "Captain William Jones" in the typescript, but Captain William H. Jones of Company M, Second Kentucky Cavalry, was killed at Glasgow, Kentucky, on December 24, 1862, during the Christmas Raid. Porter must be referring to Captain Jennings, who was sent with his company as part of Colonel Cluke's operation into central Kentucky to disrupt Federal logistical support systems, an operation described in chapter 10, note 1.

Porter and his comrades returned to Tennessee by riding east to Allen County, Kentucky, and then riding south to Macon County, Tennessee.

21. Porter reached Liberty, Tennessee, on or about February 28, 1863. Captain Hines filed a report claiming that he, Porter, and the small command of fourteen men were behind Federal lines for twenty-one days, traveling more than 150 miles. In that period of time they destroyed more than "half a million dollars" of Federal government property and caused the Federal authorities "to collect troops at points heretofore unprotected, thereby weakening [the Federal] force in front of [Bragg's] army." (Duke, *History of Morgan's Cavalry*, 358.)

12. I WAS CAPTURED FOR THE LAST TIME

1. Readyville is a small hamlet located about fifteen miles east of Murfreesboro and eight miles west of Woodbury on the old Woodbury Pike, present-day Tenn. 1 (US 70S).

2. Morgan had established a convalescent camp in Clinton County, Kentucky, as it was distant from the field of operations, remote from possible interference by Federal occupation troops, and, most importantly, in an area where horses could eat grasses to regain strength and food supplies were more readily found for the men. Central Tennessee, overrun with troops from both armies, was devoid of forage and subsistence stores.

3. Lieutenant Joseph Haycraft enlisted in Company I, Ninth Kentucky Cavalry (C.S.A.), at Corinth, Mississippi, on April 15, 1862 (Ellis and Stone, *Report of the Adjutant General of the State of Kentucky*, 2:32–33).

4. Porter generally followed present-day Ky. 100 from Tompkinsville west to Scottsville in Allen County. New Roe is probably the crossroads known today as Roary, or Oak Forest, about five miles east of Scottsville on Ky. 100. Porter probably approached Bowling Green by present-day US 231. Most likely near the present hamlet of Alaton in southeastern Warren County, Porter and his men turned north and crossed the Barren River near the village of Hardcastle.

5. Bristow is a small hamlet about four miles northeast of Bowling Green, located on the main stem of the Louisville and Nashville Railroad, near the Louisville and Nashville Turnpike, present-day US 31W.

6. The pike referenced by Porter is the Louisville and Nashville Turnpike, present-day US 31W. Porter probably followed present-day US 31W to present-day Ky. 101. That road led directly to Chalybeate and Brownsville.

Jo Mitchell enlisted in Company A, Ninth Kentucky Cavalry (C.S.A.), on September 15, 1862, in Lexington. He would be captured by Federal troops on this mission. (Ellis and Stone, *Report of the Adjutant General of the State of Kentucky*, 2:6–7.)

Jesse Grider was a sizable property owner and a clergyman in the Presbyterian Church in Warren County. Grider was thirty-five years old. His wife, Pamelia, was twenty-five. They had two children. (1860 U.S. Federal Census Record for Jesse Grider, Warren County, Kentucky, ancestry.com.)

Joseph S. Mitchell, twenty-seven years old, was the son of Henry G. Mitchell, whose wife was deceased. The Mitchell family operated a boardinghouse near Brownsville when the war broke out. It seems Joseph Mitchell had gotten married at the beginning of the war. (1860 U.S. Federal Census Record for Joseph S. Mitchell, Edmonson County, Kentucky, ancestry.com.) John M. Porter's father's deceased sister, Margaret, had been married to Henry G. Mitchell of Chamelion Springs in Edmonson County. Joseph S. Mitchell was Porter's cousin. (Porter, "Historical Sketch of the Porter Family," 5.) The "home ones" were Porter's cousins.

7. Brownsville offered Porter and his men the opportunity to forage for their horses and themselves. Foraging in enemy territory was an accepted military practice in nineteenth-century warfare.

8. Porter and his men followed present-day Ky. 259 north to Leitchfield, county seat of Grayson County, and then present-day US 62 northeast to Elizabethtown. At Elizabethtown was the main stem of the L&N. The command rode to Bardstown by way of present-day US 62. Boston is a hamlet where the L&N branchline from Lebanon Junction to Lebanon, Kentucky, crosses present-day US 62. Boston is also located near the Rolling Fork River, where Colonel Basil W. Duke was wounded during the Christmas Raid.

9. The Bardstown branch was a spur line of the L&N between Bardstown Junction, on the main stem of the L&N, and Bardstown. The Bardstown branch of the L&N generally followed present-day Ky. 245 from Bardstown to present-day Clermont in Bullitt County. Wilson's Creek, a tributary of the Rolling Fork River, meanders through northwestern Nelson County. Present-day Ky. 245 crosses Wilson's Creek at Deatsville, near the Bullitt County border.

10. The events described occurred along present-day Ky. 245, near Deatsville, Kentucky. The soldier who was mortally wounded was probably E. O. Gudgell, who enlisted in Captain George M. Coleman's Company D, Ninth Kentucky Cavalry (C.S.A.), on September 15, 1862, in Kentucky, and was reported to have "died in June 1863." (Ellis and Stone, *Report of the Adjutant General of the State of Kentucky*, 2:16–17.)

11. New Haven, Kentucky, is a small town located on the spur line of the L&N that ran from Lebanon Junction to Lebanon, Kentucky. New Haven is located on the eastern branch of the Louisville and Nashville Turnpike, present-day US 31E, just about eight miles north of Hodgenville. The Muldraugh escarpment rises at Knob Creek, and there the turnpike negotiates the steep hills in order to reach Hodgenville. It is clear that Porter was captured just south of New Haven, Kentucky, along present-day US 31E, near the Knob Creek site where Abraham Lincoln lived from 1811 to 1815.

12. Morgan would ultimately choose Brandenburg as the site where his division would cross the Ohio River into Indiana on July 8, 1863. Before arriving at Brandenburg, Morgan and his

command would fight some bloody engagements at Marrowbone Creek on July 2, Tebb's Bend (Green River bridge) on July 4, and Lebanon on July 5. The command would arrive at Brandenburg and, after seizing the packet steamboats *Alice Dean* and *John T. McCombs*, ferry the men and horses across the Ohio River to Indiana on July 8. (India W. P. Logan, *Kelion Franklin Peddicord of Quirk's Scouts, Morgan's Kentucky Cavalry, C.S.A.* [New York: Neal, 1908], 115–127.) Most of Morgan's command would be captured at Buffington Island in eastern Ohio, on July 19, 1863; Morgan himself would be captured near East Liverpool, Ohio, on July 26 (OR, 23 [1]: 642–644).

13. John A. Carter was a merchant in Louisville, Kentucky, who operated a dry goods store. He was thirty-one years old. He lived in Louisville with his twenty-four-year-old wife, Mary, three children, seventy-three-year-old mother, and his twin brother. (1860 U.S. Federal Census Record for John A. Carter, Jefferson County, Kentucky, ancestry.com.)

14. The Dry Tortugas in the Caribbean, south of the Florida Keys, was a Federal prison that was reserved for criminals who were regarded as enemies of the Federal government.

13. THE DAYS DRAGGED SLOWLY BY

1. Johnson's Island Prisoner of War Depot was established in the fall of 1861. With twelve cell blocks, it held 2,000 to 2,500 prisoners, all of them commissioned officers. In January 1865, nearly 3,200 prisoners were held at Johnson's Island. Built in the middle of Sandusky Bay, Lake Erie, it faced the City of Sandusky, Ohio, a railroad depot. (johnsonsisland.org/history/war.htm.)

2. Generals James J. Archer, Isaac R. Trimble, and John R. Jones were captured at Gettysburg. Archer was exchanged in the summer of 1864; Jones was sent to Fort Warren in Boston Harbor and was released on July 24, 1865. Trimble was exchanged in February 1865. General William N. R. Beall, a native of Nelson County, Kentucky, was captured at Port Hudson on July 9, 1863; he was released on parole in 1864. General John W. Frazer was captured near Cumberland Gap in May 1863. He was imprisoned at Johnson's Island

and then sent to Fort Warren, where he remained until the summer of 1865. General William L. Cabell was captured in Missouri in October 1864 and was not released until August 1865. General John S. Marmaduke was captured at Mine Creek, Kansas, on October 25, 1864. He was imprisoned at Johnson's Island and then Fort Warren, and was released in July 1865. (Warner, *Generals in Gray,* 11, 21–22, 41, 93, 165, 211–212, and 310–311.) Jeff Thompson surrendered on May 9, 1865, after a colorful career in Missouri. He had been incarcerated at Johnson's Island between September 13, 1863, and February 18, 1864. (Mark M. Boatner III, *The Civil War Dictionary* [New York: McKay, 1959], 837–838.)

3. One of Morgan's principal lieutenants who died at Johnson's Island was Colonel Roy S. Cluke, commander of the Eighth Kentucky Cavalry (C.S.A.), who was captured in Ohio on Morgan's raid in July 1863. He died at Johnson's Island on December 31, 1863. His remains were ultimately buried in the Lexington Cemetery, and a stone was erected over the grave by his comrades. (Stone and Ellis, *Report of the Adjutant General of the State of Kentucky,* 1:720–721.) Others from Morgan's command known to have been imprisoned at Johnson's Island were Lieutenant Alpheus L. Alcorn of Company C, Sixth Kentucky Cavalry (C.S.A.), who was killed while being transferred from Johnson's Island to Fort Warren prison; Lieutenant James H. Daviess, Company E, Fifth Kentucky Cavalry (C.S.A.); and Captain William R. Lewis, Company B, Eighth Kentucky Cavalry, who died on January 4, 1864, at Johnson's Island, four days after his commander, Colonel Cluke. (Ibid., 2:240–241, 252–253, 268–269.) In addition, James W. Bowles of the Second Kentucky Cavalry (C.S.A.), Colonel Dabney Howard Smith of the Fifth Kentucky Cavalry, Lieutenant Colonel Cicero Coleman of the Eighth Kentucky Cavalry, and Lieutenant John H. Hines of Company C of the Second Kentucky Cavalry, among many others, were confined at Johnson's Island for various periods of time. (Johnston, *Kentucky,* vol. 11 in Evans, ed., *Confederate Military History,* 284, 329, 533.)

4. Porter identifies the inmates who assisted him in the escape plan as "Hines," "Markham," and "Duncan." The Hines referred to by Porter was John Henry Hines. Hines had been the first sergeant

of "Buckner's Guides." He enlisted with Porter in Bowling Green, Kentucky, in October 1861. He then was transferred to Company C, Second Kentucky Cavalry, on June 1, 1862, and became a second lieutenant. Hines was captured at Buffington Island, Ohio, at the end of Morgan's Great Indiana-Ohio Raid. He was the twenty-three-year-old son of Ann E. Hines, forty-six, of Warren County, Kentucky. His father, Fayette Henry Hines, had died in 1847. His brothers, James Fayette Hines and Edward Ludlow Hines, served in the Ninth Kentucky Cavalry with John M. Porter. (1860 U.S. Federal Census record for John H. Hines, Warren County, Kentucky, ancestry .com; Ellis and Stone, *Report of the Adjutant General of the State of Kentucky*, 1:556–557, 2:410–411; Stewart, *Descendants of Henry Hines, Sr.*, 10.) An examination of Kentucky Confederate officers and the lists of prisoners of war at Johnson's Island that are extant failed to reveal Markham's and Duncan's identities (Joe Barbiere, *Scraps from the Prison Table, at Camp Chase and Johnson's Island* [Doylestown, Pa.: W.W.H. Davis, Printer, 1868]). Barbiere's book contains a list of Confederate prisoners of war at Johnson's Island up to December 1862. That list may be found at www.johnsonsisland.org. Also found on that website is the autograph book of prisoners of war at Johnson's Island kept by Captain C. H. Walker of the Third Tennessee Infantry (C.S.A.), who was captured at Fort Donelson.

5. It is interesting to note that Porter's kinsman, Captain Thomas H. Hines, also sought to escape his confinement in the Ohio State Penitentiary in Columbus, Ohio. Captured with Colonels Richard Morgan and Basil W. Duke at Buffington Island in eastern Ohio on July 19, 1863, Hines was ultimately incarcerated with General John Hunt Morgan in Columbus. Hines planned an escape by tunneling out of the penitentiary using the ventilation system. Hines, Morgan, and five others successfully escaped on November 27, 1863. (Captain L. D. Hockersmith, *Morgan's Escape: A Thrilling Story of War Times* [Madisonville, Ky.: Glenn's Graphic Print, 1903], 34–48.)

6. The USS *Michigan*, a steam-powered revenue vessel, was armed with fourteen large guns. The "party on their way to relieve" the prisoners at Johnson's Island was a reference to the conspiracy planned, in large part, by none other than Captain Thomas

H. Hines. From Toronto, Canada, Hines proposed a "plan for a revolutionary movement in the west" that would free five thousand Confederate prisoners at Camp Douglas in Chicago. Simultaneously, a force raised in Illinois of anti-Lincoln Democrats would free Confederate prisoners at Rock Island, Illinois, and Camp Morton, Indianapolis, Indiana. A force would also strike Chicago and Springfield, Illinois, to seize the state government. (Captain Thomas H. Hines, "Cowards Only Flee," a message in cipher sent by Hines in Toronto, Canada, to Secretary of War James Seddon in Richmond, June 1864, Thomas Henry Hines Papers, 1772 [1860–1869] 1954, Winn Collection, 46M97, Box 1a, UKSC.)

14. WITH THREE DAYS' RATIONS, WE STARTED HOME

1. Porter was conveyed by rail to Baltimore, and then by ship down the Chesapeake Bay to Fortress Monroe. Then the ship sailed up the James River to Richmond, Virginia.

2. "Rockets" is a suburb of Richmond along the James River, just south of the center city. Libby Prison was located in Rockets. Rockets was the city's shipyard and the site of the Confederate navy yard. All the "flag-of-truce boats" operated between Newport News and Rockets. (Richard M. Lee, *General Lee's City: An Illustrated Guide to the Historic Sites of Confederate Richmond* [McLean, Va.: EPM, 1987], 96–97; Stanley Kimmel, *Mr. Davis's Richmond* [New York: Bramhall House, 1958], 125–126, 170–172.)

3. The Spottswood Hotel stood on the southeast corner of Eighth Street and Main Street in Richmond. It was five stories tall, with a classic iron facade on its Main Street front. It was at the Spottswood Hotel that Jefferson Davis and his cabinet members lodged when they arrived in Richmond in May 1861. It was the most fashionable hotel in the city. (Lee, *General Lee's City,* 148.)

4. OR, 47 [1]: 1055–1057. The Ninth Kentucky Cavalry (C.S.A.), still under the command of Colonel W.C.P. Breckinridge, had remained with the Army of Tennessee while Morgan set forth on his Great Indiana-Ohio Raid. The Ninth Kentucky served with General Johnston's army all the way to the end at Durham's Station, North Carolina. (Ellis and Stone, *Report of the Adjutant General*

of the State of Kentucky, 2:5.) Elements of it then accompanied Jefferson Davis's escort until they surrendered at Washington, Georgia, on May 6, 1865.

5. Lee surrendered to General Ulysses S. Grant at Appomattox Court House, Virginia, on April 9, 1865; Johnston surrendered to General William T. Sherman at Durham Station, North Carolina, on April 26, 1865.

6. General Robert E. Lee's Army of Northern Virginia evacuated Richmond on April 2, 1865, the day Porter arrived. The Mayo Bridge was ordered burned at 4:30 a.m. on April 3. (OR, 46 [1]: 1264.)

President Jefferson Davis left Richmond for Danville, Virginia, at 11:00 p.m. on April 2. With Davis was Secretary of War John C. Breckinridge, along with the cabinet of secretaries, staff, and a military escort. Much of the industrial section of the city was set on fire. (Basil W. Duke, "After the Fall of Richmond," *Southern Bivouac* 2 [August 1886]: 163–165.)

7. The Southside Railroad ran from Richmond to Petersburg, Virginia, and then to Weldon, North Carolina; the Richmond and Danville Railroad ran to Danville, Virginia. (Robert C. Black III, *The Railroads of the Confederacy* [Chapel Hill: Univ. of North Carolina Press, 1952], 6.)

8. Washington, Georgia, is a lovely city located on present-day US 78 about forty-five miles east of Athens, on a spur line of the Georgia Railroad. (Black, *The Railroads of the Confederacy,* 6, 259.) At Washington, Georgia, Brigadier General Joseph Lewis surrendered the Kentucky Orphan Brigade along with the remnants of Colonels Basil W. Duke's and W.C.P. Breckinridge's commands on May 6, 1865. (Thompson, *History of the Orphan Brigade,* 285.)

9. Porter actually took the Georgia Railroad from Washington, Georgia, to Atlanta. From Atlanta, he took the Atlanta and West Point and then the Macon and Western to Macon. (Black, *The Railroads of the Confederacy,* 6.)

10. James Fayette Hines, the quartermaster sergeant of the Ninth Kentucky Cavalry (C.S.A.), enlisted in Lexington in September 1862. He rose to become first sergeant and was paroled at Washington, Georgia, in May 1865. (Ellis and Stone, *Report of the Adjutant*

General of the State of Kentucky, 2:2, 18, 20.) Hines was the twenty-five-year-old son of Ann E. Hines from near Bowling Green, Kentucky. Ann's husband, Fayette Henry Hines, was deceased. (1860 U.S. Federal Census Record for James F. Hines, Warren County, Kentucky, ancestry.com; Stewart, *Descendants of Henry Hines, Sr.,* 10.)

General James H. Wilson, commanding the Cavalry Corps of the Military Division of the Mississippi, raided through central Alabama to Columbus, Georgia, and then north to Macon (OR, 49 [1]: 350–353).

General Howell Cobb, a native of Athens, Georgia, and chairman of the Confederate Constitutional Convention in Montgomery, Alabama, in early 1862 was in command of Confederate forces in Macon, Georgia. He was the commander of the District of Georgia. (OR, 49 [1]: 365; Warner, *Generals in Gray,* 55–56.)

11. The Frank White of Tennessee referenced by Porter may never be positively identified. He may have been Francis Marion White of the First Tennessee Cavalry (C.S.A.), based upon that regiment's service record. (Civil War Centennial Comm'n., *Tennessee in the Civil War,* 2:428.)

Social Circle is a small town located in rural Walton County, Georgia, about forty miles east of Atlanta, north of present-day Ga. 402 (US 278) on Ga. 11.

12. Madison, Georgia, a beautiful town, is located in Morgan County, on present-day US 278, about fifty miles southeast of Atlanta.

13. Edward Ludlow Hines, twenty-three-year-old son of Ann E. Hines of Bowling Green, Kentucky, was a first lieutenant in Company E, Ninth Kentucky Cavalry with John M. Porter, serving throughout the war, and finally surrendered at Washington, Georgia, on May 6, 1865. Edward Ludlow Hines had been severely wounded in the face and hands while setting fire to the bridge over the Broad River at Columbia, South Carolina, as Sherman's army neared the South Carolina capital city. Hines actually commanded the Ninth Kentucky Cavalry that day. (Hines, "The Hines Family," undated typescript.) Edward Ludlow Hines was the brother of James Fayette Hines, and of John Henry Hines, who was a prisoner of war at Johnson's Island with Porter. (1860 U.S. Federal Census Record for Edward L. Hines, Warren County, Kentucky, ancestry.com.)

Hugh C. Gwynn was a captain and assistant inspector general to Brigadier General Basil W. Duke, who surrendered at Washington, Georgia, on May 6, 1865 (Ellis and Stone, *Report of the Adjutant General of the State of Kentucky*, 2:18–19, 420). Gwynn, at forty-nine years old, entered the war as a private in Duke's Second Kentucky Cavalry (C.S.A.) and was captured at Buffington Island, Ohio, on July 19, 1863; he was imprisoned at Camp Chase. A native of Woodford County, Kentucky, he had a wife, M. Gwynn, forty-seven, and a young son. (1860 U.S. Federal Census Record for Hugh Gwynn, Woodford County, Kentucky, ancestry.com; Selected Records of the War Department Relating to Confederate Prisoners of War, 1861–1865, Microfilm M598, Record Group 109, National Archives, ancestry.com.)

"Cousin John Porter" was actually John Watson Porter, John M. Porter's father's first cousin. John Watson Porter was the son of Oliver C. Porter, brother of John M. Porter's grandfather, Francis. Oliver moved from Virginia to Georgia at the same time his brothers John and Francis moved to present-day Butler County, Kentucky. John Watson Porter was born on April 2, 1797, and by the 1860s was one of the leading citizens of Madison, Georgia. He and his wife, the former Ann Mapp Fannin, were married in 1834 and built a magnificent Greek Revival home, complete with six Corinthian columns across the front. That house still stands. The Porters made their wealth in the banking, railroad, and woolen mill businesses. Their son, James Henry Porter, age thirty-six, served as a captain in the Third Georgia Infantry in General Robert E. Lee's army. Returning to Atlanta, James Porter was responsible for saving much of the railroad rolling stock and locomotives from destruction when Sherman seized Atlanta on September 1, 1864. (Julia Lowry Porter Block, *Illustrations of a Collection of Historical Relics of My Porter Kin* [Plandome, N.Y.: House of Peters, 1937], 15, 20–21; Porter, "Historical Sketch of the Porter Family," 3, 4.)

14. Jefferson Davis held his last cabinet meeting in Charlotte, North Carolina, on April 26, 1865. After learning of General Joseph E. Johnston's decision to surrender his army to General William T. Sherman, Davis and General John C. Breckinridge, his secretary of war, attempted to reach the Trans-Mississippi Department, where they understood Generals Edmund Kirby Smith and Richard Taylor

still remained in the field. Davis's escort of nearly three thousand cavalry included a brigade commanded by none other than Brigadier General Basil W. Duke, who had been released from prison and had taken over command of John Hunt Morgan's forces upon Morgan's death at Greenville, Tennessee, on September 4, 1864. In the cavalry contingent with Duke was Colonel W.C.P. Breckinridge and elements of Porter's old Ninth Kentucky Cavalry. The presidential caravan moved through Washington, Georgia, on May 4, 1865. Many of the troops in the escort were relieved of duty there. Duke and W.C.P. Breckinridge continued to Woodstock, where they agreed to surrender upon advice from General Breckinridge. They returned to Washington, Georgia, and surrendered on May 6. Davis surrendered to elements of General James Wilson's Federal cavalry near Irwinville, Georgia, on May 10, 1865. Davis was finally imprisoned at Fort Monroe, Virginia. (Duke, "After the Fall of Richmond," 163–165; Basil W. Duke, *Reminiscences of Basil W. Duke, C.S.A.* [New York: Doubleday Page, 1911], 469–470.)

15. The railroad from Atlanta to Chattanooga was the famed Western and Atlantic Railroad (Black, *The Railroads of the Confederacy*, 6).

16. Observed by Porter were the battlegrounds of Sherman's army in its drive to seize Atlanta. Peach Tree Creek was a battle fought on July 20, 1864, just north of Atlanta. Kennesaw Mountain was a battle fought on June 16, 1864, northwest of Atlanta. (OR, 38 [1]: 506, 607.)

17. Porter and his companions would have taken the Nashville and Chattanooga Railroad from Chattanooga to Nashville (Black, *The Railroads of the Confederacy*, 6).

18. Porter boarded the Louisville and Nashville Railroad from Nashville to Bowling Green. Mrs. Anna Hines was forty-seven-year-old Ann E. Hines, mother of John Henry Hines, James Fayette Hines, and Edward Ludlow Hines, Porter's companions who he met in Madison, Georgia. Edward Ludlow Hines recalled arriving back home in Bowling Green on June 10, 1865. (1860 U.S. Federal Census Record for Ann E. Hines, Warren County, Kentucky, ancestry.com; Hines, "The Hines Family," 14.)

19. Porter followed present-day US 231 to Little Muddy Cumberland Presbyterian Church and then Ky. 1083 to Sugar Grove.

BIBLIOGRAPHY

MANUSCRIPTS

Alabama Department of Archives and History, Montgomery, Alabama
Photographic Collections.

Filson Historical Society Special Collections, Louisville, Kentucky
Thomas Henry Hines Papers.

Kentucky Historical Society, Frankfort, Kentucky
James A. Hibben Collection. 1987PH04.
Martin F. Schmidt Collection of Kentucky Views. 2004.41.

Library of Congress, Washington, D.C.
Photographic Collections.

Bill Penn Collection, Cynthiana, Kentucky
Louisville Daily Journal. July 26, 1862.

Dr. Dan Rush Collection, Kingsport, Tennessee
Transcript. "After-Action Report of the Action at 'Ashland.'" *The Vidette*. Hopkinsville, Kentucky. October 28, 1862.
Knoxville Register. November 28, 1862.

Cora Jane Spiller Collection, Bowling Green, Kentucky
Hines, Edward Ludlow. "The Hines Family," undated typescript.
"Edward Ludlow Hines, 1842–1920," typewritten chronology.

BIBLIOGRAPHY

Transylvania University Library, Lexington, Kentucky
J. Winston Coleman, Jr. Photographic Collection.

University of Kentucky Special Collections, Manuscript and Photographic Collections
Hunt-Morgan House Deposit Photographic Collection.
Lafayette Studios Photographic Collection.
Thomas Henry Hines Papers, 1772 (1860–1869) 1954, Winn Collection, 46M97, Boxes 1a and 3.
U.S. Federal Census Records
  Census Population Schedules, Butler County, Kentucky, 1860, Reel 358, Box 6.
  Census Population Schedules, Clark County, Kentucky, 1860, Reel 362, Box 10.
  Census Population Schedules, Christian County, Kentucky, 1860, Reel 362, Box 10.
  Census Population Schedules, Hart County, Kentucky, 1860, Reel 372, Box 20.
  Census Population Schedules, Logan County, Kentucky, 1860, Reel 383, Box 31.
  Census Population Schedules, Montgomery County, Tennessee, 1860, on M653, No. 1266, Reel 102.
  Census Population Schedules, Simpson County, Kentucky, 1860, Reel 395, Box 43.
  Census Population Schedules, Todd County, Kentucky, 1860, Reel 396, Box 44.
  Census Population Schedules, Warren County, Kentucky, 1860, Reel 397, Box 45.

University of Kentucky Library, Thesis and Dissertation Collection
Coffman, Edward McKenzie. "The Civil War Career of Thomas Henry Hines." Masters thesis, University of Kentucky, 1955.

University of North Carolina Library
Southern Historical Collection.
Joseph Mason Kern Papers, No. 2526-Z.

BIBLIOGRAPHY

Western Kentucky University, Bowling Green, Kentucky, Kentucky Library and Museum, Manuscripts and Archives

Porter, John M. "Historical Sketch of the Porter Family," typescript prepared in 1872.

Record of Burials, Fairview Cemetery, Bowling Green, Kentucky.

WEBSITES

www.Ancestry.com

1860 U.S. Federal Census Record for Wm. R. Barnett, Butler County, Kentucky.

1860 U.S. Federal Census Record for William Beard, Butler County, Kentucky.

1860 U.S. Federal Census Record for John A. Carter, Jefferson County, Kentucky.

1860 U.S. Federal Census Record for Coleman Covington, Warren County, Kentucky.

1860 U.S. Federal Census Record for Samuel Garvin, Jefferson County, Kentucky.

1860 U.S. Federal Census Record for Jesse Grider, Warren County, Kentucky.

1860 U.S. Federal Census Record for Hugh Gwynn, Woodford County, Kentucky.

1860 U.S. Federal Census Record for Alanson Fidella Helm, Butler County, Kentucky.

1860 U.S. Federal Census Record for Ann E. Hines, Warren County, Kentucky.

1860 U.S. Federal Census Record for Edward L. Hines, Warren County, Kentucky.

1860 U.S. Federal Census Record for James F. Hines, Warren County, Kentucky.

1860 U.S. Federal Census Record for John H. Hines, Warren County, Kentucky.

1860 U.S. Federal Census Record for William Jennings, Madison County, Kentucky.

1850 U.S. Federal Census Record for George D. Mimms, Montgomery County, Tennessee.

1860 U.S. Federal Census—Slave Schedules Record for G. D. Mimms, Montgomery County, Tennessee.

1870 U.S. Federal Census Record for George D. Mimms, Montgomery County, Tennessee.

1860 U.S. Federal Census Record for Joseph S. Mitchell, Edmonson County, Kentucky.

1870 U.S. Federal Census Record for Mary T. Porter, Butler County, Kentucky.

1860 U.S. Federal Census Record for Eldon Sloss, Logan County, Kentucky.

1860 U.S. Federal Census Record for Sarah Sloss, Logan County, Kentucky.

1860 U.S. Federal Census Record for Nancy Sproul, Butler County, Kentucky.

1860 U.S. Federal Census Record for E. Spurrier, Montgomery County, Tennessee.

Selected Records of the War Department Relating to Confederate Prisoners of War, 1861–1865 (National Archives Microfilm M598, 145 rolls) War Department Collection of Confederate Records, Record Group 109, National Archives.

www.jesshistorical.com/Jessamine%20County%20Kentucky%20 Families/b231.htm
Luther Alexander Martin.

www.johnsonsisland.org/history/war.htm

www.rootsweb.com/~orphanhm

BOOKS AND ARTICLES

Baird, Nancy D., Carol Crowe-Carraco, and Michael L. Morse. *Bowling Green: A Pictorial History.* Norfolk: Donning, 1983.

Barbiere, Joe. *Scraps from the Prison Table, at Camp Chase and Johnson's Island.* Doylestown, Pa.: W.W.H. Davis, Printer, 1868.

Black, Robert C., III. *The Railroads of the Confederacy.* Chapel Hill: Univ. of North Carolina Press, 1952.

Blair, William. *Cities of the Dead: Contesting the Memory of the Civil War in the South, 1865–1974.* Chapel Hill: Univ. of North Carolina Press, 2004.

Blight, David W. *Race and Reunion: The Civil War in American Memory.* Cambridge, Mass.: Belknap Press of Harvard Univ. Press, 2001.

Block, Julia Lowry Porter. *Illustrations of a Collection of Historical Relics of My Porter Kin.* Plandome, N.Y.: House of Peters, 1937.

Boatner, Mark M., III. *The Civil War Dictionary.* New York: McKay, 1959.

Buford, Martha McDowell. *Peach Leather and Rebel Gray: Diary and Letters of a Confederate Wife,* edited by Mary E. Wharton and Ellen F. Williams. Lexington, Ky.: Helicon, 1986.

Castleman, John B. *Active Service.* Louisville: Courier-Journal Job Printing Co., 1917.

Civil War Centennial Comm'n. *Tennesseans in the Civil War: A Military History of Confederate and Union Units with Available Rosters of Personnel.* 2 vols. Nashville: Civil War Centennial Comm'n., 1964.

Coffman, Edward. *The Story of Logan County.* Nashville: Parthenon, 1962.

Coleman, J. Winston, Jr. *Historic Kentucky.* Lexington: Henry Clay Press, 1967.

Collins, Lewis. *Historical Sketches of Kentucky.* Cincinnati: J. A. and U. P. James, 1847.

Collins, Richard. *History of Kentucky.* 2 vols. Frankfort: Kentucky Historical Society, 1966.

Confederate Veterans Ass'n. of Kentucky. *Constitution, Bylaws and Membership of the Confederate Veterans Ass'n. of Kentucky.* Lexington: Confederate Veterans Ass'n. of Kentucky, 1895.

Coulter, E. Merton. *The Civil War and Readjustment in Kentucky.* Chapel Hill: Univ. of North Carolina Press, 1926.

Doyle, George F., M.D. *Clark County Tombstone Records.* Winchester: privately printed, 1935.

Duke, Basil W. "After the Fall of Richmond." *Southern Bivouac* 5 (August 1886): 163–165.

———. *History of Morgan's Cavalry.* Cincinnati: Miami Printing and Pub. Co., 1867.

BIBLIOGRAPHY

————. *Reminiscences of Basil W. Duke, C.S.A.* New York: Doubleday Page, 1911.

Ellis, J. Tandy, and W. J. Stone. *Report of the Adjutant General of the State of Kentucky, Confederate Kentucky Volunteers, War 1861–65.* 2 vols. Frankfort: Kentucky State Legislature, 1913 and 1918.

Gardiner, Florence Edwards. *Cyrus Edwards's Stories of Early Days in What Is Now Barren, Hart and Metcalfe Counties.* Louisville: Standard Printing, 1940.

Guerrant, Edward O. *Bluegrass Confederate: The Headquarters Diary of Edward O. Guerrant,* edited by William C. Davis and Meredith L. Swentor. Baton Rouge: Louisiana State Univ. Press, 1989.

Hewett, Janet B., ed. *The Roster of Confederate Soldiers, 1861–1865.* 16 vols. Wilmington, N.C.: Broadfoot, 1996.

History Committee. *History of the Service of the Third Ohio Veteran Volunteer Cavalry.* Toledo: Stoneman, 1910.

Hockersmith, Captain L. D. *Morgan's Escape: A Thrilling Story of War Times.* Madisonville, Ky.: Glenn's Graphic Print, 1903.

Holland, Cecil F. *Morgan and His Raiders: A Biography of the Confederate General.* New York: Macmillan, 1943.

Johnston, Colonel J. Stoddard. *Kentucky,* vol. 11 in *Confederate Military History,* edited by Clement Evans. Atlanta: Confederate Pub. Co., 1899, 286–287.

Johnston, William Preston. *The Life of General Albert Sidney Johnston.* New York: Appleton, 1878.

Jones, Mary Joseph. *The Civil War in Hardin County, Kentucky.* Vine Grove, Ky.: Ancestral Trails Historical Society, 1995.

Kentucky Records Research Committee. *Kentucky Cemetery Records.* 5 vols. Lexington: Keystone Printery, 1960.

Kimmel, Stanley. *Mr. Davis's Richmond.* New York: Bramhall House, 1958.

Kleber, John E., ed. *The Kentucky Encyclopedia.* Lexington: Univ. Press of Kentucky, 1992.

Klein, Maury. *History of the Louisville and Nashville Railroad.* New York: Macmillan, 1972.

Lee, Richard M. *General Lee's City: An Illustrated Guide to the Historic Sites of Confederate Richmond.* McLean, Va.: EPM, 1987.

Lindsey, D. W. *Report of the Adjutant General of the State of Kentucky (Federal).* 2 vols. Frankfort: Kentucky Yeoman Office, 1866.

Logan, India W. P. *Kelion Franklin Peddicord of Quirks's Scouts, Morgan's Kentucky Cavalry, C.S.A.* New York: Neal, 1908.

Matthews, Gary Robert. *Basil Wilson Duke: The Right Man in the Right Place.* Lexington: Univ. Press of Kentucky, 2005.

McWhiney, Grady. *Braxton Bragg and Confederate Defeat,* vol. 1, *Field Command.* New York: Columbia Univ. Press, 1969.

Penn, William A. *Rattling Spurs and Broad-Brimmed Hats: The Civil War in Cynthiana and Harrison County, Kentucky.* Midway, Ky.: Battle Grove Press, 1995.

Peter, Frances. *A Union Woman in Civil War Kentucky: The Diary of Frances Peter,* edited by John David Smith and William Cooper Jr. Lexington: Univ. Press of Kentucky, 2000.

Peter, Robert. *History of Fayette County, Kentucky.* Chicago: O. L. Baskin and Co., 1882.

Porter, James D. *Tennessee,* vol. 10 in *Confederate Military History,* edited by Clement Evans. Atlanta: Confederate Pub. Co., 1898.

Puetz, C. J. *Kentucky County Maps.* Lyndon Station, Wisc.: County Maps, n.d.

Railey, W. E. *History of Woodford County.* Lexington: Woodford Improvement League, 1968.

Ramage, James. *Rebel Raider: The Life of General John Hunt Morgan,* Lexington: Univ. Press of Kentucky, 1986.

Ranck, George W. *History of Lexington, Kentucky.* Cincinnati: Robert Clarke and Co., 1872.

Roberts, O. M. *Texas,* vol. 15 in *Confederate Military History,* edited by Clement Evans. Atlanta: Confederate Pub. Co., 1899.

Roland, Charles P. *Albert Sidney Johnston: Soldier of Three Republics.* Austin: Univ. of Texas Press, 1964.

Rowland, Dunbar. *History of Mississippi,* 2 vols. Chicago-Jackson: Clarke, 1925.

Russ, Lois, ed. *Butler County, Kentucky History.* Morgantown: Butler County Historical and Genealogical Society, 1987.

Saunders, Colonel James Edmonds, and Saunders Blair Stubbs. *Early Settlers of Alabama with Notes and Genealogies.* New Orleans: L. Graham and Son, 1899.

Sistler, Byron, and Barbara Sistler. *1850 Census, Tennessee,* 4 vols. Evanston: Sistler, 1975.

Stewart, J. Adger. *Descendants of Henry Hines, Sr., 1732–1810.* Louisville: Morton, 1925.

Stickles, Arndt M. *Simon Bolivar Buckner: Borderland Knight.* Chapel Hill: Univ. of North Carolina Press, 1940.

Thompson, Ed Porter. *History of the Orphan Brigade.* Louisville: Thompson, 1890.

Thompson, Kenneth C., Jr., and Nancy D. Baird. *Warren County, Kentucky Families.* Paducah: Turner, 1991.

Vanderpool, Montgomery. *Logan County, Kentucky Vital Statistics, Births, 1852–1859.* Russellville, Ky.: Montgomery Vanderpool, 1987.

War Department. *War of the Rebellion: A Compilation of the Official Records of the Union and Confederate Armies.* Series I, 128 vols. Washington, D.C.: U.S. Government Printing Office, 1880–1901.

Warner, Ezra J. *Generals in Blue: Lives of the Union Commanders.* Baton Rouge: Louisiana State Univ. Press, 1959.

———. *Generals in Gray: Lives of the Confederate Commanders.* Baton Rouge: Louisiana State Univ. Press, 1959.

Wulsin, Lucien. *The Story of the Fourth Regiment Ohio Veteran Volunteer Cavalry.* Cincinnati: N.p., 1912.

Wyeth, John Allen. *With Saber and Scalpel: The Autobiography of a Soldier and Surgeon.* New York: Harper, 1914.

Young, Bennett H. *Confederate Wizards of the Saddle.* Boston: Chapple, 1912.

INDEX

INDEX

INDEX

Hines, James Fayette, 195, 196, 265n4, 267–68n10, 270n18
Hines, James M., 189
Hines, John H., 19, 264n3
Hines, John Henry, 182–86, 189, 201, 264–65n4, 270n18
Hines, Nancy Sproule, 6
Hines, Sarah Carson, 5, 223n6
Hines, Thomas Henry, *58*, 250n8
  birth of, 5, 235n4
  as Buckner's Guide, 19
  death of, 6
  detached missions of, 97–98, 101, 102, 138–39
  family background of, 4, 223n6
  Indiana-Ohio scouting mission (1863), 165–66
  during Kentucky invasion (1862), 86–87
  legal partnership with Porter, 6, 7
  marriage of, 236–37n8, 257n5
  as Ninth Kentucky Cavalry (CSA) commander, 134
  official report of (1863), 141, 260n21
  POW revolt planned by, 178, 265–66n6
  prison escape of, 177–78, 236–37n8, 265n5
  scouting duties of, 138–39, 251n1
  in Second Kentucky Cavalry (CSA), 226–27n1
  travels to join Morgan, 52, 57–65, *60*, 223–24nn6–7
Hines, Warren Walker, 5, 223n6
Hines, William, 6, 21
History of Morgan's Cavalry (Duke), 129
Hobson, Edward H., 242n7, 244n15
Hodgenville (KY), 174, 262n11
Holland, James H., 123, 142, 147, 246n18, 251n1, 254n7
Holland, Polly A., 147, 154, 246n18, 251n1, 254n7

Home Guards, 59, 62, 67, 72, 224n7, 227n2, 229n9, 233n16
"Hopemont" (Lexington, KY), 234n19
Hopkinsville (KY), 17, 98, 102, 103–4, 211n7, 237nn9–10
Hopkinsville Road, 154
Hoskins, William A., 246–47n22
Huffman, J. M., 240n3, 243n10, 245n17
Hunt, Thomas, 210n6
Hunter, Hiram A., 80, 230n4
Hustonville (KY), 86
Hutchinson, John B., 241n3, 243n10, 245n17, 248–49n2

Indiana-Ohio raid (1863), 122
  Brandenburg (KY) as crossing site for, 170, 174–75, 262n12
  casualties in, 120, 212n10, 246n21, 251n1
  Confederate POWs from, 179–80, 264n3, 265n4
  map, *172*
  Morgan captured during, 166, 263n12
  objectives of, 170
  Porter captured during preliminary scouting mission, 170–75
  preliminary engagements, 262–63n12
  scouting mission preceding, 165–66
  troop condition, 166–67
ironclads, 214n7
Irvine (KY), 89, 233n13
Irwinville (GA), 270n14
Island Number 10, 11

Jacinto (MS), 52, 221n1
Jackson (KY), 233n13
Jackson (MS), 238n14
Jackson, James S., 208–9n2
Jackson, Thomas J. ("Stonewall"), 125

288

INDEX

Porter's travels in, to join Morgan, *55*, 57–59, *60*, 60–61, 224n7
Union occupation of, 70–71, 224n7, 226n1, 228n7
Lexington and Frankfort Railroad, 226n13
Lexington Cemetery (Lexington, KY), 224n7, 234n19
Lexington Rifles, 219n11
Libby Prison (Richmond, VA), 266n2
Liberty (KY), 86
Liberty (TN), 127, 129–30, 142, 164, 247–48n1, 249n5, 260n21
Licking River, 67–70, *69*, *70*, 227nn2–3
Lincoln, Abraham
election of (1860), 11, 13
Kentucky polling for (1860), 208n1
Knob Creek (KY) residence of, 262n11
Lincoln, Mary Todd, 221n1
Lincoln County (KY), 21
Little Muddy Creek area (KY), 2, 147, 235n5, 255n8
Little Muddy Cumberland Presbyterian Church (Sugar Grove, KY), 1, 3, 149, 255n8, 256n11, 270n19
Livingston (KY), 73
Livingston (TN), 167
Logan, George W., 20
Logan County (KY), *18*, 42–43, 54, 87, 213n1, 252n3, 254n6
Logan County (KY) Presbytery, 2
Loretto (KY), 246n20
Louisiana, 179
Louisville (ironclad gunboat), 214n7
Louisville (KY), 87, 174, 253nn3–4
Louisville and Frankfort Railroad, 170
Louisville and Nashville Railroad, 44, 142, 210n6, 252n2, 259n17

Bardstown spur line, 262n9
Confederate troop movements using, 14
construction of, 244n14
at Gallatin (TN), 230n2, 232n8
Indiana-Ohio raid (1863) and, 170
Lebanon spur line, 169, *169*, 170, 174, 262n11
main stem of, 262n8
Morgan's raids against, 52, 78, 80, 97, 100, 112, 118, 121, 141, 153, 160–61, 222n3, 232n8, 237n10, 243n10, 244n14, 247n23, 253n4
Porter's return trip home on, 270n18
Union defense of, *121*, 230n3, 231n6, 242n7, 244n14
Union supply line on, 112, 141
Louisville and Nashville Turnpike, 106, 238n12, 242n8, 243nn9, 11, 252n2, 261n6, 262n11

Macon (GA), 189, 194–95, 267n9
Madison (GA), 189, 196–99, 268–69nn12–13
Madison County (KY), 72–73, 231n7
Magoffin, Beriah, 11
Magruder, Henry C., 21
Manassas (VA), Battle of (1861), 125
Marion County (KY), 55
Markham (Johnson's Island POW), 182–86, 264–65n4
Marmaduke, John S., 179, 264n2
Marrowbone Creek, 263n12
Marshall, Humphrey, 89, *89*, 90–92, 233nn12, 14, 240n2
Martin, Ann Barnes, 61–62, 86–87, 225n11
Martin, Ann Shreve, 225n11
Martin, Lewis Young, 225n11
Martin, Luther Alexander, 225n11

291

INDEX